The

CITIZEN MARINE

One Marine's Journey of
Love, Peace, and War
Vietnam Era to Today's War on Terror

Michael G. Wenger

Roxbury Woods
Press

Roxbury Woods Press
933 Liberty Drive
DeForest, WI 53532
Phone: 608-220-2706
Email: admin@citizenmarine.com

•

Library of Congress Registration Number: TX 8-619-025

Second edition 2019. Abridged version of first edition.

ISBN-13: 978-1-7321951-1-0

Cover Design by EM Graphics

For information regarding special orders, please contact the Roxbury Woods Press.

The Citizen Marine

Living the Dream – In Every Clime and Place

A story of the fragile balance between our service members' love for home, and family and their sense of duty when called into harm's way.

Author's Note

The Citizen Marine is not a blood and guts war story. There are many of those stories already told. Its goal is to tell the story of the hundreds of thousands of service members whose good, faithful service to our nation is crucial to maintain our freedom and a good way of life. Our country has an amazing defense structure that in recent years has evolved to rely much more heavily on the reserves and guards to answer the calls of duty around the world. If you served on active duty, the reserves, or the guard, I hope my story will remind you and your family and friends of your own story!

The glossary in the back of the book will help those who are unfamiliar with military terminology.

Dedication

For Terri, our family, our friends, and for all service members and their families that continue to sacrifice so much.

Acknowledgements

First and foremost I wish to thank Terri, Kurt, and Kristin, the centers of my life, for their support of my desire to serve my country and still maintain a sense of family at home. This extends to my parents, Mike and Norma, who gave me a great start in life and stood by me every step along the way.

The Citizen Marine
Living the Dream – In Every Clime and Place

Table of Contents

Chapter One
The Citizen/The Marine: Jul 2011
US Central Command, MacDill AFB, Tampa, Fl

A Heavy Heart on Rocky Point

The evening sun was nearing Old Tampa Bay's horizon as I jogged along my favorite running path on the Courtney Campbell Causeway near Rocky Point Drive. The heavy, smothering humidity soothed each step as I took in the calm bay waters, blue skies, palm trees, and beautiful blend of Spanish and Mediterranean architecture. It was a great place to jog and think, and there was a lot on my mind.

I was a 59 year old loving husband, father, son, and working slug from Wisconsin. I was also a retired Chief Warrant Officer 4 in the United States Marine Corps nearing the end of a fourth year of retired recall duty with five trips to the Middle East under my belt.

I'd been away from my home, family, and civilian job most of that time and soon had another big choice to make. I was recently asked if I would be willing to stay for a fifth year. Would I say yes and take advantage of the opportunity to continue doing what I love as an American patriot and Marine, or would I say no and return to my civilian job, home, and family for good this time?

Like hundreds of thousands of reservists, I was called to active duty as part of the Global War on Terror on emergency call-up orders. In my most recent case, I volunteered for recall from nearly five years of retired status. This was after over thirty years of combined active and reserve service. It was very unusual for the Marines to recall a retiree to begin with, and when they did, it was only for a year at a time. Very few retirees were allowed to stay for four or more years on active duty recall once they have been mandatorily retired after serving thirty-plus years. It was an honor to have already served four years of retired recall service, and to have the opportunity to serve for yet another year, but I missed home, family and friends!

The Tug of War

My best friend, beautiful wife, and soul mate of more than fifteen years was waiting for me back in Wisconsin. Terri was supportive of my returns to active duty at every turn, and she had plenty of practice. This was my third recall since our marriage in 1996. The first was immediately after 9/11 when I was assigned as a staff officer in the Marine Central Command (MARCENT) headquarters which was co-located with the US Central Command (CENTCOM) at MacDill Air Force Base in Tampa. I served there fourteen months past my thirty-year mandatory retirement date and went back home, supposedly for good. She frequently joined me in Tampa, which we both came to love, as I never left the states on that call-up.

The second recall was nearly five years later in 2007. It was for one year to participate in the mobilization of my old reserve infantry battalion for a combat tour of duty in Iraq. While in Iraq, I was contacted by a personnel officer at Headquarters Marine Corps (HQMC) responsible for providing Marine individual augmentees to CENTCOM. The gears were put in motion to cut a set of orders for a third recall as soon as I got home from Iraq.

With most of the world's problems currently focused in the Middle East, the op tempo at CENTCOM was grueling for both active duty members who did three year tours, and for individual augmentees who spent anywhere from six months to a year there. The normal staffing level at CENTCOM is around 1,500, but the permanent staff was bolstered with upwards of 3,000 temporary augmentees. This was to handle the vastly increased workload generated by two wars and wide spread unrest in the Middle East. It was difficult for the services to attract staff members, as most of them already did several tours of overseas duty with their services. They knew duty at CENTCOM would mean more deployments, and avoided it as much as possible. As a volunteer, I was readily approved for another year of recall.

That one-year recall at CENTCOM had by now stretched to nearly three years, and it was looking like yet another year. As long as I stayed in Tampa, Terri and I would see each other regularly, but there was no guarantee I wouldn't be sent back to the Middle East. It was common for staff officers in CENTCOM to routinely be sent anywhere in the CENTCOM area of responsibility, which was 20 countries in the Middle East for varying tour lengths. My duties pretty much guaranteed me another trip to Afghanistan of indefinite duration if I stayed another year.

In all this, she never failed to support my sense of duty. Every time the calls and extensions came, she gave me that special, understanding look of love and compassion that said "I love you, I'll miss you, but I support you." Her biggest concern was my safety in combat zones. I always countered that I was safer there with Marines and soldiers to protect me than on an icy Wisconsin road with no protection! I also pointed out that after five trips to the Middle East, I never suffered a scratch, but one visit at home with my two Grand Runts, and I ended up with bruised ribs! Even though that logic never flew for some reason, I always had her love and support.

So, once again, I was feeling the emotional pain that every one of the thousands of military men and women are constantly torn between duty and family feel. Whether it is a reservist called away from family, friends, and a civilian job for a period of time, or an active duty member that gets orders with little or no choice of their next assignment, the price paid to answer the call of duty is the same - separation from home, loved ones, friends, and a safe job.

A 40 Year Journey in Three Miles
The sight and sound of an airliner climbing over Tampa from the nearby international airport stole my attention as I jogged. Suddenly I wondered if the next one would take me back home to Terri, my family, friends, and work, or right back to the Middle East.
As I thought about the different paths my life could soon take, my mind started drifting back over the forty-year tug of war between my love of home, family, and strong sense of duty...

Chapter Two
The Beginning: 1971-73
Lodi, MCRD, San Diego, Camp Pendleton and Beyond

The Dream

The Vietnam War was still raging when I approached high school graduation in 1970. Although it had peaked with the major TET offensives in 1968/9, the protests on the University of Wisconsin Campus were still constant and intense. There was a bombing at the university's Sterling Hall, killing a researcher. Nixon was president, and Simon and Garfunkel's "Bridge over Troubled Waters" was on top of the music charts. In Lodi, Wisconsin though, folks were more concerned about what impact the weather was going to have on this year's crops.

Vietnam and the Draft

Like every male of my age, I had to decide how I was going to deal with the draft. The draft as it had been known through the sixties was changing. There was a great deal of unrest throughout the country decrying the unfairness of the old draft system. Therefore, a new lottery system was established to determine who would be drafted.

The new system would create three lottery drawings to get through the next three years. Each year, the needs of the military would determine how many new inductees would be required. On the day of the drawing, each day of the year would be drawn one at a time and put in a sequence of 1 through 365. Each month after, the military would determine how many draftees would be needed, go down the list of birthdays until they had enough. If you had a low number, the chances of being drafted were pretty high. If you had a higher number, you wouldn't go. While the military was drawing down and the requirements were becoming less, they still needed people.

The first drawing would be on 1 July, 1970 for those born in 1951. The next drawing would be on 5 August, 1971 for those born in 1952;

and what would become the last drawing would happen on 2 February, 1972, as the draft ended on 1 July, 1973.

I was born in 1952 and would have to wait over a year and a half to see what my number would be. This was agonizing to me after watching my future go to the winds, and realizing I had to decide what I wanted to do with my life. I became very restless. I didn't feel ready for college. I took only the minimum courses necessary to graduate high school to focus on our family business. There were no more deferments for college students anyway. It now came down to how to handle the draft, and how to deal with all the fear, hatred, and uncertainty that had become Vietnam.

I made my decision. I would sign up for two years and would be nearly done by the time they drew my number! Things suddenly changed for me, as now I not only wanted to join, I wanted to join what I thought was the best. Some of my friends had already joined the Marine Corps, and I was impressed with what I saw when they came home. It was finally settled!

Upon my parent's return, I broke the news to them. Dad was extremely upset. He was drafted into the Army and sent to Korea. His duty was grueling. He served with the US Army 13th Combat Engineers in direct support of the Marines, and spent most of his time "in front of the front" in harsh conditions of weather and terrain. He escaped death more than once, and he saw how the Marines lived and how they operated. He didn't want to think of his son going through that as well. I respected my parents more than anything in life and couldn't let them down, so I backed off.

My restlessness continued and got even worse. Even though Mom and Dad understood, I felt it necessary to find a good compromise. I joined the US Marine Corps Reserve for six months and would return for normal drill weekends. I left with Mom and Dad's love, but not Dads' full approval.

This seemed like a good plan. I would be back in a few months, wouldn't have to actually go to Vietnam, and could still challenge myself to become a Marine like my friends that I thought so highly of. So, I covered all the bases. I honored my parents, would be a Marine, and would be done before I knew it. Brilliant plan!

Marine Corps Boot Camp

Armed with a large yellow envelope containing my orders, I boarded a plane in Madison and headed for San Diego on 8 February, 1971. The departure was a tear jerker. Dad was the worst. He wasn't good at articulating his feelings, but nobody had a hard time knowing how he felt then. It was all clear and well understood in the hug he gave me at the departure gate. Mom was strong, my brother sad, but there was understanding in his eyes. My little sisters were too young to say much. They knew I'd be back, so what was the big deal?

I heard a lot about the reception of recruits at San Diego, but I didn't think it would start at the airport right in the public eye. It did! I found the spot my instructions led me to, and found other recruits standing with that same look of uncertain anticipation, each holding the same large yellow envelope. We weren't kept waiting long. A Marine with a Smokey the Bear hat walked up to us and informed us in a loud and thunderous manner that "the smoking lamp is out." I knew what that meant, but I didn't smoke. The guy next to me smoked and apparently didn't know what it meant. It was a real attention getter to the rest of us when the Marine went to him, took the cigarette out of his hand and put it out in his eyeball! At least we all thought he did. It sure looked like it!

Well, he had our attention and after that all he had to do was whisper. But, whispering was not in his DNA. We received very loud, clear, concise instructions that landed us on a bus in front of the receiving barracks at the fabled Marine Corps Recruit Depot in just minutes.

With his helpful guidance we amazed ourselves at how fast we could get off the bus and find an empty pair of yellow footprints to take up! We were quickly formed into a very well organized formation, but didn't know how to march as a unit yet. Leave it to Marines with two stripes and a Smokey hat! They had us lock arms and used commands we could understand, like "forward march" and "turn to the right" and "mob stop." They were careful to leave spaces between the words to prepare us for proper execution of real commands. How thoughtful of them!

The first stop was the barber shop. Within minutes, everyone was bald! As long as anyone with a mole or wart pointed to it, there wasn't any blood. Those barbers were good! Then we were issued our training uniforms and lined up in front of changing tables. Within a few more minutes, our civvies were in boxes to be returned to our families. Now we are all the same! Nobody had hair, everyone was dressed the same, and all we had for any sort of identity was our scarlet and gold platoon flag with the number 2017 on it. This would be our platoon number. Everything we did, didn't do, and were supposed to do, from that moment to graduation, was identified by that number. We would all know that number to the day we die, Alzheimer's or not!

Not long after dark, we were back to where we started for our first night…the fabled reception barracks. My platoon was assigned to the second deck. They don't have floors in Marine Corps buildings; they have decks like a ship. The Marines that were so helpful in showing us how to get us off buses fast were again helpful in showing us how to make racks the Marine Corps way. Then the lights went out. Life was good. We got through the first day! Or so we thought.

There was a sudden rumbling action on the deck above that shook our racks. Oh no! This was like the stories you hear about Marine DI's making recruits get in and out of their racks until they do it fast enough. It sounded like it was happening on the third deck, and it would soon be our turn. In the morning we were told that wasn't the case. It turned out to be the big 1971 earth quake in Los Angeles. If it was like that in San Diego, what was it like in Los Angeles? Geez! This doesn't happen in Wisconsin! Is there a 24-hour return policy?

Three months of recruit training went fast once it got started in earnest. The first few days included forming and were limited to administrative and medical requirements, until four full platoons are formed. That happened on day twelve, and off we went for real.

We drilled and we drilled. We went to class after class, and we constantly changed uniforms for the training at hand. We learned how to save lives, and how to take lives. We studied every facet of being a United States Marine. But always in the background was the harassment designed to inflict unfairness and distraction while teaching us to focus on the mission.

My drill instructors and primary marksmanship instructors each had a good impact on me in their own way. Even after more than forty years, I remain thankful we had people that knew how to find the balance of respect, toughness, and clarity necessary to prepare you for combat, while never forgetting what and who you represent as a US Marine. They all would have a profound and very positive effect on my long active and reserve career. I would develop a full appreciation for what they say about Marines, "No better friend, no worse enemy."

Before I knew it, Platoon 2017 was within a couple weeks of graduation. To my great surprise, I received news that Mom and Dad, my brother Ron, and sisters Judy, Tammy, and Cherie were coming to the Marine Corps Recruit Depot (MCRD) to see me graduate! This wasn't easy for my family. Money was tight and the farmers my parents served always had an urgent need to get something fixed before it rains or the crops go to waste.

I was elated!! The decision to do all this was hard to begin with, and I loved my family more than anything. It was very understandable if they felt I'd abandoned them. This was the greatest feeling in the world! I would be the Marine I wanted to be, and my family would be there to see it! Most of all, my Dad would be there and would be full of pride in his son! That day will live in my memory as one of my very best ever!

Infantry Training Regiment (ITR)
The next step for every Marine in those days was a month at the Infantry Training Regiment (ITR) at Camp Onofre, a smaller camp within the larger Camp Pendleton area. Infantry training was part of every Marine's training, regardless of specialty. Nowadays, they get it as part of recruit training, which includes "The Crucible". This is a grueling multiple day and night march in impossible terrain, under extreme pressures, resembling what they may expect in the harshest combat conditions.

Perhaps the most important lesson I learned from a Navy Corpsman in ITR was to wear two pair of the cushioned soles socks that are still issued today. The first pair should be worn inside out and the second pair should be worn normally over the first. This stops the feet from sliding during long marches in hot terrain. This came in handy over many years, especially when again I donned combat boots for duty in Iraq and Afghanistan in the years to come.

Aside from blisters for those who didn't heed the Corpsman's advice, shin splints were the most common injury during ITR. My last name started with "W" so I found myself in the last of four platoons, way back in the third squad. The last of the last! Any infantryman will tell you that when you move as a company the first platoon moves at whatever pace they set, but the last platoon has to react to the accordion effect when the first platoon varied its pace. I always wanted to change the order so those guys would get it! I was overruled. Bastards!

Towards the end of ITR, we finally would be confronting the famed and feared "Mount MF." I'll leave what MF stands for to your imagination. Its real name was Old Smokey, but it was the steepest, longest hill the Marines had to tackle as part of ITR then, and still today during the Crucible of today's boot camp training. As I endured the inevitable steep march in full combat gear, I remembered the advice I got from a Marine who had already done it.

He said, "Just make sure all your gear is high and tight on your back, get a good grip on your rifle sling, and look down at the Marine's boots in front of you. Just put one foot in front of the other. Don't worry about anything else - just one foot in front of the other." It worked! I found it easy to look at the boots of the Marine in front of me because it was so steep and they were right in my face! That guy was a genius! It felt like it might have killed us, but now we were among those who have taken on Mount MF! Great to be in the club!! Ask any Marine!

In one month's time, 211 Marines learned how to be members of an infantry fire team and participate in every form of daytime and nighttime attack (supported or unsupported with air, artillery, or armor). We fired every weapon in the Marine Corps infantry arsenal, and we were introduced to the harsh realities of terrain, weather, and war in every possible way, short of actually being shot at. Even so, there were times where we were crawling under live machine gun fire!

Graduation day came and we were all on our way to our specialty training. Those Marines whose specialty was infantry would stay for another month of even more intense infantry training. Those Marines going to Vietnam, regardless of specialty, would come back to Camp Onofre for yet another month of "Staging" after that. They would brush up their infantry skills and prepare in the best way they could for Vietnam. But as Roger Maier, one of my Lodi high school classmates said after his tour in Vietnam with the Army in 1971, "You can't prepare for that!"

Artillery School, Camp Delmar
My first specialty was artillery. When I got back home, I would be a member of the 4th 105 Howitzer Battery. It was a fiercely proud reserve unit made up of Vietnam draft dodgers that chose six years of reserve duty over two years of active duty with a likely Vietnam tour. I was not a Vietnam draft dodger, and I wasn't sure that I wanted to go back to this unit. However, I promised Mom and Dad that I wouldn't take the two year route, so that pretty much put me in that crowd.

I packed my sea bag and waited for the plain green bus to meet us at the bottom of the terraced Quonset huts that had been home for the past month. Now I would go to another place in Camp Pendleton, called Camp Delmar, for training with the 105mm howitzer.

It was a place for many specialty schools back then, including Navy Corpsman qualification. I took pride in learning artillery. To get a projectile out of a steel tube and move it to a place up to seven miles away, within a few meters of where it was needed, presented a learning challenge to me. I'll always remember the quote on my manual, "Artillery lends dignity to what otherwise would be a brutal brawl."

Going Back Home
My active duty was over, and I was on my way home to Lodi. Along the way, military pay had been increased over 100%! I didn't know what to do with all the money! The $33 every two weeks was already great. Now it went to $66! I saved the extra money and paid off my '66 Caprice that I bought from my Aunt and Uncle Janice and Lonnie Pease.

As was required in those days, I traveled in uniform. I wore the tropical uniform, which would be discontinued in the mid seventies in favor of the current green trousers. My flight was late in the evening. I anxiously passed the long hours at the LA International Airport shining the bill on my frame cap. A young girl from India came up and gave me a hand-crafted neck piece. Her mother smiled as she came up to me, and I could see they were very sincere. It is still a pleasant memory for me, as by that time I had already felt the scorn and furrowed brows of most Americans. They were so tired of a war they never felt was justified, necessary, or even legal. I often wondered if the neck piece that young girl gave me brought me luck through the many years of Marine Corps service that unknowingly lay ahead.

When I got to Chicago after flying all night, I changed into a set of dress blues that I bought for $35. Somewhere in doing so I lost my plane ticket! Thank goodness the airline personnel put me at ease and printed another one.

I arrived to a very proud and happy family and was now ready for college. I was signed up and ready to start a two year course in computer programming at Madison Area Technical College (MATC). But, being home didn't last long.

Before school started in the fall, however, I would embark on one more mission. It was an intense mission, but I did get back in time to start school. We had conducted an amphibious landing and day-after-day of shoot and move artillery tactics utilizing all 24 hours of every day. Once again, I was amazed at how much could be done so far away in such a short time!! I would often think back on this one!

4th 105 Howitzer Battery and School

As expected, my duty with the 4th 105 Howitzer Battery was filled with mixed emotions. I was home, and that was good. However I took great pride in my Marine Corps training and felt good about doing my part supporting my fellow Marines still in Vietnam. I loved being a Marine! Most members of the unit had no particular pride in being Marines, and the benefits of avoiding two years of active duty were now lost. Having to attend drill weekends had by now become very inconvenient. Our friends were going to weddings, hunting, fishing, and doing much more interesting things than taking 105 howitzers to the field and shooting them. My fellow Marines were sloppy in their uniforms and in their attitudes. I was having problems feeling any pride to serve in that unit. It was the only time in Marine Corps history where reservists were allowed to wear wigs! That didn't last long and was fixed with President Reagan's presidency.

School and Marriage

My life was brightened by school and home life. My classmates at MATC would become lifetime friends. One of them, Gary Wipperfurth, was caught in the lottery and had to quit school to attend Air Force basic training. He joined the Air Guard to avoid two years of active duty. He missed the second year of school, but we have remained friends and still see each other regularly. Ron Guenther and Jon Schumann graduated with me and also have remained close friends for over 40 years. Life was good other than duty in the reserves when Vietnam was still raging, although with much less press coverage.

My relationship with my girlfriend Judy was going well after a rough start upon my return and we became engaged. As I needed to make more money, I had to work a summer job in the local canning factory in addition to helping in my parent's farm machinery repair business. To satisfy Judy's parents, who clearly stated there would be no marriage in their eyes if I stayed Presbyterian, I took lessons in the Catholic faith. My parents had no problem with that and said it was more important to be focused on what keeps us together than to quibble about religion. I took special note of that! Another of life's lessons! Who was really closer to God?

We were married on 14 October, 1972 in Lodi, Wisconsin. Our wedding gift from my classmates was wrapped in a computer core dump, which only a true computer programmer of the era could appreciate. It was what you got when your program didn't work and was printed in hexadecimal. Better friends are hard to find! We honeymooned in the new Disney World in Orlando during spring break. We took $500 and put $300 back in the bank when we got back. We were young, but we were very frugal.

The second year of school went quickly. We were a young couple in love and back in the days it seemed it was the role of the wife to please the husband. My waist line quickly expanded! We only had one car and Judy had to use it for work, so I hitchhiked in the cold of winter. I worked at Sears to help with groceries and expenses. One day while waiting for the bus on a cold January day, I noticed the newspapers showing pictures of Vietnam Prisoners of War being released. It was 27 January, 1973 and Vietnam was over for the United States! It was a date I would remember forever. What I couldn't have known was that it wasn't quite truly over for the United States and I would be in Okinawa in 1975 when South Vietnam fell to the North.

The Tug of War Begins

Graduation came in May, 1973. Another big day in my life! I was a Marine, and now I was a computer programmer! It was the best of both worlds! But, my Marine Corps experience with the Madison reserve unit wasn't what I wanted. Should I take a civilian job, or should I go back to active duty? Four more years of reserve drill weekends had become even more unappealing to me. Now with Vietnam over, at least for the United States, perhaps I could get my specialty changed to COBOL (Common Business Oriented Language) Programming and get my weekends off! At least sometimes...

In the last days leading up to graduation, I was doing a lot of soul searching. One night while enjoying some beer in our apartment, my friend Ron Guenther said to me, "So when are we going?" I had pretty much decided to apply for a commission and return to active duty, and now Ron was ready to join me!

The job situation in Madison was not great, and I was convinced that I needed to get out of the reserves. In hopes of getting a systems officer specialty, I applied for a ground commission and Ron applied for commission as a fixed wing, fast mover (jet) pilot. I was shocked when Ron was accepted and I wasn't! With the end of Vietnam, the ground forces were drawing down, but the air side still needed pilots.

By now I was determined. I wanted to get back to active duty and pursue a new career there, at least for a few years to get some experience. Judy and I discussed it over a pizza in a restaurant near our apartment, and it became our fateful plan. I worked with the recruiters and was on my way back. On the day I went to Milwaukee to process, the paperwork was fouled up. I was livid, as I was still working at Sears and lost a day's wage! When the recruiters said they would do whatever they needed to do to get me back, I said, "Okay, then come re-enlist me at Sears!" They did it! The next day, I was re-enlisted with Judy by my side and a crowd of on-looking shoppers and lots of pictures. For better or worse, off we went!

I was once again an active duty Marine. It felt good after all the anxiety of deciding. Our parents were settled with it, although we would all miss each other. Plans were made for my parents to visit, and off we went. Judy's parents weren't the traveling type, so letters and phone calls were the plan for them.

It took a couple of months to get my orders, and I worked with the local recruiters until they came in June. I was able to request my duty station, and chose the Marine Corps Recruit Depot in San Diego. There would have to be a three month COBOL programming school in Quantico, Virginia first.

Back at Rocky Point
The tug of war between love of family and sense of duty would last for forty years. It was just getting a good start in my mental journey. As I settled into my three mile run, the familiar Tampa scenery that I loved made it easy to drift back to the past...

Chapter Three
The Active Duty Years: 1973-80
San Diego, Okinawa, Camp LeJeune

A New Direction

The three month Marine Corps computer school went well. I finished second in the class, which worked out good for the number one student. I was already a Corporal and couldn't be promoted, whereas the number one guy was a Lance Corporal and ended up with a promotion. He was a good guy whose promotion was well-deserved. We would serve together several years later. Judy and I were now ready to start our new life in San Diego!

Duty, Love, and Heartbreak in San Diego

We got to San Diego no worse for the wear. We found a place we liked in Pacific Beach and had to find some help to unload the truck. The apartment manager suggested offering the Mexican car wash workers around the corner a few bucks. It worked great! They were happy for the pay, and the job was done quickly.

We loved the apartment, and we loved San Diego. It is such a beautiful city, of which I still never tire of visiting. I was soon promoted to Sergeant and Judy found work. We were enjoying life! But it was short lived. I would soon receive orders for Okinawa to satisfy my overseas control date requirement.

Okinawa

The Tiger Airlines flight was nineteen hours and stopped at Anchorage, Alaska for refueling. Tiger Airlines was the airlines for many of the troops headed for Vietnam. My memory of the flight includes a Navy Corpsman that taught me how to play chess on his miniature board. Apparently I knew more about chess than he thought because he became very upset when I kept beating him! If only I could remember my ingenious moves!

We finally landed in Kadena Air Base in the southern part of the island of Okinawa and were then transported to Camp Butler in the central part of the island. The entire island was sixty-five miles north to south and only an average of five miles wide, with the exception of the Motobu peninsula, which was fifteen miles wide. I was pleasantly surprised at all the vegetation after picturing "The Rock" in my mind for so long! This wouldn't be so bad after all! I just missed my bride.

The admin office opened early and got us on the way. It was then that I would meet another Mike from Random Lake, Wisconsin. He was Sergeant Mike Sauter. The two of us would be roommates and stay in touch for many years. We would become known as the "Double Mikes" to the hostesses of Kitamae, the village outside of Camp Foster.

During my Okinawa tour, several members of my III Force Automated Services Center (FASC) unit ended up jumping on 4th Marine Regiments trucks that were frantically trying to gather all their Marines to get them to their ships or aircraft in order to shuttle them the short distance to Saigon to support Operation Eagle Pull, the evacuation of Americans and allies from Saigon. North Vietnam was moving south much faster than predicted, and the 4th Marines were needed immediately instead of the anticipated two or three weeks.

The FASC Marines that joined them were met by very stern reprimands upon their return. The fear of lost stripes was looming over them, but the admonishment was limited to words such as "good initiative, poor judgment." I would have those words repeated to me several more times before the end of my career…

Half way through the tour, Judy came over for a month long visit. The timing was perfect because I had been asked to watch the home of the local American school principal who was taking a thirty-day leave. We had a beautiful home in Awase overlooking the beautiful coast, and we had the use of the family Mustang. It was a huge car for Okinawa, but it was great to have! We fit in a ten-day tour of Taiwan and Hong Kong, which remains a favorite memory. I always hoped to go back there someday.

I was disheartened at the overwhelming distaste the Japanese held for Americans after dropping the bombs in Hiroshima and Nagasaki in World War II. The bombs were terrible, and killed in the vicinity of 250,000 civilians. What seemed to be forgotten is that the Japanese killed between eight and ten million Chinese prior to that in their Imperialistic thrusts leading up to World War II.

It was a long thirteen month tour. I had a two man room outside of the squad bay where the more junior Marines stayed in bunks and wall lockers. I remember walking through the squad bay in between paydays. There would be dead silence with all the young Marines lying in their racks and passing the lonely hours. One time sticks out in my mind in particular. The eerie silence was there as always, but someone was playing Simon and Garfunkel's Sounds of Silence. It seemed so perfect for the mood. I think of that day to this day every time I hear that song!

The Freedom Bird and Home

Our long awaited Freedom Bird finally came to get us. Our flight took us through Yokosuka, Japan and on to LA International Airport. As was the case in those days, we all had to fly in our dress green uniforms. As was still the custom in 1975, military members in uniforms were treated as the enemy by the great American civilian establishment. Garbage was thrown and someone would yell "baby killers" from the crowd.

I arrived home to the warmth and love of a close family. After more leave, Judy and I once again packed up the apartment and were on the road with great trepidation of what Camp Lejeune would be like. We would have loved to return to the San Diego duty we both loved, but it was Marine Corps policy to make the shortest, least expensive moves between duty stations.

Camp Lejeune and Parenthood

Judy and I made the drive to Jacksonville, North Carolina and Camp LeJeune. We weren't impressed upon our arrival. Jacksonville was not an impressive city, and we were already missing San Diego and home in Wisconsin. It was truly in the backwoods of North Carolina, but at least it was close to the coast. We picked out a colonial style apartment and settled in for what we saw as a long year and a half, to finish our four-year commitment.

Another Hitch

Despite the backwards nature of Jacksonville, Judy and I decided it was a good place to stay and start a family. Camp Lejeune had always been known as the married man's heaven, and single man's hell. We knew if I re-enlisted after my overseas tour, we would be left alone for at least three years. By now, that seemed like an eternity! And there was a bonus! It was enough for a new Sears washer and dryer! I called it Judy's "pregnancy bonus package." Not the kind of bonus new parents look for, but on our income, we were very happy!

It was a special re-enlistment ceremony. My sister Judy was visiting from Wisconsin. She and my wife were welcomed by all my office Marines. Brigadier General John Phillips did the re-enlistment ceremony and swore me in for another three years. Another decision made, another life plan laid out.

A Family Begins

Kurt was born on 3 January, 1978. I made a mental note to kick his ass at age 18. His actual due date was up to six weeks later. If he was going to come that early, he could have just as well come when the tax credit would have been helpful! Somehow that mental note was lost in sure awe and pride. I swelled with more love than I knew could humanly exist! The sight of Kurt in the incubator, shortly after his pre-mature birth, will be in my memory forever. I absently clutched the pillow intended for an extended labor stay and couldn't take my eyes off the little guy!

Back to School

My decision to pursue a bachelor degree was a big deal. College education was rare in my family. My parents were brought up under very austere conditions during the depression. College planning just never made the list when they made priority decisions in child rearing. Being truly impressed with Marine Corps leaders in my early years I knew the importance and value of good leaders. But, to be an officer, you had to be a college graduate.

My Pepperdine courses were finished in fourteen months and I attended the first graduating class at Pepperdine's new Malibu campus. The Marine Corps flew me out and back on orders. Judy and Kurt had to stay back as we just didn't have the money. That was a huge disappointment, and Judy took it in the best light she could, but it hurt a lot.

A Surprise Promotion

My duty at II FASC was going well. Judy and Kurt had made friends in our Tanglewood neighborhood and time passed quickly. I was surprised to get a call from Master Sergeant Rix at Headquarters Marine Corps (HQMC) congratulating me on my selection to Gunnery Sergeant! I worked with him in Okinawa and Camp Lejeune before he got orders to Headquarters Marine Corps (HQMC). My memory of him was powerful as he had pull up bars over his desk. You had to do pull ups before you could talk to him. I thought the call was a joke and didn't appreciate it. That year, 1979, was not good for promotion in my specialty. Normally, there would be up to 150 or 200 Staff Sergeants selected for promotion to Gunnery Sergeant. But, in 1979, there would only be three, courtesy of the Carter administration! I completely gave up any hope.

Turned out it was not a joke, as I was one of the three selected…must have been the Pepperdine degree! I was very junior on the list and it would be a good year before my number would come up for the actual promotion. Even so, it was a still a great feeling! Making Gunnery Sergeant, E-7 in the Marine Corps, in those days in less than ten years was rare!

Going Back Home for Good

We stuck to our plans to return home and raise our family there. We returned to Wisconsin in February, 1980. Another decision made, more plans set. The family back home was excited to have everyone in one place again.

Judy and I eventually settled in Sauk City, twelve miles from Lodi. We raised Kurt and our soon to arrive daughter, Kristin there. Both would choose to stay in the Sauk Prairie area for years to come, to marry and raise their own families. With so many life decisions to make and so little time, we could always feel good about this one. I still love driving through Lodi!

Leaving the Seventies

The eighties were looking good for us, but the world around us was by no means calm. The fight against communism brewing before World War II was only put on hold during it. Nazism and Japanese Imperialism were beaten, but many parts of the Far East were still up for grabs as to what form of society and government they would choose. Ho Chi' Minh in Viet Nam felt communism was right for his country. Not all Vietnamese agreed, and the ultimate results were history.

When allies of WWII took up their stations for the new battle as the war ended, France went to Vietnam and the UK went to Malaya to stem the renewed growth of communism in the Far East. When France pulled out of Vietnam in desperation, the US understood the necessity to maintain a global free market and took up where they left off. The British adapted successfully to guerilla warfare in Malaya and achieved support from the populace. As such, they were also successful in integrating them into the global political and economic community.

The US did not adapt as well to guerilla warfare. The monolithic approach and big army strategies weren't working in the jungles. The continual build up of more force with less and less success lost the public's support until we pulled out entirely for political reasons. The Vietnam War was over for the US by the mid-seventies with over 58,000 dead, but the killing had just begun.

Led by Pol Pot from 1975-1979, the Khmer Rouge Cambodia killed somewhere between 1.7 - 2.5 million citizens. They killed anyone with ties to the previous government or other governments, professionals, and intellectuals. US efforts weren't sufficient to deter Pol Pot's killing fields in 1975. His form of brutal, totalitarian dictatorship isolated his country politically and economically.

The US pullout took victory away from Vietnam Veterans at a time when we were winning. Their war was much more warranted, and they had much more success, than people will ever know. While Vietnam won the ability to form their communist government because we pulled out, their people remained impoverished under their political and economic isolation. It wouldn't become reintegrated into the world economy until 1986, when they finally realized economic and political reforms were necessary to survive. The price of democracy and free global markets is high, but seldom attached to why we need to fight to keep them.

It would take over thirty five years, but I would take great pleasure to hear our citizens thank service men and women for our service, including Vietnam Veterans. If we would have finished the Vietnam War in earnest, the world would have benefited economically from Vietnam's participation ten years earlier, and maybe millions of Cambodians would still be alive.

As the eighties approached, I loved home, I loved Judy, I loved watching Kurt grow, but I knew deep down inside the peace was only temporary. I was a Marine, and a Marine's business is war. I'd maintain my affiliation with the Marine Corps as a reservist until the dreaded business of war returned as I knew it would.

Back to the Present and Rocky Point

My Vietnam era memories snapped me back to the present. I wasn't ready to stuff all this inside and just let it go. It was killing me. I still loved being a Marine, and I knew the world wasn't ready to settle down even, if I was ready to just be a loving husband, father, and son. It was still early in my three mile run and I again took note of the bay and surrounding beautiful Tampa Bay. When will it all be enough, and when can I just enjoy this beautiful world? My memories persisted.

Chapter Four
The Reserve Years: 1980-2001
Sauk City, Wisconsin

Home, Work, and the Reserves

The eighties had arrived. My love for all my family was stronger than ever. I would enjoy the continued company of good friends. They were there for every important event in my life, military and civilian, and the fun and laughs we had through the years were what life is all about.

I wanted to pursue my civilian dreams like every other red-blooded American, and Rayovac was a good company and employer. My job was very enjoyable, and I rose quickly in the ranks. Nothing was more important to me than raising my children in the same kind of loving environment that I grew up in, but I wanted to maintain my association with the Marine Corps too. The world would someday need a force in readiness. Little did I know how right this logic would be twenty-one years later when the events of 11 September, 2001 would impact all of our lives.

Being in the National Guard or Reserves was not popular in the early eighties, and was certainly not well understood. Those that chose duty as a guard or reservist had to be intrinsically motivated by a desire to serve or earn college benefits. The desire to enlist at all had to come from within, as the country was moving away from Vietnam and didn't see any form of a draft in the future. I imagined several different ways the world situation was heading for conflict, and so did the nation's leaders. President Reagan started rebuilding the military that had been nearly gutted to the point of ineffectiveness by the previous administration. Every Marine, every soldier, every sailor, every airman, and every Coast Guardsman could feel the re-energizing surge.

For now, I was content to make a good start of our new home and civilian career. Judy and I settled on a house in Sauk City after an exhaustive search for affordable homes nearer to Madison. My gross salary went up $500 per month, but after taxes, it amounted to $90 per month, as much of my military pay wasn't taxable. Judy didn't have steady income, and her expenses for selling her calligraphy far outweighed the cost. Our house payment went from $250 per month to $600. It wasn't like the change to civilian life was a get rich quick scheme, and I took a part time job at the local Ace Hardware to make up the difference.

Another Miracle

After a year to adjust to the changes, Judy, Kurt, and I welcomed Kristin to our world. Like her big brother, she was in a much bigger hurry to join us than anybody realized. It was way too early, but Judy knew it was time. We drove the few blocks to the Sauk Prairie Hospital with much less fanfare than we did for Kurt back in North Carolina. My tires stayed intact. Experience was the key!

What looked like hours of labor after checking in to the hospital suddenly erupted into an urgent recall for the doctor who had gone on his calls and a much harried trip to the delivery room! Dr. John McAuliffe got there just in time to have his shirt literally torn off by one nurse as another put his gown over his already outstretched arms. Kristin was in those same arms moments later. Talk about teamwork!

When I saw Kristin's plentiful red hair and her fine, beautiful facial features, I saw beauty in a way I never dreamed possible. She looked so grown up for her age. Her tiny lips were so perfect, and she looked like she'd waited a long time for this moment. She had a mind of her own then, and has had it ever since. I was so proud! No greater love can there be than parent's love for their newborn children! It is almost as if an unspoken connection, that never goes away, was made then and there.

Judy and I didn't know what the sex of our baby would be. In those days, only special circumstances, sufficient to risk the use of technologies of the day, could be used. To have a boy and now a girl, we were beside ourselves! Judy was truly happy, which was reflected in her tears, as we shared the most special moment any mother and father can share.

Balancing Civilian and Marine Corps Life

I was feeling whole. At Rayovac, I wore a three-piece suit, and once a month or more got back into my camouflaged utilities and trained as an infantryman. I had been selected to the rank of Gunnery Sergeant while still on active duty, but had to wait until my number came up to receive my actual promotion. Since I was one of only three selected in my specialty, and was very low on the list, it would take nearly a year to receive. Between that and the fact that I had been away from the infantry for so long, it was decided to make me the Company Gunnery Sergeant (a billet that required primarily strong leadership ability). The platoon sergeants and officers would bring the infantry skills necessary to operate effectively as a unit. In late 1980, I received my promotion to Gunnery Sergeant.

Never giving up on my dreams to become a Marine officer, I applied for an appointment to the Warrant Officer ranks and was promoted Warrant Officer 1 in October, 1981 in the specialty of 4010 Data Systems Officer. Because I was a reservist serving in an infantry company, however, I actually was serving as an infantry officer.

My years as an infantry officer remain as my proudest Marine Corps years. When I hear the Marine Corps Hymn I feel a special, deep-down pride when they sing "every clime and place." All infantry Marines can truly claim they have been to every clime and place as our hymn proclaims! Woe be it to anyone who looked down their nose at an infantryman from any service in my presence!

The Citizen Marines

Delta Company Marines were civilians all but forty-eight days a year. Yet we endured the searing desert heat and terrain in places like Camp Pendleton, Twentynine Palms, and Iraq. We sweat under the unrelenting summer humidity, chiggers, fleas, and sweltering heat of Camp Lejeune and the deep woods and hills of Fort McCoy and Fort Riley. We climbed the steep, jagged cliffs of Marine Corps Mountain Training Center in Bridgeport, California in both summer and winter conditions. We used cross country skis and snowshoes in freezing temperatures to traverse the hills, pastures, and slopes of Fort McCoy, Bridgeport, and Narvik, Norway. We lived aboard ships like the USS Iwo Jima and USS Saipan before conducting major amphibious landing operations. We became proficient in urban warfare, and we used every available second, of every available minute, during our weekend drills honing infantry skills while balancing our civilian lives.

We were challenged to the toughest tests the Marine Corps requires of every infantry battalion. We became the first reserve battalion to pass the Marine Corps Combat Readiness Evaluation System (MCCRES). Lieutenant Colonel Braun, the battalion commander at the time, and I would meet briefly over twenty years later as I departed an aircraft. He was the captain greeting the departing passengers. Lieutenant Colonel Braun was a pilot in both the Marine Corps and civilian world. He took on the infantry assignment to broaden his Marine Corps skills and made history doing it. Just another example of a great Citizen Marine!

I could have quit anytime. I never saw reserve retirement as anything that would amount to enough to cover the commitment it was taking. What started as a plan to get my military service out of the way, and over with quickly, had wormed its way into my heart and soul! When I was tired, some other Marine who should be more tired, kept going. When I hated to walk into the locker room in my suit with my seabag to change for yet another drill weekend, and be away from Judy, Kurt and Kristin, somebody like Staff Sergeant Brenton would come up from behind and nudge me out of the way so he could get to his locker and get going. If he could do it, I could do it!

Leaving Delta Company

Reserve officers were allowed to serve two years and you had to give up your billet to make room for any incoming officer. This was how the Marine Corps maintained a force in readiness. I had been in the unit for nearly nine years when some young Captain wanted to join. The new Delta Company commander had to decide between one of the three Warrant Officers to make room for the Captain.

It was a gut-wrenching event. The new company commander knew that I and the other Warrant Officers had been the glue that kept the company going while regular officers came and went. But he also knew he couldn't have too many officers. We knew from experience that if he waited a month or two, he wouldn't be over strength in officer numbers. Once the incoming regular officers saw the op tempo of the unit, it was more than they wanted in their lives and they would drop out. But he was new and felt compelled to make a decision and make his mark.

I was resentful, but felt confident as I knew I could find something. I volunteered to leave to make the new commander's life easier. I told him he could not afford to lose Dave Snyder who was truly a cornerstone of the rifle company. After one phone call, I had an assignment the next day in Marine Air Control Group 48 (MACG-48) at Naval Air Station, Glenview, Illinois.

Marine Air Control Group 48, NAS Glenview
As I drove to Chicago the next day to join my new unit, I was full of anticipation. I had been in the Marine Corps for over seventeen years at this point, close enough to be concerned about making the twenty-year mark, which would make me eligible for a reserve retirement pension at age sixty. Even more so, I wondered if the reserve air wing would live up to my expectations as a ground Marine. Would I feel like I did in the Madison unit in the early seventies if the Marines of my new unit didn't take pride in their service?

The answer became obvious upon arrival in the office spaces of the large hangar of MACG-48. The Marines looked sharp and were crisp in their actions. I could be happy here! I wasn't looking forward to the monthly drive to Chicago, but I felt good in many ways. It was a fresh start! Not that I really needed one, but it was coming someday one way or the other. Very few reservists stayed in the same unit as long as me and my fellow Warrant Officers in Madison. It was good to know that keeping my Marine career going was an option for me.

I would spend over six years with MWCS-48. The duty was demanding, and when looking back on my records, there were many months when I spent two or three weekends in Glenview and was lucky to spend one or two of them at home! I would become close with a new set of officers. One of them, Major Bill Hamerstadt and I would end up serving together for many years and would become good friends.

Brief Call to Duty
After a couple of years acclimating to MWCS-48, Saddam Hussein crossed into Kuwait and started the Gulf War. My old unit, 2nd

Battalion, 24th Marines, was called to active duty and served in first line combat roles in Operation Desert Storm in Saudi Arabia. My new unit, MWCS-48 was organized into two groups. Half would be activated to support units on the East Coast and Norway for a NATO training mission led by Major Bill Hamerstadt. I would be part of the other half of the squadron that would be sent to California to join a newly created Marine Expeditionary Force, whose duty was to provide support to a temporary Naval Amphibious Group that had been formed as a contingency if Desert Storm escalated. Our commander was Colonel Craig Hullinger, who would also become a good friend in the future.

I left Judy and the kids and my job at Rayovac to be on the advance planning team. Judy was not happy with my decision to stay involved in the service, as it would mean being away from home with Kurt and Kristin at such young ages. Judy had been becoming more and more restless as Kurt and Kristin grew. She was struggling with her role and what she wanted in life. She was now studying marketing and would join the corporate work world. The situation wasn't good, and her demeanor was changing. I realized this, but was committed to both the family and to my Marine Corps responsibilities. Duty called and I had to go.

The orders wouldn't come, and I didn't have to leave Glenview. The Gulf War ended so quickly that all other plans for mobilizing reserves were reviewed and cancelled within a week. I was kept on active duty to help bring the other half of the squadron home after their mobilization, and was home in less than two months.

Back Home with Change in the Air
I returned to my Rayovac job and an increasingly restless wife. It was getting more difficult to maintain a good balance. I asked Judy if my Marine Corps duty was the reason for her very obvious unrest. She said that wasn't it. Even so, I sensed that wasn't the extent of it...something was very wrong.

Empty House and a Note
Things soon came to a head with Judy. Our marriage clearly needed work, but I couldn't stand the thought of giving up. We had come so far together! Kurt was fifteen and Kristin was twelve, and I couldn't

stand the thought of a divorce. On the way home from a drill weekend in Chicago in 1992, my heart was heavy. I knew our relationship was close to over, even if she said the Marine Corps wasn't the problem. I had come to peace with calling it a day. By then I had twenty-four years of service and had done my part. Knowing that I had come as far as I could was somewhat satisfying. I stopped at the Wisconsin/Illinois border rest stop to focus my thoughts. It was settled. I would go home and tell Judy I was quitting the Corps.

There was an eerie early evening sky and Jim Croce was playing "Lover's Cross" on the car radio as I drove the rest of the way home to Sauk City. There was a strange feeling from all this, but I was resolute in my decision. I arrived home early that July Sunday evening only to find it empty. There was only a very short note telling me where the divorce papers could be picked up. My emotions ran amuck. It was three months short of twenty years for us!

It had become obvious she didn't know what she wanted in life, but it was equally obvious I was the reason she couldn't find it. I was overwhelmed by conflicting emotions of confusion, fear, and exhilaration. The fear of losing everything important to me was horrifying, but thoughts of relief and a chance to rebuild without the daily drama and intensity that had become the norm kept breaking through.

I thought Judy was sincere saying that it wasn't the Marine Corps causing her emptiness and restlessness. I wanted more than anything for her to come back, but she never looked back. We started yet another path, this time separately. After a year of sharing time with Kurt and Kristin between her apartment in Madison and our home in Sauk, she would move back to Sauk. They finished their high school years sharing time between our places just a few blocks apart.

Moving On

I set a new course for myself. I committed to keeping the house near the kids, deal with the unpleasant changes at Rayovac, and ended up staying in the reserves. The months passed and I was healing, but I didn't want to give up on getting Judy back. I had read M. Scott Peck's "Road Less Traveled," and thought if I would invite her to a seminar about it that was coming to Madison, maybe it would somehow interest her in coming back. My hopes were dashed when she came with a girl friend, both hoping to meet interesting guys there. My disappointment was immediately softened when I met Terri that night.

I loved the book and knew and liked the speaker, and signed up well in advance. I registered early and went into the Sheraton's bar to have some appetizers. It was the divorced guys' eating plan. I left my seminar books at the bar and went to forage for food at the Hors D 'Oeuvres bar. Upon my return, I was delighted to see a beautiful blond woman, with a set of seminar books next to mine! The whole bar was empty. She had to want to meet me! She denies this yet today...

I introduced myself, and we chatted about small stuff. I was intrigued by Terri from that moment. It was as if I could sense the depth of her soul through her eyes. It must be divine intervention! I signed up weeks earlier, but she signed up at the last minute. This had to be a plan! Two good, lonely people pining away in Wisconsin. That had to be a chip shot for a loving God! Judy and her friend left empty handed that night, but I thought I may have just found my new soul mate!

We decided to sit together at the seminar, and the rest is history. Our friendship and love grew as the months passed. Her husband had left her a year earlier, so both of us had divorces in process. Within a year, both divorces were final and Terri and I embarked on our life's journey. We promised each other that we would support each other's goals and allow each to pursue them as necessary. Little did we know how prophetic it would be that we met at a seminar which was basically about how to be "together separately."

Judy would go on to meet and marry Vince several years later. Both Vince and Terri would be accepted warmly by our family and we would all enjoy family birthdays, ball games, and weddings as Kurt's and Kristin's families grew.

Things were going well with Kurt and Kristin. Judy's home was nearby and they found it easy to go back and forth on agreed upon schedules. Terri and I continued to grow, learn and love together. I continued my Marine Corps duties with MWCS-48 at Naval Air Station Glenview, but Rayovac was getting harder.

It was becoming clear there wasn't room for two directors and a vice president in the information systems department. I received a very enticing offer from a consulting company I frequently dealt with, although it would mean living in Chicago. I would keep my house and come home on weekends to see the kids, but I would be gone all week.

They say all experience is good, but some of it is painful. It turned out to be one of the hardest years of my life. Ironically, even though I was now closer to my Marine Corps reserve unit and had decided to stay, the demands of the new job made it impossible. I left MWCS-48 and my twenty-four year Marine Corps career came to an end. This killed me because I really loved being part of it, especially since my unit was right in Chicago, and it would no longer require me to drive back and forth from Madison, like I did for so many years.

Terri knew I was hurting. One night as I lay in my Chicago apartment, she called while she was in Washington, DC for an American Diabetes Association conference. She had visited the Marine Corps Monument that day, and was inspired by the inscription that reads "Uncommon Valor Was a Common Virtue." It was a quote from Admiral Nimitz watching a Marine landing in WWII. She called me just to say "…You'll always be a full-fledged Marine to me." It touched me deeply, and I knew through my tears that I had a very special friend.

After two exhausting large scale projects in Kansas City and Houston, I could clearly see the business model of the new Comdisco division was not going to work. My love for Terri back in Madison flourished, and I asked for her hand in marriage at the Firehouse Restaurant in Prairie du Sac in 1995. We were engaged and planned to marry in May, 1996.

Home Again, Re-Marriage and Back to the Corps
Being in contact with several Madison information technology consulting firms, I was very confident in landing something back in Madison. I readily accepted an offer from the Compuware Corporation in Madison that January. The second job change in a year rattled my confidence. I asked Terri for an extension on the marriage date. The request was swiftly and soundly denied! She wasn't going to let this one get away! My love and admiration grew deeper.

Terri and I were married on 11 May, 1996 after three years of mutual love and friendship. We ended up with a full scale Wisconsin wedding, even though it was the second one for us both. Before we walked down the aisle, she read the look of apprehension on my face. She did the only reasonable thing in such circumstances and snorted at me! Terri! Snorting!! All my questions, all my doubt and all my problems went away instantly and we walked into what was to become one hell of a journey together. Our reception was at the Dorf Haus in Roxbury and it was a very joyous day!

Several of my old Delta Company Marines came to the ceremony in their dress blues and performed the traditional welcome ceremony for Marine wives. They lined up in front of the Dorf Haus in Roxbury for the reception and drew their swords. On command from my old platoon sergeant, Harold Carry (who once taught me the ropes of leading an infantry platoon and was now a First Sergeant), they sharply created the hall of swords guiding the bride and groom to the reception hall. As Terri reached the end of the hall of swords, First Sergeant Carry performed the traditional formal welcome for all new Marine wives by swatting her rear end with his sword and exclaiming, "Welcome to the Corps Wench!" Terri was highly honored! I'm pretty sure…

At the Dorf Haus, we had the traditional cake cutting ceremony. Terri insisted on using my Marine Corps Mameluke sword for the cutting! It is the sword officers wear today dating back to the Barbary Wars. Marine Lieutenant Presley O'Bannon was awarded the sword for bravery during the Tripoli campaign of the First Barbary War, giving the Marines' Hymn its line "to the shores of Tripoli." I was pleasantly surprised, and knew once again I had a true soul mate. The Mameluke sword is also used to cut cakes in the traditional Marine Corps Birthday ceremony, but I hadn't been the oldest or youngest Marine, so I was inexperienced in the fine art of Marine Corps cake cutting. She guided me through it all.

We honeymooned in Hawaii. I had never been there, and didn't really care about going, but Terri had been there and loved it. Enough said. We had a beautiful honeymoon and enjoyed the tours. On Oahu, the tour bus took us past the Kaneohe Marine Corps Base and I felt a sharp pang. I missed my Marine Corps duty. As fate would have it, a letter came soon after our honeymoon looking for reserve Marines who would be interested in reserve duty at the Marine Forces Pacific Command (MARFORPAC) headquarters at Camp Smith, Hawaii.

Terri had already read it, and when I looked up after reading it, she was smiling. Enough said again! After six months of meetings in Chicago, I was among the first group of seventy Marines selected. My Marine Corps career was back full swing!

Marine Forces Pacific Command

I was assigned as the Assistant Director of the Systems Integration Hub (SIH) for MARFORPAC. I would be an Individual Mobilization Augmentee (IMA) reservist. Instead of a weekend a month and two weeks a year, I was actually integrated into the chain of command and would agree on duty schedules with my active duty counterparts. My role as a reservist was to become familiar with the information technology support operations for the command and be prepared to assume the directorship should the active duty director be required to deploy.

I would travel to Oahu two or three times a year and Terri would come at least once a year. Terri understood my duties at MARFORPAC had to take priority. Not one to whimper, she would make many friends on her own and explore other islands while I worked at Camp Smith. We would still have plenty of time together in Waikiki in my off hours. She would eventually be my tour guide after my Marine Corps retirement. Kauai would be her favorite, so it was on the mandatory list of things to do and places to see.

As things in life happen, the Compuware job was getting stale after five years. My boss Dave was gone, and the business was changing. I had a nice office that I had decorated with Hawaiian art and Samurai swords. I found out much later that we weren't supposed to have swords in our office, but nobody had the nerve to tell me. Good! I liked them! Dave would always come in to select one when he wanted to kill himself. He was there a lot and we enjoyed good humor together! They wanted me to get an assignment and move out of the office, so I finally packed up my office, moved out, and found a permanent assignment with IBM. Not exactly what they had in mind, but it was best.

Another New Job and 9/11

I was ready for the next step in consulting, and thought IBM had a better chance of offering it. The ironic part is that my first day with

IBM was the first day of my working experience that I didn't wear a suit! IBM was notorious for formality with its employees, but this assignment was with the State of Wisconsin, and they didn't like consultants making them look bad in their casual wear. I wore better clothes when hauling manure than some of those people wore to work! I settled on casual wear that still had some semblance of respect in the office.

On 11 September, 2001, I was at the meeting to go over a project's status. My boss's wife interrupted the meeting with several calls and increasing intensity from their home in Tennessee about the news she was watching. I knew the first plane that hit the twin towers was not an accident. I had by now read extensively of the Arab/Jewish struggle and the growing radical Muslim problems, which led me to further Middle East readings. I knew immediately this was a very significant event that would change America forever, and I wondered if my senior officers at MARFORPAC were putting the gears in motion for a recall of reserve officers. My question was answered within days.

I couldn't help but think back to my early school days and reading about the Crusades of the fifteenth and sixteenth centuries. Images stuck in my mind of massive armies clashing back and forth, sometimes with Arabs smashing Christian societies, and sometimes with Christians slaughtering Arab societies. Was that ever stupid! Glad we don't have that anymore! Or do we? Was this Islam's turn to attack Christianity in the see-saw battle that had been raging through the centuries?

The days of Islamic and Christian attacks and counter attacks with large armies and horses had been replaced with technology, mass communications, and infiltrated theological influence. We couldn't be beaten militarily on the field of battle, but we offered the opponents of our society every weapon necessary to fight us effectively, including our principles, our values, our press, and our political correctness. Our very strengths were our most vulnerable traits as a nation.

I left work that day and watched the news with the rest of America. Anxiety prevailed in the office, our cities, our state, and our nation. If this was war, and it was, how long would it be before the call came from MARFORPAC? They would be sending all the primary staff officers to Bahrain to support the US Central Command

(CENTCOM) to which our three star general also reported, and I would have to backfill. Terri and I spoke about the inevitable. Her love and support was absolute! She understood the "higher calling" of those who serve. She thought at that level herself and, as fate would have it, her turn would come years later. If she only knew then how it would impact our lives, she may have had more questions, but for the time being, she knew I would be called and was bracing.

Back to Rocky Point

My mind shifted back to my run in Tampa Bay. I had covered an entire half mile leg since I last drifted off! With all that happened in my life, it boggled my mind to think the ten years since 9/11 had just as much life packed in! As I plodded forward, I wondered if it would all finally settle down and I'd be home with Terri and my family for good, or if I'd be right back in the Middle East and away from home for yet another year. My thoughts drifted back to 2001 when the balloon went up for many of us that served on active duty, in the guard, or in the reserves...

Chapter Five
Call to Active Duty: Oct 2001-Nov 2002
De Forest, WI, US CENTCOM, MacDill AFB, Tampa, Fl

Another Call to Duty

Terri and I wouldn't have much time to prepare for the call to active duty to come. At the time of the 9/11 attacks, I had been in my reserve assignment with the Marine Forces Pacific Command (MARFORPAC) at Camp Smith, Hawaii for over five years. By 2001, I had gained a very good knowledge of the operations and had actually produced a manual to hand over to government and military inspectors that came around and to indoctrinate new arrivals. When the expected call came, I was ready and was confident I would be able to perform my duties successfully, as the active duty director had been deployed to Bahrain along with other key staff members of the command.

Both Terri and I had distinct memories of the call. It came from Lieutenant Colonel Ed Zelchak, the deputy director of MARFORPAC G6 (Systems). As soon as I hung up, I looked at Terri who had overheard the conversation. The reality was setting in for both of us. I was worried about how we would organize our finances to make do with less income. For Terri it was who was going to shovel the driveway in the winter!

As we stared at each other, I broke the silence by saying "I've got to sit down and make out a budget." After slinging her purse over her shoulder, Terri's first words were "I'm going to buy a new snow blower" and out she went! It paid off too. The winters of 2001 and 2008 were wicked! She would send a picture standing on a snow pile higher than the stop sign on our corner.

After a few days, we were settling into plans that would get us through the six months of involuntary call to active duty. The orders included a couple weeks of notice, and we were becoming more comfortable with it every day. By now Kurt had finished his degree in Radio, Film and TV at the University of Wisconsin, Oshkosh. Kristin was studying Human Resources Management at the University of Wisconsin, Whitewater.

Kurt decided on taking a shot at his own business. Since I had been spending most of the weeknights at the DeForest house with Terri since our marriage, I offered Kurt my home office to start his business. Kurt would do all the house maintenance to pay his way. This turned out to be a good arrangement for the next ten years! So, with the homeland secured, I made my plans to join now Colonel Bill Hamerstadt and his Marines in Camp Smith.

Change of Plans

The phone rang again. Again, it was Lieutenant Colonel Zelchak. This time he asked me if I could find a secure phone in Madison and get back to him as soon as possible. I found one at the local Air National Guard's F-16 Squadron's headquarters. It was only half duplex which meant you had to say "over" after you were done so the other end knew when they could talk. It also had poor quality, but I heard more than I wanted to. My heart sank and my confidence was shattered.

I was being diverted to Tampa to become the Deputy G6 (systems officer) at the Marine Central Command (MARCENT). The US Central Command (CENTCOM) was responsible for all military operations in the Middle East, and MARCENT was the Marine Corps component providing Marine Corps staff support to CENTCOM. Both were located at the MacDill Air Force Base in Tampa. This was the very place I was ordered to in 1980, but decided to leave active duty instead. Was this fate or what?

All the work to prepare to take over the directorship of the systems integration hub at MARFORPAC at Camp Smith was out the door. I was now being assigned to a totally new and unfamiliar command which happened to be in charge of the most active combat operations in the world! It is the way of the Corps!

Tampa and MARCENT

Terri dropped me off at the airport and went to her Luther Memorial church. The organist played "Seek ye first the Kingdom of God" and Terri broke down crying. We loved it at our Sauk City church, and she wasn't sure if I would ultimately end up in a combat zone somewhere. She already learned that Al-Qaeda and the Taliban were fond of slitting people's throats.

I arrived in Tampa on 22 October, 2001. My first concern was to find a place to stay. The base quarters were overflowing and we all had to find our own billeting. I had made reservations at the Hyatt in the Westshore area of Tampa on the Courtney Campbell Causeway. After being told not to commit to a six-month apartment, I decided to stay put at the Hyatt. They kindly gave me a monthly rate equal to the current per diem rate, and I would have all the flexibility to quickly deploy without the last minute hassles of breaking apartment leases, storage, and airport transportation challenges. I would spend significantly more than allowed for my meals and incidentals, but the flexibility was most important to me.

I was sure I would be ordered to Bahrain with other MARCENT Marines soon. It never happened, and I ended up staying in the hotel for over fourteen months before it was over. The beauty of the Rocky Point area would become a permanent part of my life for years to come, but that wasn't high on my mind at that point.

For over three months, there would be no time off. The op tempo after 9/11 at CENTCOM and MARCENT was grueling. On a daily basis, I left the room at 0600 and wouldn't be back until at least 2100, and often later. I quickly learned the ropes from Major Tom Ivan, the Assistant Chief of Staff, G6 at MARCENT. If Tom would be forward deployed to Bahrain, which could be the case any time, I had to be prepared to assume his duties. My first 24 years of Marine Corps experience was at the battalion level or below. Five years at MARFORPAC taught me about the United State's higher level global command structure.

The world then was divided into US military regions commanded by Commander in Chiefs (CINC's). They had since been renamed to Combatant Commands (COCOM's). There were six primary regional COCOM's then; North, South, Europe, Central, Pacific, and Korea. Africa would be separated from the Central Command and assigned its own command later. There were also supporting Combatant Commands, including the Strategic Command, Transportation Command, and Space Command.

Each Combatant Command was staffed by the joint services and was headed by a four-star flag officer. Their role was to support US policies and provide security for Americans abroad. Their chain of command would routinely flow through the Joint Chiefs of Staff at the Pentagon. Dotted line relationships would be added as appropriate for contingency operations. This could lead directly to the National Command Authority (NCA), comprised of the President, Vice President, Sec of Defense, Sec of State, Chairman of the Joint Chiefs of Staff, and various intelligence directors.

Each COCOM four-star flag officer had a three-star flag officer from each service reporting to him or her. These officers head up what are called Component Commands that provide the staffing, logistics, and all provisioning of forces from each service, as appropriate, to meet the needs of their parent COCOM's.

CENTCOM had 26 countries located between the European (EUCOM) and Pacific (PACOM) Commands until Africa became a new Combatant Command named the Africa Command (AFRICOM). Nearly every major conflict in the last twenty years had been in CENTCOM's area of responsibility, hence the eventual breakout of the African continent to the new AFRICOM.

As a unified United States military command, CENTCOM was also augmented by a global coalition of allies. After 9/11, there were 72 countries represented at the CENTCOM headquarters in Tampa. I was irritated every time I heard someone saying, "Why are we the police force of the world?" Nearly ten years later in Afghanistan there would be 49 countries sharing the mission.

That our country was at war was evident in so many ways. Security was at its highest at MacDill Air Force Base. The building signs and numbers were covered, and the op tempo was intense. I never thought I would see such a high potential for attack on our home soil!

Settling In

There was no time off at MARCENT. The daily meetings were intense. There were early morning intelligence reports from CENTCOM, and very demanding planning sessions for soon-to-be conducted Afghanistan operations. The days were long, and duty was grueling. Terri and I established a routine of Friday night phone dates. IBM was very supportive. They had many reservist employees called away after 9/11. They treated us well with guaranteed continued employment upon our return, and they paid the difference between the military and IBM pay. This took a huge burden off of Terri's and my shoulders and made the recall easier to handle financially.

Operation Enduring Freedom (OEF) was launched as America's response to radical Islamists who attacked our shores. Camp Rhino was the first US-led coalition foothold, making the soon to follow ground war in Afghanistan possible. At 430 miles from the Arabian Sea and 120 miles southwest of Kandahar, it was the largest and longest inland movement of Marines in history.

I was on duty in CENTCOM's joint operation center one night early in the operation. Our special operations positions were compromised and they had to ride on horseback to the pre-designated hot landing zone for extraction. CENTCOM monitored their movement closely. After a harrowing escape, they were on helicopters and out of harm's way, but a highly sensitive radio was missing. It was close to midnight Tampa time, and an immediate decision had to be made whether or not to change the codes that connected all US units worldwide. I saw this as sufficient cause to alert the MARCENT Chief of Staff at home.

If the Taliban would have found the radio with the current KEYMAT codes, it would be worthless to them as long as the codes were changed. (The hardware is no good without the codes.) A decision was quickly reached to not execute the world-wide change, since it would only be thirty minutes before the codes would automatically change on the prescribed schedule.

Of significant note to me was that the Special Forces members riding the horses were Army and had the radios in their ruck sacks and not on their bodies. Marines would never do such a thing, as I told the Army Major next to me in the operations center who also had years of infantry experience. The ensuing friendly discussion kept both of us and several others awake for the rest of the shift. I was joking of course. The Special Forces conducting that operation were the best of the best. Some of them had to learn to ride horses just for this mission, and did a damn good job of it!

Getting Accustomed to Higher Headquarters Duty

CENTCOM was a joint command, meaning it was staffed from all the services. The Marines were by far the smallest force, but still the best combined air, land, and sea force. It was task organized into three basic sizes called Marine Air Ground Task Forces (MAGTAF). The smallest was the Marine Expeditionary Unit (MEU) which was comprised of a ground battalion with air, artillery, armor, and logistics support tailored to anticipate immediate missions while deployed in naval fleets.

Next was the Marine Expeditionary Brigade (MEB), comprised of a ground regiment and supporting air, artillery, armor and logistical forces ready to react within hours or days, in any clime or place. The MEB would typically be formed and sent to a large scale contingency operation within days or weeks anywhere in the world.

The largest was the Marine Expeditionary Force (MEF), comprised of a ground division, air wing, artillery regiment, and all appropriate supporting logistical units. The MEF would participate in large scale operations worldwide and typically blend in with other services as either a supported or supporting unit in the task organized command, established by the Joint Chiefs of Staff.

After over 30 years of service at every level of command by now, I really did have respect for all services as I learned how joint operations worked. It was very impressive and I was proud just to be an American, but I was most proud of my service. The Marines have always been fast moving, hard hitting, and provided the best "bang for the buck."

After a few months, things at CENTCOM were settling down somewhat and allowed Major Tom Ivan me to cover each other for some days off until he left for Bahrain. The Afghanistan operation went well, and planning for a potential Iraq operation was in process.

Kristin and her fiancé Mark came to Tampa for their planned visit. They had gone to the parks in Orlando and were late returning. I was getting worried. They finally got to the hotel and told me they missed the Westshore exit on 275, and had ended up across the Franklin Bridge in St Petersburg. This wouldn't have been bad by itself, except they were nearly out of gas! They did make it, but we never stop worrying do we?

Terri and I were able to maintain regular contact. We emailed each other regularly and continued our Friday night "dates". We would make it a point to talk with each other after a long week and start our weekend "together separately". It was so good to hear her voice, so steady and confident. It brought strength to me. We had no idea this would be our way of life much longer than we could ever know in the years to come!

Forced Retirement
Not to let me go too long without another shock, fate offered up yet another one. Some genius at Headquarters Marine Corps (HQMC) noticed I had passed the thirty-year mandatory retirement mark. I wanted to stay, and Lieutenant General Hailston wanted to keep his team intact. They couldn't afford to lose any one of the small Tampa staff. The MARFORPAC headquarters at Camp Smith in Hawaii was also understaffed, so they couldn't easily replace me. After a great deal of angst amongst the bureaucrats in Washington, they came up with a plan that pleased all concerned. They would administratively retire me as of 1 July, 2002, and keep me on active duty on the "retired retain" list.

My retirement package arrived while I was still executing my existing active duty orders. I had to be the only Marine I knew that received his or her retirement letter and certificates addressed to a hotel room!

The Marine Corps was very limited in the number of Marines they could keep on this list, so they did it very reluctantly, but Lieutenant General Hailston turned around and endorsed a request to extend me for six more months just to keep them on their toes! So, I would stay "in the game" for another six months!

A Medal for Terri
In the meanwhile, Colonel Bill Hamerstadt and my fellow Marines back at MARFORPAC in Camp Smith, Hawaii were fighting the war from there. They had deployed much of the staff to Bahrain to support their forward headquarters. Bill was the Assistant Chief of Staff G6, but it was a much bigger organization than my small team in Tampa. For years, Bill thought I should have been put in for a medal for all I did during my reserve service there. Since he was on active duty now too, and had the time and motivation to do so, he submitted for the award. It was approved and sent to Tampa for presentation.

I knew about it, and wondered why they weren't presenting it to me. There were award ceremonies held all the time in the small headquarters building in which we were located. One day, Colonel John Tempone, MARCENT's Chief of Staff, asked when Terri was coming down for another visit. It just so happened she would be coming for a visit in just a couple of weeks. He said, "Great", and moved on. It all became clear when he invited Terri to the medal award ceremony that would occur after her arrival. Nice touch! But, it wouldn't be that simple.

As Master Sergeant Rupinski read my award citation, Colonel Tempone stopped him cold and said, "…Yeah, Yeah, Yeah! We all know and love Mike, but we all know who REALLY deserves this award! Do we have a medal we can give Terri?" Master Sergeant Rupinski just happened to have an extra Navy & Marine Corps Commendation Medal lying around and handed it to the Colonel.

Colonel Tempone called Terri to the front and presented her with the medal with some very kind words about having to put up with me, all of them, and the Marine Corps. He acknowledged her important contribution to what made it all work, and Terri was so shocked, shy, and very proud! The medal and pictures of Colonel Tempone presenting it to Terri are framed and hanging proudly in our DeForest house today!

The 9/11 attacks changed Terri's life forever. Like the rest of America, she was afraid at home and afraid to travel. She had been traveling to Washington, DC for the National Academy of Sciences working on a food safety committee. During the flights, passengers were prohibited from getting out of their seats during the last 30 minutes of the flight. Doors to the cockpit were gradually getting reinforced, and passengers were encouraged to help take down anyone who tried to interfere with the flights. When she arrived, the streets were dead. She saw firsthand how business had slowed down and how the street traffic was much less and taxis were much fewer than what she had become accustomed.

John Lee Malvo and John Allen Muhammad were committing murders in connection with the Beltway sniper attacks in the Washington, DC Metropolitan Area and were still at large. It was dangerous to stop for gas anywhere in that area. Terri saw the news clips of beheadings of Americans and an Anthrax scare, which had paralyzed the city as well. She was afraid to open packages that came in the mail as the country watched people die as a result of the "white powder" in the envelopes. Postal workers were in an especially dangerous profession! After a few months of this, federal government mail all went to a special mail handling facility to be "sanitized" before delivery. This added about a week to normal delivery time. This limited federal government's communication to almost exclusively email.

Nonetheless, Terri wouldn't be deterred from seeing me in Tampa. This made it worth the risk and made her feel a part of it all. She flew into St Petersburg instead of Tampa in hopes to avoid problems at Tampa International. She felt the smaller airport was safer, as the planes weren't quite as big as those that a hijacker might be interested in. All the passengers would be eyeing each other up as they waited for their flights. Who was the next hijacker? Who was the air marshal?

At MARCENT she got to meet US Army General Tommy Franks, the head of CENTCOM. She also met several senior coalition officers, including a Swedish general who was openly smitten by her, and kissed her hand right in front me. It was the way of the Swede! My Hyatt family and Armani's loved her, and John and Joanie made sure she got her Lobster Bisque that she loved. She would have liked to lick the bowl clean! We truly made the best of our separation with our visits!

A Scare Back Home
The war and being away from home was enough for me, but life wouldn't stop there. My Dad had been diagnosed with bladder cancer. They thought they caught it early enough, and could get it all, if they removed the bladder before it metastasized. The operation to remove the bladder was successful in getting rid of the cancer, but the operation itself damn near killed him, at least three times over, during the following nine months! My mother called me thinking it could be my last chance to see him. By the time I got to Theda Clark Hospital in Neenah, Wisconsin, the rest of the family was exhausted, so I took over the watch to allow the others to get some rest.

I spent a week with Dad while the family rested. Before leaving, I was able to thank the doctor that saved his life. I would now return to my duties in Tampa, but the family would have much ahead, with many more fears of losing Dad. He came through it all, and would have ten more years of building oak furniture, before it would all catch up with him again. Without the great doctors, nurses and staff at Theda Clark, he would have left us far too soon. Where do we get such people! My sister Tammy's daughter Carlie was suitably impressed as well, and as a result would become a nurse herself years later. I never miss an opportunity to thank a doctor or nurse for all they do…it is all too often questioned or unappreciated.

Another Career False Ending

Back in Tampa, CENTCOM continued to monitor operations in Afghanistan and, as was customary, made contingency plans to prepare for anything the National Command Authority and Joint Chiefs of Staff may direct them to do. The Taliban had been ousted within weeks. Osama Bin Laden had been cornered in Tora Bora, but had escaped to Pakistan. The North Atlantic Treaty Organization (NATO) had established an international headquarters in Kabul with three major areas of involvement to address the issues in Afghanistan: security, governance, and development. The headquarters would be called the International Security Assistance Force (ISAF).

The remnants of the Taliban forces, including the Haqqani network, would begin insurgency operations against the ISAF, while the US looked not only at rounding up the key players of the 9/11 attacks, but containing radical Islamic terrorists as a whole. When viewed as a whole, the problem was much bigger than just a few guys that decided to attack Washington, DC. The radical Islamic element was asserting itself globally, but predominantly in countries such as Syria, Iraq, Iran, Pakistan, Somalia, Sudan, and many more in CENTCOM's twenty-six country area of responsibility. However, Iraq quickly became the alligator closest to the boat.

There was clear evidence of weapons of mass destruction (WMD), and Saddam Hussein already had a track record of using it against Iran and his own countrymen. Sarin gas, and other highly concentrated chemicals that could be transported by artillery or long range missiles, became the concern. One needle-point sized drop of sarin gas could kill a human being. Iraq had known stockpiles of sarin, and was suspected of even more sinister capabilities.

The United Nations had become an even more feeble organization than the now defunct League of Nations. The US had a hard choice to make. Should we go in while the intelligence and evidence was fresh and nothing had been moved, or should we wait for UN approval? The CENTCOM planners were working on a plan. The President went to the UN in an effort to garner support, but everybody at CENTCOM and MARCENT knew it would be months, before we went. In my opinion, if the politicians had the courage to name the real enemy, it would have been named "radical Islamic terrorism", and there would have been many other places that would have been targeted for intervention. Coalition participation was important enough for President Bush to wait, and the planners needed time, but the delay would alter the outcome.

To me this meant the justification to keep a retired Marine on active duty was no longer viable. There would be time to adjust staffs in CENTCOM and component commands before anything big would happen. The discussions to extend me ended with plans for a retirement ceremony for 18 December, 2002. I began to make plans to retire and return home to Terri and my IBM job.

In the meantime, the annual Marine Corps Ball was nearing. Marines throughout the world gather to celebrate their beginning on 11 November. Terri loved the balls and we invited her friend Kathy to attend. I invited my friend Eugene to attend as well. Marine Corps balls would be held wherever Marines are in the world, whether they celebrate in full dress or battle uniforms. On several occasions, I had C-Ration pound cake in the field to celebrate, but never missed one.

We got a table in the rear of the ballroom. Our Guest of Honor, Army General Tommy Franks, the CENTCOM Commander, came through the door. When he noticed me at the table, he stopped by to shake our hands. My stock raised out of sight with Terri, Kathy, and Eugene! A moment to remember forever!

Back at Rocky Point
The memories were flowing as I continued my Rocky Point run. My heart pumped heavily now as it propelled me along the familiar path. How could I have known I would be back in Tampa and CENTCOM seven years later, especially after I thought I was once again leaving for good? Would my service continue this time, or would I go home soon? The vivid journey through time continued.

Chapter Six
Reserve Retirement/Life at Home: 2003-2007
Sauk City, De Forest, Madison, Wisconsin

A Farewell to Arms

This time it really looked like the end of my Marine Corps Reserve career. I felt fortunate that I stayed after nearly quitting at the 24-year mark. The extra years gave me experience at the highest levels of command, and I took pride in serving at every level, in every rank from private to Chief Warrant Officer 4.

Many of my friends that had accomplished so much and sacrificed so many weekends and summers were in my thoughts. They went unrecognized after twenty or thirty years of service. The reserves just didn't hold ceremonies. Some of the most deserving reserve Marines I ever knew went quietly into the sunset with no recognition of the long, arduous service and great sacrifice. I was sure that the reservists in the other branches could claim the same injustice.

But, the Marines of the Marine Central Command (MARCENT) weren't going to let my thirty-two years of active and reserve service go unrecognized. The time for the ceremony came quickly. Terri, Kurt, Kristin, and her fiancé Mark were coming to Tampa for the ceremony and plans were made to get me back home for good. My good friends Denny and Schumann would also surprise me!

Retirement in 2002

The ceremony to mark my service was held with the most important people in my life present to witness it. The MARCENT Marines, led by Master Sergeant Gabriel Casas put on a memorable, full Naval retirement ceremony traditionally conducted for retiring Marine Corps officers and Staff Non-Commissioned Officers. It included the ship's bell, a Bosun's Mate and his whistle, and side boys. The side boys represented the path ashore for the last time. Most of the time, they would be comprised of enlisted sailors or Marines.

At MARCENT, enlisted Marines were in short supply, as they were needed in places like Bahrain and Afghanistan. I was honored to have senior officers such as Lieutenant Colonel Gordy Bellview and others from the staff on our six-member team. Seven years later, Gordy and I would meet again when I returned to CENTCOM, and needed a partner in order to take the new Marine Corps Combat Fitness Test! It would certainly be a unique reunion!

Lieutenant Colonel Chuck Peterson, whom I served with for the past fourteen months, was the Master of Ceremonies. He was an F-4 fighter pilot with more than a couple of "hard landings" on his record and on his body. He advised the Iraqi Army in their war with Iran in the eighties and had a prominent place in the recent Iraq invasion planning. It truly was a high honor to have a Marine like this in charge of my last Marine Corps ceremony.

The Bosun's Mate blew his whistle, piping Chuck and me aboard. The standard ceremony starts with the presentation of retirement awards, letters, and gifts. I was honored with the Legion of Merit Medal, which was very unusual for Warrant Officers. Tom Ivan nominated me for the award, but I never actually expected to receive it. It was usually awarded to colonels and generals, or very senior enlisted members. I certainly took great pride in receiving it, and again felt very fortunate not to have been forgotten like so many of my friends in the reserves, who simply quit drilling and never got so much as a thank you.

I was also presented with a flag that was flown over the USS Arizona (near my prior duty station in Hawaii), and a plaque inscribed with the CENTCOM area of responsibility map, the MARCENT emblem, and my dates of service. My retirement orders were then read, and by tradition, I faced Lieutenant Colonel Peterson, and requested permission to go ashore for the last time. The Bosun's Mate piped me ashore, as I circled back around to take Terri by the hand. I then led her, Kurt and Kristin back through the Side Boys. It was all over. I was now free to go home and start putting USMC (Ret) after my name and rank in official correspondence. Courtesy of Kurt, the ceremony was all on tape.

Rest in Hawaii and Back to Work and Wisconsin

Kristin, and her fiancé Mark, drove my car back to Wisconsin. Terri and I flew home to be together for good. We started our reunion in life and love with a return to Hawaii, where it all started. We enjoyed all our favorite spots; and many of the friends we made during my Marine Forces Pacific Command (MARFORPAC) service greeted us back. I especially enjoyed my afternoons at their favorite spot, Moana Surfrider's Beach Bar and the Banyan Tree.

Then it was back home to resume civilian life. We enjoyed our traditional family Christmas at my Sauk City house with my parents, and all the family. I was technically still on active duty until midnight of 31 December, 2002. Terri and I would have one more private ceremony. I dressed in my blues, and Terri put on her best gown. We then went to our favorite place, the Dorf Haus in Roxbury, to mark the formal end of my Marine Corps career, or so we thought.

It was good to be home with family and friends, but my sense of duty was still strong, and I wasn't satisfied to be on the sideline after all those years of intensive training and pride of belonging. My desire to continue my service was strong, but suppressed as I worked hard to re-establish my civilian life and career. It was cold. I grew up in Wisconsin's climate, but through the years drifted in and out of warmer climates so much that I had to adjust again. I liked the climates of California, Okinawa, North Carolina, and Tampa, but just being home kept me warm where it counted, in my heart.

I turned my attention back to my civilian career. IBM had been very good to me and supported me well for 14 months of military leave. But there were big changes in the wind, and I never got started with what I was originally hired for. Mercifully, I was not assigned to the State of Wisconsin KIDS project that I was helping with when I was recalled.

However, the consulting side of IBM's business was in turmoil. As of 1 January, 2003, they had acquired the IT consulting practice of Price Waterhouse Coopers and I was getting lost in the transition. Never receiving any IBM training, I was concerned about representing the company properly in high level consulting assignments. More importantly, assignments were not given to me during all the confusion!

Taking charge of my own fate, I skillfully arranged a six-month assignment with the US Navy's Network Centric Innovation Center (NCIC) in Coronado, California. I had very fond memories of my San Diego days in the early seventies, and relished a chance to return. When IBM acquired Price Waterhouse Coopers, they inherited the contract, which had six more months to go. Being accepted onto the contract, I was back on track with my civilian career.

San Diego

I loved living in San Diego again and chose an apartment on Cortez Hill overlooking downtown and the Gas Lamp district. My work took me to Coronado every day. It felt strange to be in a room full of naval officers and not being in my Marine Corps uniform. But I quickly established my own personal "battle rhythm," and enjoyed my assignment. It felt good to stay involved, even if it was with the Navy! Truth be known, the Navy and Marines get along very well, but of course they have a reputation of competition to maintain. I held my own in the office place!

I missed Terri, but we stayed in touch and she approved of the assignment. We would be together every two weeks, whether I came home or she came down. IBM was great that way! I loved my apartment. Terri got me started on W.E.B. Griffin books, which I read in the evening hours. The daily drive to work over the Coronado bridge was very enjoyable. Great memories, great view, and great job!

The six-month Navy assignment went fast. My next assignments were troubling. IBM has a high reputation to uphold, and I still didn't have any training! They were looking at me for a couple of very high level assignments. These would be 100% travel, and would entail contacts with very senior people either at the City of Kansas City, or the Chase Bank in New York. I just didn't feel qualified to represent IBM at this level without training, and didn't want 100% travel after all I'd been through.

I had not only a great immediate family, but the extended family was great as well. My cousins were great to grow up with and I still loved seeing them. My cousin Debbie worked at Wisconsin Physician's Service (WPS) and seemed to take pride in her job. I knew they were getting a new TRICARE contract and thought applying for a job in information technology might be worth a shot.

TRICARE is the military's health care system. Working for WPS would allow me to take pride in serving in a different way!

Terri and I had lots to think about during our Hawaiian vacation spot. Debbie came through and a WPS job offer was imminent. A decision would have to be made before the vacation was over. If I accepted the WPS offer, I would miss the excitement of travel and the flexibility of consulting, but I'd be home every day.

Once again, the balance of love of home, and what had become a desire to travel, was haunting me. As I swam in the South Pacific waters of Waikiki and gazed upon the view of the famous pink Royal Hawaiian hotel, and my beloved Banyan Tree, I decided it was time to take the WPS offer and stay home.

New Job at Home, Buyer's Remorse and the Doldrums
My first year at WPS was the most miserable year of my working life. It wasn't bad enough that I was now on the sideline of the battle against radical Islam, and forced to listen to all the civilian talking heads on TV who thought they knew more about how to deal with the threat than the generals and policy makers. I also had to deal with WPS company executives who thought they knew more about how to run a mainframe computer system than the team of professional technicians I was leading.

Still, my longing to be back "in the game"' was largely offset by the benefits of being home. While work life was not good, I still liked getting home every night to see Terri. I loved the balance of seeing the world and getting back home to the hilly, wooded country roads where I grew up.

Kurt and Kristin were out of college and stayed right in the Sauk Prairie area. We were close enough to see my parents in the Wisconsin north woods regularly as well. I was especially enjoying my weekly golf outings with Schumann and Kurt. None of us were great golfers, but just being together on the Devils Head course in the Baraboo Bluffs every week made up for it. The beautiful rolling hills, trees, rivers, lakes, sunsets, and camaraderie made all the pain go away. If laughter is the best medicine, the three of us would live forever. Is this a bad thing?

A Marriage Made in Heaven

Kristin married her high school sweetheart, Mark, and their reception was at the Dorf Haus. The most memorable moment for me was when Mark had to give his speech. He's not a speaker. At one point in his short talk, he talked about liking Kristin, and after a short search for words, all he could say was, "Well…who wouldn't like Kristin?" I had tears as the crowd clapped wildly. They bought their first house in Dane and soon welcomed little Dylan into the family. Terri and I were now grandparents, which weighed heavily in favor of enjoying being home!

A Family Crushed

My youngest sister, Cherie, was diagnosed with advanced brain cancer. It was a crushing blow to the family! We had been fortunate up to that point, not having to suffer any sort of shock of this nature. Cherie was nearing forty years old with five children ranging in age from three to twelve. Her husband Chris had a good job, but his salary alone barely covered their basic needs.

I had been frequenting VFW Post 8483 in Madison. Sue Haack, the Commander, also grew up in the Lodi/Dane area and knew my family. When she heard about Cherie, she and the Auxiliary President and good friend, Kathy Steensrud, planned a fund raiser. Along with many close friends in the post, they raised over $6,600 in one day. It was a great success and made a family trip to Disney World possible. We wouldn't know it then, but it would turn out to be the last trip they got to take as a family.

Back to the Future and Rocky Point

As my thoughts returned to the present, I was well along in my early evening Tampa run in Rocky Point. I had come a long way since being recalled after my Marine Corps retirement, and four years of civilian life at home, and my return to Tampa. If I returned home, I would still miss CENTCOM and being an active Marine, but I also knew the time had likely come. Staring straight through the beautiful view of the bay, my thoughts drifted back to my journey through the past.

Chapter Seven
Call to Active Duty - Iraq: Sep 2007
Sauk City, DeForest, Wisconsin/Camp Pendleton, California

An Enemy Grows While a Nation Sleeps

I had become very disillusioned with my decision to leave IBM and join WPS, as the culture just didn't seem to be a good fit for me. Did I do the right thing? Additionally, I missed the adult leadership and camaraderie of the Marine Corps. The daily intelligence briefings at the Marine Central Command (MARCENT) and my work with the US Central Command (CENTCOM) were missed with all the things going on in the Middle East. I just wasn't ready to feel like an old elephant walking to the caves to die just yet!

I started volunteering for a return to active duty, but Headquarters Marine Corps (HQMC) has always been extremely tightfisted about bringing retirees back. It was the opposite of the Army that was involuntarily recalling retirees that didn't want to return. As a retired Marine, just wanting to come back wouldn't get you there. There had to be specific needs for your specific skills, and you didn't call them, they called you. To be eligible for retiree recall, you had to be within five years of your retirement date, and I was within just two months of going past the point of no return.

My time was realistically up, and I was just glad to have such a great family and great home. There was real trouble brewing in the world, and all I loved could be threatened in the not so distant future. Nobody seemed to be paying attention to all the signs. What bothered me most was that the leaders of our great nation were trying to hide it in the name of political correctness. As a firm believer that problems can be fixed, there first has to be an acknowledgement that the problem even exists. I dealt with reality, and the politicians dealt with intellectual concepts they willed to be real.

A religious war didn't fit neatly into the liberal leadership's intellectual world view, but it was real, and it would come. I watched with disgust as the United States stood in front of the United Nations for six months arguing about whether there were weapons of mass destruction in Iraq or not back in 2002. It was as if they were expecting cement missile silos that couldn't be easily moved! Thousands of containers of old sarin gas had been found by now at places like the Muthanna Chemical Complex near Iraq's Lake Tharthar. It was no secret there was more as well. For some reason a chemical that could kill a person with a drop smaller than a pin head didn't count? And that was just what was left behind during the six months we gave the Iraqis to move things around!

Radical Islam

In my opinion, we were well overdue to start dealing with radical Islamic terrorists. Not Islam - radical Islamic terrorists! There was a big difference, and it was disgusting that our leadership was more worried about the backlash of mainstream Muslims (or at least those claiming to be mainstream) by the mere inclusion of the word Islam when describing the radical's actions. The true battle as I understood things was between radical Islam terrorists and Christianity.

Terri actually corrected me one day pointing out that the battle was actually between radical Islam and anybody who wasn't. She was very open-minded, but understood the threat of the radical form of Islam. We saw radical Catholics in Ireland and radical Protestants in England in our own life times. When they were killing people in the passionate pursuit of their religious beliefs, they were dealt with. Until we were willing to call radical Islamic terrorists what they were, and treat them accordingly, we continued to give them more time to grow stronger.

In my own informal research at the time, the world population was roughly 31% Christian, which was shrinking rapidly, and roughly 27% Muslim, which was growing rapidly. The Muslim population was at roughly 1.8 billion during my active duty years. The best estimates of the time were that one to five percent of the total Muslim population was radical, which amounted to over ten million radical Muslims spread around the globe, some active, some dormant. It became extremely important for me to understand what radical Islamic terrorists were about.

Allah, the same God that Christians, Jews, and Muslims alike worshiped, chose the prophet Muhammad to make his final revelations to the world through the angel Gabriel in approximately 610 AD. The revelations went on for approximately 23 years. It is widely agreed that Muhammad was illiterate, and worked with his family and trusted associates, to record the revelations that would eventually become known as the Qur'an.

At the beginning of the 23 year period, Allah's instructions were to tolerate the non-believers as long as they were mono-theistic, meaning they believed in one god, and that one God was him. The revelations indicated the "People of the Book" (Christians, Jews, etc.) were mostly correct, but a few things were interpreted wrong along the way. Allah's revelations to Muhammad would set things straight and were to reign with holy infallibility as his final revelations. This is much like the Catholic doctrine considered to be holy of substance and infallible in the eyes of man.

The revelations agreed that Jesus was a prophet, like Muhammad, but he was not divine. There is but one god, no Mary, no Spirit, no Holy Trinity. The more radical element of Muslims is the belief that towards the end of the twenty three years, Allah abrogated and said non-believers were impure and deserved death. The radical interpreters of the Qur'an believe Allah made this abrogation and charged true believers with killing non-believers, thereby promising a place in paradise for those that martyr themselves in Allah's name.

Mainstream Muslims either weren't sure, didn't admit it, or just wanted to ignore it so everybody just got along. In any case, the history of the Qur'an has many twists, and it was eventually assembled but not in chronological order. The question of Allah's abrogation would be left unclear in the final assemblage of the Qur'an. It stands as the key difference between how a mainstream and radical Muslim interprets the faith today. The world would be in the cross fire as they sorted it out.

Did Allah change his mind about non-believers? Did he truly say they were impure? And was it the duty of true believers to kill them? To the radical, there is no place for non-believers, and no place for civil state governments. To them Islamic Sharia Law was the law of the land and directed all of mankind's social, cultural, legal, ethical, and moral conduct of life activities. It was the duty of the radical to re-establish Islam to global dominance and influence as it had been for over 800 years after Muhammad's death in 632 AD. Until 1500-

1600, Islam dominated what we know as the Middle East today. The goal of the radical Muslim is to restore first the most holy of lands, then the world.

Radical Muslim terrorists are not "I'm OK, you're OK" kinda guys. I was appalled at the shallowness that the "blame America first crowd" displays when they assert that we are at fault for the clash of religions. They insist the radical Islamic fundamentalists wouldn't be bothering us if we hadn't angered them with our global expansion and interference with their lands and their ways.

I also shook my head when I heard someone in America say it is just a matter of educating them. My own studies of the Middle East and of the religion convinced me the average radical Muslim has spent far more time educating themselves in their religion than the average American spent even understanding Civics 101. Say nothing of religion that is of little concern to so many of our population in the first place.

Mainstream Muslims claim a desire to co-exist. This might be true. Those that claim this desire may be sincere, but it will come to a true test someday when they are forced to take a position between their radical brethren and the non-Muslim world. When we start seeing more condemnation of radical Muslim's actions from mainstream Muslims, it may signal a positive change, but it is dangerous to assume their sincerity. Every time I heard a Muslim claiming not to be radical, and decry the very mention of Islam in terrorism, I wondered if it was a radical in disguise. Our very principles of a nation and nature of a peace loving people make us an easy target for deception.

In any case, I believed the only way to stop radical Islamic terrorists was, in fact, the mainstream Muslim population taking a stand against them. The sheer numbers of radical Muslims, even if they were only one to five percent of the 1.8 billion total Muslim population, would overwhelm any sort of military engagement on a field of open battle, like was done during the Crusades. Thankfully those days are over, and today's battles are fought on the air waves long before smaller numbers of combatants meet in the field. Today's radical Muslim is living in neighborhoods, and blending into the societies of the countries in which they settle. They are waiting for their chance for martyrdom, and can achieve it with a single act.

Others were joining international groups like Al-Qaeda, or regional groups like the Taliban, focused in Afghanistan, or what would become the future group seeded by our pull out in Iraq-the Islamic State of Iraq and Syria or the Levant (ISIS/ISIL). These would become household names, but if anyone would care to do minimal research, they would find hundreds of Islamic groups internationally, regionally, and locally in countries scattered throughout the globe.

For our leaders to think we could go to Afghanistan, shoot up a few guys that we know were involved in the 9/11 attacks, come home, have a ticker tape parade, and get on with solving our own social issues, was unacceptable to me. I was having a very hard time listening to the news channels and being around my otherwise well rounded friends back in small town Wisconsin who thought we should just get out of the Middle East and let them kill themselves.

The Sound of Distant Drums

Word came that my old reserve infantry unit in Madison was being mobilized as part of the reserve battalion headquartered in Chicago. This was for a second combat tour in Iraq and they were woefully short of officers. Again I found myself torn between staying home to enjoy my family, friends, and beautiful countryside, and responding to my strong sense of duty and responsibility to my country.

I was retired, and wouldn't be involuntarily called this time. Terri and I talked it over, and as always, she would support me. Her concern was for my safety, and for the first time in our marriage, my duty would likely take me into harm's way. But, she knew me well, and reluctantly gave her concurrence and support to seek a chance to go back with my old unit. Had she known at the time it would be much longer, she may not have so readily agreed!

I had some old contacts at 2nd Battalion, 24th Marines, my old reserve infantry unit, and before long got word they would like very much to add me to their deployment roster. This was in July, 2007 and the long process to get me back on active duty began. HQMC was being very resistant. My formal specialty was data and communications systems, and they didn't seem to care about my nine years of infantry experience with the very infantry battalion that was requesting me.

They were also concerned about my age. At 55, I would be one of the older infantry officers at the battalion level. At any level for that matter! And, in the spirit of true bureaucratic character, they didn't like "by name" requests. They preferred to find more appropriate officers to fill requirements their own way. The problem with that was they weren't getting it done and I had strong backing from the activated battalion commander.

Moving past the uncertainty, I was on the path of preparation. I increased my daily workouts, and put myself on a healthy eating plan with Terri's guidance. My battalion contact, Chief Warrant Officer 5 Jim Roussell recommended some reading for me. One of the books he recommended was "Learning to Eat Soup with a Knife" by Army Lieutenant Colonel John Nagl. The book focused on counterinsurgency operations and it really hit home. It would suit me well through Iraq and later through Afghanistan.

I ordered a couple pair of the new Marine Corps desert MARPAT utilities (uniforms) and desert boots not knowing if I would be issued any, or if I would even be called. Officers usually had to buy their own uniform. I had every utility uniform the Marine Corps issued since 1971 in my closet, with the most recent being the older chocolate chip desert utilities from my MARCENT days. Things had changed in five years!

Navy Corpsman HM2 Salter arranged a rush physical for me with the Air Force 440th Air Wing Headquarters Medical Unit in Milwaukee. I made sure to arrive early, and when reaching for my ID card to be allowed through the gate, realized I had left my wallet at home! I called Terri at her State Department of Trade and Consumer Protection Food Safety office back in Madison. She rushed home and found it on the bathroom floor. She then dutifully charged off to meet me half way between Madison and Milwaukee. With her help, I still arrived early enough for the Air Force medical team to complete the physical. Is that love, devotion and support beyond the call of duty or what! If she didn't want me to go, that could have ended my chances right then and there!

Time was quickly passing and it was getting late. The battalion had already mobilized and had begun their pre-deployment training in the Marine Air/Ground Combat Training Center in Twentynine

Palms, California. If I didn't get orders soon, it would be too late to finish pre-deployment training!

I decided to call in the artillery and contacted Major General Drew Davis who was once one of our 2nd Battalion, 24th Marines staff officers, and my commanding officer at Marine Wing Communications Squadron-48 in the Glenview Naval Air Station. This got some traction. With the support of the current battalion commander, Lieutenant Colonel Frank Charlonis, Colonel Mark Smith of the 24th Marine Regiment, and Major General Davis's contacts at HQMC, we began to beat down the bureaucrats.

I received orders the first week of October. The orders were for a year. I would join the battalion for pre-deployment training already in progress at The Air/Ground Combat Training Center at Twentynine Palms, California. My Marine Corps career would be re-kindled after nearly five years of retirement. I couldn't have been happier to get "back in the game," away from the oppressive atmosphere of my civilian job, and all the talking heads on cable TV!

I worked with Tony Konkol, my boss at WPS, to arrange for military leave and was surprised at the level of support I would get from them! Tony would take on my duties himself and they would keep my position intact for me. In addition, they would pay the difference between my civilian and military salary! I got my old Delta Company Marines together for a going away party, and things were set for my departure.

On 22 October, 2007, I was officially back on active duty. Terri and I made a tearful departure at Madison's Dane County Airport. I had already said my goodbyes to Kurt, Kristin and her family, and Mom and Dad. Everyone was concerned with Cherie and dealing with her brain tumor, so my departure wasn't center stage for them, but it was still emotional.

Once again leaving my wife and best friend Terri, a very comfortable, stable life, and a great, loving family, my emotions were mixed. I felt terrible about leaving Terri alone and worried about how Cherie's illness would impact the family, but I was excited to be back on active duty and given a chance to contribute in the country's great time of need. The last few days at home were filled with some people chipping away at my reasons for wanting to return to duty. They kept asking "what was in it for me?" They just didn't understand. It wasn't about me. It was about our country, our freedom, and our way of life! They had no capacity to appreciate the world situation and my desire to serve. Terri did. That is why we were best buddies!

The flight to San Diego was smooth and on schedule, but the threat of wild fires was prevalent. I had been watching them on the news. I wondered how it may impact my ability to get around Camp Pendleton to process before heading up to Twentynine Palms to meet the battalion. The drive from the airport to Camp Pendleton was very smoky but traffic moved quite well. The Fallbrook area near Camp Pendleton was burning. I recalled navigating around that area during my Non-Commissioned Officer School field training in 1972, thirty-five years earlier.

Camp Delmar and Camp Talega

I would need to process back to active duty at Camp Talega, a small camp in the far northern end of the sprawling Camp Pendleton. During the time it would take for processing, I would be billeted at Camp Delmar, forty-five minutes south of Camp Talega.

I checked into the Camp Delmar officer quarters known as Harborsite. It was memory lane immediately. I had artillery school at Camp Delmar in 1971 and the same buildings were still there! They had been fixed up quite nice. The old transient barracks I stayed in and hated back then were now the Non-Commissioned Officer (NCO) School for Lance Corporals preparing for promotion. The government sure got their use out of that old building!

My room in the Bachelor Officer Quarters was somewhat depressing. It was cinder block construction, not well lit, had no internet, and the phone was very poor. I met Chief Warrant Officer 2, Chuck Andrews, who had also volunteered from retired reserve status and successfully fought the same battles with the HQMC that I did. He just finished three years of voluntary active duty with the Walter Reed's Hospital Wounded Warrior Regiment in Washington, DC, and worked for Midway Airlines in Milwaukee in his civilian job.

Chuck and I joined forces for dinner at Joe's in Oceanside and got acquainted. We would serve in close proximity over the next year, and would return to Camp Delmar and the officer quarters to process back to retired status afterward. We talked of how difficult it was to get the orders and how much we both wanted to get involved again.

My first night was spent making sure my new uniform was ready. The MARPAT utilities were new to me. Only a Marine could know the details of uniform preparation which would make an old dog look for new tricks. First the Irish pennants, then the perfect sleeve fold. This was a combat tour and all the Marines left their dress uniforms back home. Only utilities were to be packed for this mission. I was impressed by the new utilities! They would require no ironing, and the desert boots were actually very comfortable and would never need shining! This alone was amazing after over thirty years of starching utilities and shining black boots!

After all the effort to get back, it was really happening! I had Terri's love and support, and my family was as settled as they could be as Cherie's brain tumor persisted. Now I hoped to make the grade as an infantry staff officer on a combat mission. It had been over seventeen years since I had been with the battalion, and all of my experience was at the platoon level. Serving at the battalion staff level would be new to me and I just hoped to carry my own weight. My staff experience at MARFORPAC and MARCENT would help, but it wasn't infantry.

After four days of dodging fires, we were able to get to Camp Talega by 0740 and the medical team arrived shortly after to clear us for duty. We returned in the afternoon for final endorsements and made final preparations to drive to Twentynine Palms. The next morning we were on our way! We were both full of anticipation of what was ahead, and we were ready to get started.

Chapter Eight
Pre-Deployment Training: Oct 2007-Jan 2008
Marine Air/Ground Combat Training Center, 29 Palms,
California

Pre-Deployment Training

We arrived at Twentynine Palms Marine Corps Air/Ground Combat Training Center at 1100 on 26 October and checked in with our battalion's S1 Officer. We drew our 782 gear (field equipment), and started integrating into the battalion staff and joining the pre-deployment training process.

Every military staff at the battalion level or higher uses the same numbering scheme to identify their function to facilitate coordination in combined or joint operations. The Battalion Staff consists of S1 (Admin), S2 (Intelligence), S3 (Operations), S4 (Logistics), and S6 (Data/ Communications Systems).

Chuck was assigned to the S4 Logistics staff and I was assigned to the S6 Systems staff in the Information Management Officer (IMO) role. The IMO function became more important as information technology became integrated into every facet of the Marine Corps, including infantry battalions.

As the IMO, I would coordinate between the S3 Operations and S6 Systems and Communications areas as necessary. This would be tricky, but that seemed to be my fate wherever I worked. Every assignment I ever got, as a civilian or as a Marine, was outside of norms in some fashion. I guess I'm just a tricky guy! Months of anxiety and uncertainty were over and destiny would be fulfilled!

I called my sister Cherie who had been dealing with her brain cancer now for a couple of years. So far, she was beating the odds. I had been to doctor meetings with her and her husband Chris, and was doing what I could to help before I left. My other sisters and parents spent a lot of time with the five kids, which was a far more demanding task. Her spirits were good and she would never give up hope. All of us learned a great deal from her!

The initial training classes were held throughout the mainside area of Twentynine Palms. Later in November, the entire battalion would move out to Camp Wilson for the 30 day Mohave Viper field training exercise that all deploying battalions had to undergo. It would entail living in mock Iraqi villages, and involved emulating duty in Iraq as much as possible. They even had actual Iraqis acting as villagers. The young Marine would encounter every sort of challenge expected during actual combat patrols.

Chuck and I were quickly brought into the training currently in progress. For me, this included working with our S6 Systems Staff Non-Commissioned Officers, to provide communications support for the battalion's various training events, while also fulfilling personal pre-deployment requirements. Nothing's changed that way! We had to find ways of doing the impossible with nothing. Damn it was good to be back!

Our young Marines were getting a chance to rehearse patrols in a studio down in Miramar called Stu Segall. The rehearsal included actual Iraqis, actors, role players, and all the sight, sounds and shocks of an Iraqi village. It was going very well. I couldn't have imagined this type of preparation in my early days when Vietnam was raging.

All officers had to introduce themselves at a "Hail" celebration conducted by Lieutenant Colonel Charlonis as the battalion was being formed. Most of the time a unit would have "Hail and Farewell" celebrations, but we were all coming together for this mission, and nobody was leaving, hence it was just a "Hail." I made sure everyone knew Chief Warrant Officer 5 Jim Roussell and I had quite a history together with the battalion. We were both coming off retirement, so I thought this should be mentioned. I was certain he was too modest to mention the fact that we were both road guards at the parting of the Red Sea under the command of Moses. As far as I knew, we were still friends after I mentioned it. Old friends are great to have!

Every Marine is a rifleman. Even me at my advanced age! All Marines going to Iraq had to not only conduct their routine annual requalification duties on the known distance course, but also had to qualify on additional ranges in preparation for combat called Tables 2, 3, and 4. We did them all in one day! Only in America! I was very impressed with the proficiency and organization the Marines put us through to meet this demanding requirement. It was hot, and we all had full body armor and ammunition.

Unlike the routine qualification course where we had shooting positions at the 200, 300, and 500 yard lines, we all stood in two long, tight lines and responded to commands to move forward and engage targets as we walked. The Marines in line behind the shooting line ensured safety was maintained. We would get commands to shift left, right, take a knee, go prone, move forward, etc. all while shooting. Each phase was well choreographed and we were strictly directed to shoot "two to the chest, one to the head" on the target in front of us. I called it line dancing with an M-16, but it was not as well received as it was intended for some reason. Serious guys these Marines!

Our mainside training was coming to an end and we would soon be testing our skills at Camp Wilson and Mohave Viper. The remaining training included high technology capabilities such as Biometric Automated Tool Set (BATS) and Handheld Interagency Identity Detection Equipment (HIIDE) used for obtaining and storing identity information. Command Post of the Future (CPOF) for Operations Center support, SharePoint for use in exchanging information between higher and adjacent commands, Live Tissue training for burn treatment, and Improvised Explosive Device (IED) Training, Tactics, and Procedures (TTPs) were also included in the training.

One of the things I took special note of is how much emphasis is put on Post Traumatic Stress Disorder (PTSD) before we went into combat. In the Vietnam days, all Marines had boot camp and thirty days of Infantry Training Regiment (ITR). Those going to Vietnam had another thirty days of staging battalion. There wasn't a lot of emphasis on how to handle the stresses of combat back then. As we started Mojave Viper, we were given a session on "Killology" by retired Army Lieutenant Colonel Dave Grossman, a well-known and highly respected author and lecturer. Topics included not only how to recognize and treat signs of PTSD, but more importantly, how to prevent it.

Camp Wilson - Mojave Viper

Camp Wilson was huge, flat, and sandy for the most part, with some rocky hills. No trees, no bushes, no grass. K-Spans were newer buildings replacing the fabled old A-Frame structures. Each would hold about twenty Marines, depending on how many had wall lockers or other furniture beyond a cot. There were a lot of them! The shape of them was like a Quonset hut, but they were built using newer materials. The floors were cold, dirty cement. My space consisted of a cot, my sea bag, and my pack. I had two beautiful homes back in Wisconsin, and here I was living like a mud Marine. Again, why do I do this to myself?

At first I was excited, thinking the new K-Span structures would protect against intense summer heat and crisp winter cold of the high desert. Wrong! They may have been designed to be insulated, but they must have not included the insulation. November brought the harsh, biting winds of winter to the high desert. The next thirty days would be the coldest, most miserable days and nights of all my years in the Corps! Norway was cold, but we had cold weather gear. Not here! I swore at times during my night shifts in the combat operations center the K-Span material actually radiated and amplified the cold! I would waste no time taking off my uniform and getting into my sleeping bag when I got to my cot! My wool shirt made a nice pillow though, and the bag was warm. Home sweet home!

As I stood in our battalion area one of the first nights, I noticed a full moon rising between two high mountain peaks in the crisp, clear skies. The sounds of high caliber machine guns and mortars took me back to the many prior times I had seen these sights and heard these sounds. Here we go again! The dense morning clouds over the high desert roads and peaks, the pure night sky with bright stars and moon, the whiteness and softness of the sand under foot. The intense op tempo of Marines, trucks, tanks, amtraks, helicopters, and fixed wing fast movers engaged in some very serious training emitted a rush of adrenaline. Ah the memories!

We were joined by two seasoned Israeli officers who briefed us on urban combat. They were all of twenty-six years old, but were very seasoned combat vets. One was an urban combat specialist who talked about how they root out terrorists from the populace, and how they plan to kill or capture enemies in the middle of very congested urban areas. The other was a guerilla warfare specialist who talked about how they fight the Hezbollah in Israel. No PowerPoints from them!

They brought actual footage of whacking bad guys in crowded city streets in Israel. These guys were good!

I made a point to stay in touch with Terri, even though we were now in the field. I could tell she felt better when receiving my call every night before our nightly meetings. Cell phone signals were weak in the desert, requiring me to walk out to a dark, open spot in the sand near our operating area to catch a signal. The signal was better if I faced a certain way, but the frigid cold would force me to turn out of the wind. Terri would raise hell with me because she could tell the signal weakened.

To add to the challenge, my battery was going dead. My cell phone died one night just as I was saying how interesting the machine gun fire and tracers across the valley looked and sounded. That got her attention! If you know nothing about Terri, know that when she makes her mind up about something, she sees it through. I had a new battery back at mainside in the overnight Fed Ex delivery! We stayed connected the entire month. With the new battery, I never had to turn out of the bitter wind and lose the signal. If I did, I was protected by my cozy new scarf. She really did love me!

The battalion's Marines practiced speaking into an English to Arabic translator. We also had a good number of Arabic speaking Marines that took it upon themselves to study the language before their call up. We also had "terps" assigned when we got into the country. It was vital that we could converse and establish relationships. All the companies honed their kinetic skills, but paid particularly close attention to the civil action and police skills that would be required.

Major Mann was interested in integrating me into the shift schedule as a combat operations center Watch Officer to help spread the workload within the S3 staff. I wasn't sure how confident I was, but I was there to serve. If that is what they needed, I'd give it my best. It had been seventeen years since my infantry experience, but my more recent higher headquarter staff experience built up my self-assurance.

I started on the night shift as a Watch Officer in the combat operations center on 3 December. After each night of Watch Officer duty, I had to find a way to get my personal training requirements met before we left for Iraq. Chuck and I, and all others who were late joining the battalion had to complete all the individual training requirements the battalion had already met through drill weekends and Annual Training Duty periods. These drills and training included MK-19 Grenade Launcher, First Aid, M-240 Machine Gun, 50 Caliber Machine Gun, Vehicle Familiarization on the 7-Ton Truck, Humvee Mine Resistant Ambush Protected Vehicle (MRAP), the Human Dimension of Combat, Targeting Effect (Kinetic/Non-Kinetic), Foreign Military, Rules of Engagement, Law of War, Escalation of Force, Combat Hunter, and many more.

Mother Nature even helped out in her ever thoughtful manner! We knew wind and sand storms would be a factor in Iraq, so we had to learn how to operate in them. We all had goggles, scarves, and even bought condoms to protect our rifle barrels. However, maintaining operation control and awareness was a challenge at a different level. One night during my shift, we got hit with winds, rain, and blowing sand that would never be matched in my tour in Iraq. The K-Spans were not sealed, and the wind and sand came through with little blockage. I kept the laptop my employer was kind enough to allow me to bring along in my "office" in the K-Span next door. It was only a few steps away, but I thought I'd better check to see if it was okay. It wasn't. I couldn't even find it under the sand! Worse than that, my favorite coffee mug suffered the same fate, as did my cell phone that I had been charging for my next chat with Terri!

As part of our personal requirements for combat certification, I took part in the High Mobility Multipurpose Wheeled Vehicle (commonly known as Humvee) roll over training, plus a couple of other vehicle familiarization classes. The Humvee Egress Assistance Trainer (HEAT) puts four Marines with weapons and gear into a Humvee chassis. They then roll you about three times, like a rotisserie BBQ grill. Once stopped, you have to find your way out. Anyone that has been in a Humvee knows how many foot grabbing traps there are in the cramped quarters! Depending on the stopping position, getting out can be a real trick!

Once out, you were expected to maintain your situational awareness and provide security, while getting the others out. A Quick Reaction Force (QRF) consisting of the next four trainees rush to assist. They would designate someone as unconscious or with a broken leg, and they couldn't use the injured part of their body. By the pace of my heartbeat and need for clean underwear, I would have to say "Good Training!"

We finally entered the last phase of the Mojave Viper exercise. We conducted patrols and encountered all sorts of obstacles such as planted IEDs and small arms/RPG attacks. Additionally we had to establish relationships with the local Sheiks and general population, in order to gather Intel to root out the bad guys. We worked heavily with various Intel systems, close air support, arty, mortar, tanks, tracks, etc. Very intense stuff!

During training, the Battalion Commander and key staff members received daily updates on the real world Intel and daily news for Camp Habbaniyah, our assigned area of operations in Iraq. We had a good handle on the Sheiks, their levels of political and tribal influence, bad guys to watch out for, etc. This was Jim Rousell's game, and he played it extremely well!

The final exercise scenario included insurgents being forced out of their previous operating areas into three towns and embedding themselves into the general population. We would practice more meet and greet and establish relationships with the tribal, civil and political key figures, as well as the average person on the street until ENDEX was sounded. We would then have three days to get all the weapons, vehicles, gear, ammo, etc. cleaned, accounted for and turned in, get the sand out of our ears and asses, and head for our airports to start Christmas leave.

ENDEX came and Lieutenant Colonel Charlonis called for a battalion formation, summarized our training results, and set the pace for returning after Christmas leave to tie up the loose ends, and finalize preparations to deploy by the end of January. With that, the mass exodus began.

Christmas Leave

I still had my rental car I was paying for on my own since my arrival. It came in very handy throughout the training! Chuck and I both got flights out of Las Vegas and would ride together through the narrow, jagged, and at times, steep highways between Twentynine Palms and the Las Vegas airport. On the way back, he would not be with me so I would have to navigate the poorly marked route on my own.

We got to the airport and our flights were delayed, so the drinking lamp was lit. It was several hours before my flight. I was enjoying conversation with some fellow Marines and an Army Staff Sergeant from Fort Irwin, where they have similar training for deploying Army units. I was extremely happy to be going home. It was hard to even think of the return trip in ten days. That was a lifetime away! By the time my plane took off, it turned into a Red Eye flight, and I slept the whole way!

I had often told Terri that Major Mann chewed my ass, and that I was freezing my ass off during the Mojave Desert exercise out in Camp Wilson. One morning she caught a glimpse of me walking to the shower from behind and started chuckling. Apparently I had no ass! Good training for sure!!

Our Wenger family tradition was to have Christmas Eve at our Sauk house. We would go to Terri's family which was an hour and a half north in Larsen, Wisconsin, on or near Christmas Day. Our leave was centered on these traditions. To make them work under these unique circumstances, we had a lot of decorating, gift buying, and snow shoveling to do! We did it all together and enjoyed it. The winter of 2007/8 was especially snowy and cold. Terri's snow blower had sure come in handy for this call up too!

Kurt was living in my Sauk home and was maintaining it very well. I never had to worry about it! Between him there and Terri in DeForest, they picked up my duties and worked tirelessly to keep the houses in shape. Where do you get a wife and son like that? Kristin and her husband Mark were living nearby in Dane with their first son, Dylan. My parents were up in Wild Rose, Wisconsin, an hour and a half away, and came to my house on a regular basis. They set the bar for Grandpa-dom and Grandma-dom way too high. Terri and I didn't think we could ever match them, but we'd spend our lives trying. They had a secret weapon that hardly anyone knew about! They paid attention to their grand children, listened to them, and always made them feel special. If that's all it takes, shouldn't someone write a book on the topic?

Back to Duty
The time at home went quickly, and it was hard leaving Terri at the airport. We were hoping she could visit before the battalion departed

later in January. The return flight was delayed and took away the daylight driving time I was counting on to navigate the mountainous desert highways from Las Vegas back to Twentynine Palms. Nevada roads were quite good, but as soon as I crossed the California line, they became dipped and curved, with brush, wolves, and coyotes crossing in front of me. I missed my navigator Chuck, but got to Twentynine Palms in about three and a half hours.

The last days of pre-deployment training consisted mostly of catch up medical and administrative matters. I bought some international calling cards at the PX and reserved an officer quarters room and rental car for Terri's visit. Small pox shots were given to those that required them. They were messy. You had to go through complicated lengths to avoid contagion with your room mate. I was exempted from the shot because of my age and danger of infecting Terri as we were planning on her coming down before we left. I thought what a nice gesture on the doctor's part! Or was he insinuating that I had lived long enough already, so what would it matter if I got infected? Nice guy! I think…

We treated our cammies with insect repellant provided by the Corpsmen. The doc gave us the solution to wash them, which should keep Iraqi bugs away for the times we would spend on the desert floor. Nice touch! I worked on how to get all my armor, gas mask, 782 combat gear, uniforms, and other items into my sea bag and pack. For the first time in my many years in the Marine Corps, I bought some subdued Chief Warrant Officer 4 bars. The Marine Corps didn't have them in any of the prior wars.

We all got new dog tags and filled out battle cards. Battle cards were new to me. They would hold all the important information that would be needed to identify you and provide corpsman with vital information. We would fill out several and keep one visible at all times. Anytime we would travel, we would give the convoy or flight leader a copy as well. Good thinking!

I had "Officer of the Day duty" the night we sent the Advance Liaison (ADVON) off to Camp Habbaniyah. We would all follow in a couple weeks, but they would get there early to begin coordination with the 1st Battalion, 1st Marine Regiment. It wasn't much of a sendoff at 0400 on a cold, rainy morning, but I guess it was better that way.

As we got closer to our own departure, they started assigning Plane Captains, and I was tagged for my flight. When I told Terri, she immediately sent me a link to a cat herding super bowl commercial. No respect!

She arrived for a visit on Thursday, 11 January. She would pick up a rental car and drive to Twentynine Palms from Palm Springs. It was getting late, so I called her on my cell phone. She was delayed, but on the way. I asked her how she liked the countryside. After a brief silence, and in a sweet, thoughtful way only she could pull off, she said, "God must have had a bad hair day here." You gotta love that woman!

We enjoyed Breakfast at Denny's, and I made sure to get her to the Twentynine Palms Inn for dinner where Chuck, Major Barnhill, and I went a couple times. It was a real oasis with a rich history going back to the days of the earliest settlers and American Indians. I took her all around mainside and gave her a tour of Camp Wilson she heard so much about, and also showed her the very spot in the open sand where a weak signal allowed me to call her every night, facing the right direction of course! We very much enjoyed this! On her last day, we enjoyed a scenic drive through Joshua Tree National Monument and watching the Packers lose a playoff game to the Giants at Applebee's in Yucca Valley on Sunday.

I would never want to live in Twentynine Palms, but met plenty of people who wouldn't want to live anywhere else! My sister Judy and her Marine Corps husband, Ken, were assigned to the 7th Marine Regiment and lived in Yucca Valley. They still have great friends there and still love it.

On Monday we drove to Palm Desert and stayed at the JW Marriott Desert Springs hotel and had our last night together before my deployment. The good bye was tough, but our love and friendship was strong, and we spoke of being able to be together for good in eight months. I always felt her presence where ever I was, so in a way we never parted.

On 24 January, the battalion gathered at the designated area to meet the buses that would take us to March Air Force Base. Several Marines and I were appointed as Guardian Angels and were issued live ammunition. We parted Twentynine Palms on schedule at 1600 hours. Our deployment to Iraq had finally begun.

Chapter Nine
Arrival in Iraq/Relief in Place/Transfer of Authority: Feb 2008
Camp Habbaniyah, Iraq

March Air Force Base and Kuwait

The two-hour bus trip from the Twentynine Palms Marine Corps Air/Ground Combat Training Center went quickly and uneventfully. We arrived at March Air Force Base on schedule at 1800 hours on 24 January. As Plane Captain, I double checked the rosters and ensured that we had 100% accountability of personnel and ammunition. There were always a couple glitches, and I spent most of my time at March working with the stick leaders to nail down the last roster adjustments.

We were soon on our way to Budapest, Hungary which took about six and a half hours. We would only stop there for an hour and a half, so we had to stay on the plane and wait for the remaining four-hour flight to Kuwait.

We arrived at Kuwait at 0730 on 26 January and were bused to Camp Virginia for temporary billeting and in-country processing. It was a large area with huge tents. With virtually no delay, we were herded as one large group into a briefing tent where we received our general orders and were briefed on conduct expected in a combat zone. Our ID Cards were gathered and swiped, starting the clock for our overseas time. We were surprised to hear there would be two flights to Al Taqaddum Air Base, known as "TQ" that same night. From there it was a short truck ride to Camp Habbaniyah. Before we knew it, we were on buses to Ali Al Salem Air Base and herded into "ready tents."

The first flight left on schedule at 2000 hours, but our flight was cancelled at the last second. We had literally gotten right up to the C-17 in our buses and could see the well-lit American flag over the entry ramp to the aircraft, when the heavy fog rolled in! We were bussed back to the ready tents we came from with no idea when we would be making the short trip to Camp Habbaniyah. It would turn out to be several days of monotonous hell.

Forward Operating Base Camp Habbaniyah
We finally arrived safely at Camp Habbaniyah at 0530. The short trip took us over a bridge crossing the Euphrates River. The river scenery was eerie. There were eroded mounds of dirt everywhere as a reminder of biblical days when the Euphrates and Tigris were broad and flowing. The whole area was once under water. Centuries of war and destruction of irrigation canals left the rivers narrow and shallow with only the mounds remaining. It almost looked like a junior version of our badlands.

We all slept until 1100. We got back up for in-briefings and went to the nearby rifle range to draw our combat load of ammunition and battle-zeroed our rifles. After more rest, we gathered in the combat operations center at 2100 for an area familiarization. I found the AT&T call center that I would stop at every morning at 0730 or so to call Terri. It was on my long walk to the chow hall, so it would become part of my morning routine. It was in very rough condition. The crappy, wooden floors were uneven and ready to break-through. The wood phone stalls had been nearly carved through by all the rotating units, but the phones were in fairly good working order. If I called by 0700 or at least by 0730, she would still be awake back home.

Nights in the combat operations center were taking shape for me. Staff Sergeant MacNally of the battalion we were replacing had patience and was teaching me the trade. He really had it down to a science. We would have to react to any Significant Activities (SIGACTS), handle any other phone, radio, or email traffic that came in, and have the Battalion Commander's reports ready for him by 0600 every day. We had progressed in our left seat/right seat routine, and now I was in the right seat, which meant he sat back and watched me. Overall, I was doing okay, but I had trouble with handling counter fire missions fast enough.

As soon as the radar batteries established throughout the area of operations would detect some type of launch, whether it would be a mortar, rocket, or anything else, we would plot the point of origin (POO). Then the artillery support folks would very quickly determine point of impact (POI) based on the radar supplied trajectory information. Our job was to plot the POO and POI on the automated system and determine whether or not to authorize return fire. Throughout the tour, we would get an average of ten counter-fire drills a day and never responded to one with real counter fire. Our predecessors said they only returned fire a couple times as well. Most of the time the radar was picking up a flock of birds taking off, or as I surmised, perhaps a bunch of camel farts...

Mail started reaching us now, too. Terri sent me a projector clock that worked out great for me in my room. It shined on the plywood ceiling so I could see it from my rack anytime of night. It was a great idea! That's my Terri. Always thinking! It was a constant reminder of her steadfast love and support.

RIP/TOA and a New Assignment
On 6 February, our Relief in Place/Transfer of Authority (RIP/TOA) with the 1st Battalion, 1st Marines was scheduled. We would take formal control at the stroke of midnight. Our Operations Officer, Major Mann, and their Operations Officer, Major Grahm were standing over me as the hour approached. At exactly midnight, I was to send the formal transfer of authority message out to all our higher, adjacent, and subordinate units. I had it all teed up for hours knowing it was important, and I was ready! At the prescribed time and upon Major Mann's order, I hit the send button.

The 2nd Battalion, 24th Marines was now in charge of Camp Habbaniyah and our area of operations as assigned by Regimental Combat Team 1 in Fallujah.

I finally got to the BAS and after cleaning the wax and sand out of my ears (I was having a hard time hearing) and they arranged a trip to the nearby Al Taqaddum air base to get my broken tooth checked. It was a Naval Expeditionary Dental Unit. They couldn't fix my tooth properly, but did put a bonded restoration in that should last until I got back home in seven months. It felt good, and plugged the gaping hole in my head that bothered me. I was good with it!

Major Bourland, the assistant operations officer to Major Mann, thought I would be of value if I could help the battalion commander with his Daily Intentions Report, keep our SharePoint page up to date with the regimental headquarters, organize all the requests for information coming in from the companies, prepare the weekly Battle Update Brief (BUB) slides, coordinate electronic warfare route clearances, and maintain the battle drill manual. You know - all his stuff! Major Mann agreed and I was reassigned.

I dug right in. They wanted the Battle Drill Book done in a few days. I worked around the clock to get it the way they wanted. Battle Drill Books provide detailed guidance for nearly every circumstance a conventional infantry unit might encounter including, but not limited to, Counter Fire, Casualty Evacuation, Troops in Contact, Mass Casualties, Missing Marines, Improvised Explosive Device/Possible IED, Unexploded Ordinance, Detainees, Downed Vehicle/Accident, Escalation of Force/Defensive Action, Blue on Blue Incidents, and Green on Green Incidents. I was in my element! An old Marine writing new tricks! Plus, I had my secret weapons - Gunnery Sergeants Welton and Hight. I could do this!

Daily Life in Camp Habbaniyah
I quickly adjusted to my new routine and kept very busy. I definitely felt like I was contributing! I settled into a battle rhythm of getting up at 0630, getting to the call center to call Terri by 0645, having morning chow by 0730 and in the combat operations center by 0800. I would ensure that the companies were sending in their daily reports so I could put Lieutenant Colonel Charlonis' report together for an on-time submission to the regimental headquarters. The afternoons would be spent making sure all the battalion records and SharePoint website were up to date.

Outside the Wire
About three weeks out on 19 February, I would embark on my first combat convoy to Camp Fallujah and our regimental headquarters. Gunnery Sergeant Smithson, Staff Sergeant Matthews and I were in an armored Humvee. I was pretty much safe as a FOBBIT on Camp Habbaniyah. Traveling is where the danger came, but I had to do my duty. Everyone had to go "outside of the wire" sometime!

Our convoy leader's briefing laid out everything we needed to know in the event we ran into trouble of various sorts. Everybody would know exactly what route we took, exactly what frequencies to call if we got hit, exactly how to call for support, and exactly what to do until help arrived. Every convoy that left the wire would conduct this briefing. We would maintain constant contact with the combat operations center. I was usually on the receiving end of these reports, so this was an interesting switch.

All the Main Supply Routes (MSR) had names known by every command and every driver. We would take MSR Michigan on a couple connecting routes to our destination to the far side of Fallujah where the regimental headquarters was headquartered. Going through Fallujah for the first time was fascinating to me. I could see the famous bridge where insurgents killed the Blackwater agents and hung them from the supporting structures. The buildings were all basically dilapidated, but not from war. The war damage was evident, but not predominant. Every building looked like it was falling down or had fallen down from disrepair. The streets were littered with trash, debris, and dirt. This is just the way these people live! It was a different world. Most men were wearing robes, and all the women had burkas. Some children wore western clothes.

Arriving at Camp Fallujah was eerie. There was a sand storm. The air around us was red and the sky was yellow. We parked and agreed to meet at a prescribed time. I felt strange walking around the headquarters in my flight suit and boonie hat, but I soon learned it was expected and understood by the inhabitants, including the regimental commander. That was the main thing I guess! Tents, antennas, and barriers were the main features! Seeing this flat, non-descript, and dull camp made me appreciate Camp Habbaniyah. At least we had interesting street layouts and palm trees, albeit they were filthy with dirt and dust. But home was home!

Back in Wisconsin

The brutal winter persisted back home. Terri said the snowfall accumulation for the season was just a little over one half inch from the all time seasonal snowfall record of 76.1 inches. It would far exceed that before it was over! She had started going to a personal trainer and was very disciplined about getting to her workouts. They were in Lodi, so she was getting a good look at the little town where I grew up.

Return to Rocky Point

Memories of my Iraq tour's early days dredged up the familiar feeling of starting an overseas tour. There is always the adventure and sometimes danger of being in a foreign land and it always starts with a time line, the end of which seems so far away. Was I ready to go back and start yet another long countdown to the day I would come home?

The Citizen Marine
Living the Dream – In Every Clime and Place

Chapter Ten
Combat Operations Center: Mar-May 2008
Camp Habbaniyah, Iraq

Camp Habbaniyah and Combat Operations

We were on a phased schedule to turn more and more of Al Anbar Province over to the Iraqi Army (IA) and Iraqi Police (IP). It was likely that as this was happening, other units would leave. As a result, we would assume a larger battle space and evolve more and more into a back-up roll to the IA and IP. At the time, we expected to pull out of Camp Habbaniyah by May and turn it over to the IA. That would not transpire.

Overall, our morale was quite good. While Counterinsurgency Operations isn't what Marines are truly trained for, our Marines knew the importance of the civil portion of our duties. We were much more suited to kinetic ops like the original push, but there just weren't enough police to do what had to be done in a massive counterinsurgency. So the Marines and Army had adjusted to the task. We also knew it could change overnight, and we would remain ever vigilant.

On the first of March, Lieutenant Colonel Charlonis and Major Mann headed to Combat Outpost (COP) Hawas to supervise combined cordon and knock operations with a reconnaissance team and Navy Seals. Cordon and knock had become a routine way of raiding homes based on actionable intelligence, resulting in the discovery of fake walls and tunnels. Several adults and children came out of the home, but just as the Seals left the building, there was a grenade explosion resulting in nine Enemy Killed In Action (EKIA) and no friendly casualties.

Cordon and knock was a common practice, but it was particularly noteworthy that the Navy Seals and a conventional infantry battalion cooperated and coordinated. All too often the special operations teams would come into an area of operations owned by a conventional battalion without notice or coordination. Too many times it didn't work out well. This was a tribute to Lieutenant Colonel Charlonis and Major Mann and their relationship building skills. I personally took a small part of the credit for the good relationship after getting their Senior Chief's 'kill house' rebuilt when our enterprising young Marines stripped all the interior wall wood to improve their living quarters at Camp Habbaniyah.

A Touch of Home

One day after returning to the combat operations center for evening chow, I spotted a huge poster taking up all the space on a long hallway wall within the combat operations center building. It was a huge banner of notes and signatures for everyone in Headquarters & the Service Company from our Chicago Key Volunteer group and all of our families. Terri had been driving down a few times, and I figured she would have signed it. It took up the entire length of the long hallway, and it would be very difficult to find Terri's signature if she had signed it.

As I thought about it, I knew Terri was very detailed, and on something this big, she would go for something small to send her message to me. It ended up taking me zero time to find it. On the tip of a large star on one end of the banner was a special note to me from my favorite Devil Doggette. Did I know my Terri or what? What a great idea the banner was! We all loved it, and it was there until the end of our tour. Every time I entered the combat operations center, I would have a greeting from Terri! What a steadfast group of family patriots!

Easter time was upon us. I got Easter cards from Terri, my family, and even got a couple cards by name from families in Madison's Golf Company. Nice touch! It was a special day in the chapel. The busted up cement floor, plywood altar, plastic lawn chairs, and guns still made me feel at peace and appreciate my home and family, especially for Easter. I thought of my sister Cherie and her family, all they were going through with her brain cancer, and it brought me closer to them.

Additional Duties/Fallujah

Major Jeff Strey, Executive Officer extraordinaire, informed me late on 29 March that I was assigned as the battalion's safety officer. Major Barnhill was our safety officer, but he had been reassigned to a billet in Bagdad. Lucky bastard! He would have his own trailer room with his own sink, shower, and toilet! That was the good news. The bad news was that he had a higher likelihood of getting blown off his private toilet by mortar rounds that were coming in regularly…

Wasn't this great? I was now a safety officer in a combat zone! I took it as a distinct indicator of the Executive and Operations Officers' faith in my excellent ability to keep higher headquarters out of our hair with my brilliant report writing skills. The regimental headquarters was pushing hard on safety. The reality was that even if it was a combat zone, the statistics of non-combat injuries were way too high and had to be curbed. The regimental headquarters Executive Officer made that very clear. Now my pucker factor was really up! Could I have my infantry platoon back?

I had to attend a regimental safety meeting in Fallujah the following Monday. That meant another combat convoy. This time it translated to a three-day trip. My meeting wouldn't be done in time to leave with the convoy, so I would have to stay in Fallujah and wait for their next trip. This time I rode in a 7 Ton and followed the same route as I had several times before. Sometimes, we would take a route that required us to cross the Euphrates on Army Combat Engineer ferry boats.

We arrived on schedule, without incident, but as soon as we arrived, we realized they were in "River City," where all communications are shut down until a casualty's next of kin is notified. There was no way to communicate with Habbaniyah or with Terri! Just three hours before, a Marine Corps Major had been killed in an Improvised Explosive Device (IED) attack. It was a fairly new tactic. Apparently, a truck leaving Camp Fallujah was able to release an explosive device using a specially rigged glove compartment chute on a supply delivery truck. It was simple. The chute had been built, and the bomb was let down using a string as the truck left the base. It was especially tragic because the Major was trapped in the burning up armored Humvee and died.

On 1 April I finally caught a ride back to Camp Habbaniyah with the battalion commander's Personal Security Detail (PSD). Traveling in Iraq was dangerous for members of headquarters, but for the rifle companies and platoons, danger came with every step they took in the streets and in the countryside they patrolled every day and night.

Either way, these Marines faced danger everyday and had to make sure they didn't let their guard down for even a second.

Life at Camp Habbaniyah

In order to keep our companies supplied with food, ammo, fuel, and operating supplies, we conducted several Log Trains every week. There were logistic trains consisting of seven-ton trucks, Mine Resistant Ambush Protected Vehicle (MRAP's), and up armored Humvees. One of the Log Trains hit an IED and survived with little damage to the MRAP and no injuries. We were finding IED's and caches daily, but it was a cat and mouse game as they adapted to our techniques and we adapted to theirs. This was the third one that detonated on us, and it kept everyone sharp. It hit the front of the MRAP.

I talked to the Lieutenant who was sitting right where it hit, and he said it was a very quick, dull thud, and he hardly felt anything. It caused damage to the transmission case and shaft, but overall, the MRAP did its job quite well. The other two were a seven-ton truck, and a M1114 up armored HMMV. The trucks were protecting us quite well so far.

My IMO duties were expanding and I started getting more involved in the Biometric Automated Tool Set (BATS) systems, used to record biometric data on facial, retina and fingerprints of suspected insurgents. The database was growing vastly and was becoming quite effective in finding wanted insurgents. If there was reason to initially record their information, we would also load fake names and any other information we had, to see if they had been involved in any prior bad behavior. We had several operations coming up that would require an expansion of our existing inventory, and Major Mann asked me to see if I could dig up some more BATS systems. Another Fallujah trip took shape.

Fallen Heroes

On 14 April we suffered our first casualties. Two Marines from Milwaukee's Fox Company were killed and one wounded near their combat outpost (COP) 569. Up until then we had been fortunate. But this time fate looked the other way.

Corporal Ricky Nelson and Lance Corporal Dean Opicka were in an up armored Humvee as part of a Fox Company convoy when they hit an IED. Corporal Nelson died instantly in the blast. Lance Corporal Opicka died after several attempts to save him. The turret gunner was blown clear of the wreckage. He would later receive the Purple Heart medal for his wounds and the Bronze Star Medal for heroism trying to save his fellow Marines. River City was sounded immediately, and for the first time, it would be our own Marines that were involved. All external communications were shut down until the notification of next of kin.

It was very somber in the combat operations center as the reports came in. Everyone went about their jobs. We all knew it could happen, and we knew it could happen again. I will never forget the respect that was rendered for these three Marines in Fox Company, at the battalion headquarters, and all the way up the chain of command.

Terri was in Hawaii, so our calling routine was an additional four hours off. We had been through many River City communication blackouts by now, but this time she was very worried, and very upset. We both were at loose ends because we hadn't been able to talk as often as we were accustomed. The technology that made it possible for us to talk frequently was a double edged sword. If we weren't used to it, times like this wouldn't bother us.

We had a memorial service in a big, empty warehouse. The young Marines were very highly thought of by their officers, NCO's, and fellow Marines of Fox Company. Corporal Ricky Nelson's first tour with the battalion in Iraq and his participation in this, his second tour, would later be chronicled as part of a movie called "Perfect Valor". They got a good send off and their pictures would remain in our combat operations center on our Hall of Honor.

The Mission and Sand Storms Continue

I had to return to Fallujah to do some safety officer work, and to scrounge for BATS equipment to support the upcoming operations Major Mann had up his sleeve. Getting back there seemed too soon, and at the same time, too long. On my last trip we were only three hours behind an IED explosion that took the life of Major Hill. It had only been days since we lost Corporal Nelson and Lance Corporal Opicka. All of us traveling had them on our mind.

It would be a one-day round trip with the battalion commander's PSD. The trip would incorporate a stop at combat outpost (COP) Golden far north of our Battalion combat operations center. We started early and were turned back shortly after crossing the Euphrates River due to blinding rain and sand storms. We couldn't see past the hood of the vehicles! We got back to the combat operations center on time for me to get my morning chores done. We tried again in the afternoon and made it.

We arrived without incident, but Camp Fallujah was in River City upon our arrival again. I soon found out that 1st Battalion, 9th Marines got hit in their new area of operations just as we arrived at Camp Fallujah. The last report I received was that there were two KIA and two surgical evacuations. They went through Mojave Viper just before us back at the stumps, but didn't deploy here until just now. They were still in their Relief in Place/Transfer of Authority (RIP/TOA) with 2nd battalion, 8th Marines and already took casualties. It would be a rough tour for them. Our Intel told us we could expect increased enemy activity as it got warmer and as the elections (both US and Iraq) approached. It was pretty much on target.

I went about the business of my BATS equipment hunt requested by Major Mann. After a long day, I had amassed a good inventory of BATS systems to support Major Mann's future operational plans. It felt good!

Al Qaeda Cat

It was a time of calm, but a time of edginess. We felt danger, but we couldn't see a face or describe a reason for our concern. Enter Al Qaeda Cat. Major Bourland and a few of us spoke of him over the fire pit. Cats at Camp Habbaniyah were everywhere. The story of Al Qaeda Cat spread like wild fire to incoming battalions. They say his stealth was legendary. One second he would be rubbing against your leg purring and before you knew it, he would slit your throat with a single swipe of his sharp claws! All who sat at the pit made sure their weapons and K-Bars were at the ready. Who would be the first to pooh-pooh the legend of Al Qaeda Cat?

Family and Friends

Terri was in Hawaii at our favorite spot in Waikiki. Me being in a combat zone was no reason for her not to go, right? It was good for her! I received a package from her containing a very nice looking and comfortable pillow with Marine Corps patterns. She made it with the Chicago Key Volunteers. It was placed at the head of my rack and made a perfect reading pillow. It complimented the cagey reading light she bought me. Does she love me or what? She was very surprised when I came home and it was still so clean!

The next day my daughter wrote that they saw an ultrasound and her "Little Beaner" was going to be a boy. Wow!! Grand Runt II would join us about the time I got back home! My immediate thoughts were that Daddy Mark would almost have enough boys to have his own little fire-team! He was probably thinking he would have enough boys for a good deer drive. In any case, I had one happy daughter and son in law, and they had one happy Dad! The "Little Beaner" made all we were doing worthwhile, and reminded us all of the preciousness of life.

The War Continues

On 1 May, Major Mann was promoted to Lieutenant Colonel. The ceremony was held in an informal semi-circle by the combat operations center's flag poles. Our uniforms were mixed between desert cammies with eight point covers, flight suits, and boonie covers, depending on our traveling status. Combat zone promotion ceremonies are the best!

The business of war quickly reminded me of where we were. A recent operation resulted in six detainees. Some were in our retention facility, and some were whisked off to higher headquarters if their BATS profiles indicated any reason to do so. Milwaukee's Fox Company had another IED hit, but suffered no casualties or equipment loss. All the same, we found ourselves in River City again. The 2nd battalion, 3rd Marines just east of us suffered three KIA and one MIA.

Early May brought the issue of Sadr City to our forefront. Our nightly operations brief indicated a potential that we may be tapped to assist the Iraqi Army in the taking of the Sadr City section of Baghdad. The op tempo around Camp Habbaniyah had increased significantly. We had tanks brought in to rehearse tank/infantry coordination in urban combat. We were within a day or two of being called into the Sadr City operation.

It was cancelled at the last minute, but the pucker factor was up and stayed up. The Sadr City threat combined with what was going on down south in Basra, and the Al Qaeda activity that Major Bourland was dealing with up north, kept us on our toes. We could go in any direction at any time! Lieutenant Colonel Mann planned several operations that would have us positioned to react accordingly.

It was now 11 May, our wedding anniversary and Mother's Day. Once again, we were in River City! Nothing happened in our battalion area of operations, but I was feeling the anxiety of not being able to call Terri on schedule, especially on our anniversary! Terri was at loose ends this time, more than usual in River City. She had several rings, but the phone was dead by the time she answered. She thought it may have been me on the satellite phone. Again, the River City blackout brought home the sadness that so many mothers wouldn't be hearing from their sons on Mother's Day while they were in harm's way.

When we finally connected, much later in the day for Terri, we enjoyed our call, but I was feeling very empty afterward. I could sense her sadness, fear, and depression. What was I doing to her? I sat in my room late at night listening to Enya and Dennis Kamakahi music and enjoying a mental journey of us in our DeForest home listening to the same music. It was a long night…

The "Ground Hog Day" effect was setting in. Every day was the same. But a routine was good. As long as I kept my energy level up, I liked it. I was still very disciplined in my eating and exercise routines. There was always the danger of a rocket, mortar, or ground attack, but our security was very good so I didn't worry much. As little as six months before we got there, it wasn't that way. Our predecessors just started going slick (no armor) around the camp not long before we arrived.

There were plenty of events to keep the traveling Marines and the companies on their toes. One of our convoys was near a Vehicle Born IED (VBIED) that detonated as they traveled through Fallujah. The Captain in charge reported muzzle flashes right after the explosion and the turret gunner returned fire. None of our Marines were hurt, but the sources of the muzzle flashes in the top story of a building probably had their "Man Night Thursday" ruined! The young Captain seemed to draw fire wherever he went. He was truly a lead magnet! He did the right thing and protected his Marines. All was right with the world.

Our tour was down to eighty days left! In my early days as a Marine in Okinawa in 1975, we would have countdown calendars in the shape of the island to our Freedom Birds and would fill them in one day at a time. Tours were thirteen months then. Once you got below a hundred days, you were a two-digit midget! I congratulated everybody on being a two-digit midget, but they didn't get it. They would have if we were there for thirteen months!

Madison's Golf Company got an interesting mission. Air Force Captain Nancy Lester, a reservist from Milwaukee, was a veterinarian stationed in Baghdad in a Civil Affairs Group. We were constantly looking for ways of connecting with the local citizens to gain their support, increase their confidence in their Iraqi Army and Police, and provide inroads for intelligence gathering to help us cut the bad guys out of the populace. For three days, Golf Company conducted what we called a Combined Veterinary Event (CVE) in rural areas of Abu Bakit/Btiri, Abu Aifan, and Abu Taha with Captain Lester.

She was quite excited to get "outside the wire" and was very comfortable when she found out the Marines that she would be working with were from Wisconsin. They distributed fifty-nine bags of livestock feed, and forty five human food bags, with numerous school supplies and candies to the children who came. They vaccinated and de-wormed 244 sheep, 56 Holstein cattle, and 15 goats. And we were able to run a large number of the local citizens through our systems and check our BATS databases for insurgent activity. A win-win for all!

It was a great day for me to talk with the young Captain from Milwaukee on how the Marines from Golf Company eventually learned to walk up to the animals with increasing confidence. The good Captain had to be quick! The animals fought the young Marines with great vigor. She confided in me that it was possible that not all the de-worming medicine made it into the animals! I suddenly knew of some young Madison Marines that shouldn't have any worm problems for awhile!

Every day was filled with a very impressive array of activity ranging from combat patrols and convoys with the threat of going kinetic at any moment, to civil affairs work like this. While every now and then I felt like it was ground hog day, I realized you just have to take notice of the things like this that make every day unique.

As May came toward the end, the temperatures were reaching 105 degrees. We would leave in August before it reached 130 degrees, but we would get a good taste of the heat before we left. Sand storms were now the norm, and the feeling of a constant layer of powdery sand was to be expected. It meant cleaning my rifle and pistol more frequently. You didn't need them often, but when you did, you needed them NOW and they needed to work!

The Surge was working. Al Qaeda for all practical purposes was losing Iraq's support. They had a huge break in their lines of communications, ease of movement, and available recruiting/training areas. But they were resilient and strong in other areas. They were also very patient, and they fully expected the world-wide return to Islamic rule to displace civil governments would take more than a hundred years. They were watching our elections back home knowing they would determine the battleground in the short term (five to ten years). They could easily wait things out if the elections went their way.

Back in Wisconsin

For the first time in the years since my return to Wisconsin from my early days of active duty, the snow was breaking all records. In the eighties, we were lucky to get two or three good snowmobile runs in per year. Now that I was gone, Terri was overwhelmed trying to keep up with the snow removal and was very glad to have that new snow blower! The snowmobile trails were humming. I missed snowmobiling, but not driving on slippery roads. I was glad to be in Iraq surrounded by armed Marines in a combat zone, rather than being subjected to every jackass that doesn't think you're driving fast enough in the snow and ice!

Terri was putting in long days. She missed her best friend and soul mate, and he missed her. She was commonly staying up until 1-2 AM, partly to keep up with things, and partly because she couldn't be sure of my safe return. She found good friends at the Imperial Garden on

Madison's east side. It was close to our DeForest house, and they treated her like family just like the people at the Dorf Haus in Roxbury near our Sauk house.

Mom kept up the letter writing, which made me anticipate mail call just as I did thirty-five years earlier in boot camp, and through the seventies, while away from home. She would read my emails to Dad and it made him think of his Korean War days. He was plenty busy with Memorial Day woodworking projects.

Cherie was starting to have problems bothersome to our family and close friends. Her brain cancer was persisting. She was getting lost driving short distances, and the kids weren't getting the supervision they really needed. She was still in charge and was blocking attempts to get help. She had so much respect and love from all of us, but was nowhere near ready to give up control or life in general. We had to respect that!

As it warmed in Wisconsin, Terri was ready to plant her DeForest flowers, and did a fantastic job with them. I always enjoyed thinking about driving up to the house and seeing them along the driveway, around the bird bath and street light, and everywhere. She had good taste in flowers and men!

So all was well back home. I realized that everyone back there was running way harder than me in my safe, cozy, comfy, forward operating base in Iraq! It made me think of being away from the rat race. It may sound nuts, but it was good to be in a combat zone with only the mission and your fellow Marines to think about! Temporarily of course.

Back at Rocky Point

It all seemed so surreal as I reeled my thoughts back to the present. I was about half way through my Iraq tour and enjoying my mental journey through the forty-year tug of war between love of family and sense of duty. As I enjoyed the Tampa scenery and pondered my uncertain future at CENTCOM, my memories continued to flow.

Chapter Eleven
Combat Operations Center: Jun-Jul 2008
Camp Habbaniyah, Iraq

Camp Habbaniyah and Combat Operations

By 1 Jun things were settling down even more as the Iraqi Security Forces improved. Our battalion was put into an over watch status. Security was good and the week before an Iraqi Police unit stood fast in a Fallujah engagement. There was talk of elections being postponed, which we thought may be a problem if they were prolonged for too long. The locals were looking for direction, as they had lived under the oppression of the Saddam Hussein and radical Islamists for too long. Either an election would determine democratic leadership or they would strengthen their tribal ties, which would make it harder to bring in a unified government.

Lieutenant Colonel Mann stressed the importance of not losing focus. It is at this time in a combat tour when lethargy can set in and people start making mistakes. The key to success for our area of operations was to maintain security between Ramadi and Fallujah. Our concerns centered on a recent release of prisoners from the Bucca prison camp. We wanted to track the prisoners in our Biometric Automated Tools System (BATS), so if any of the prisoners became involved in further illegal activity, we would have what we needed to properly classify and process them.

Bridges Over the Euphrates

The US Army's 814th Engineers continued operating the ferry that took us across the Euphrates River three Mine Resistant Ambush Protected Vehicle (MRAP's) at a time. It was always somewhat troubling when we found ourselves spinning around in the mid-river current, but the small "tugs" would quickly come to our rescue and put us back on course to the right river bank. One night, a sand storm got the tug boat drivers disoriented. They ended up landing our teams on the same side of the river on which they started! We often complimented our Army brethren on the great job they did on the river crossings. By now we had made several crossings with them and this one mistake did not dilute our respect for these heroes.

They had fifteen month tours and this crew was on their last few months. Even though the heat was unbearable, they still had to wear full combat gear, including armor. Their work loading, unloading, and navigating was arduous. They stood by their ferry 7 X 24, day on/stay on, and were always there when you needed them. What particularly impressed me was the fact they wore life preservers over their armor! As long as they didn't thrash about in the water, the preservers would actually hold them afloat, armor and all! Another great feat of engineering giantry!

But trouble was brewing. The reeds on both sides of the river were growing and blocking the view up and down river. My visual of the biblical story of baby Moses floating in a basket down the river was certainly intensified! We started noticing increased small boat traffic with photographers. Since this wasn't exactly Disneyland, and the locals weren't wearing Mickey and Minnie T-Shirts, we made the brilliant observation these were insurgents preparing to make our river crossings more difficult.

Major Malone was assigned the mission to deal with the reeds. He coordinated with an engineer unit that had flame throwers. He recruited me to assist and we arranged a ride on the ferry bridge for the flame thrower team. I witnessed the expertly delivered flames that greatly increased our fields of vision up and down river. The Major was a genius! It is another great memory. We couldn't help but feel we saved some of our fellow Marines and valiant Army Engineers' lives. Our own included...

Life in the Rifle Companies

Our rifle companies patrolled, and they patrolled and they patrolled. They patrolled the streets of the cities, and they patrolled the fields of Anbar Province. I don't know which was more dangerous. The streets held danger with every Iraqi, and the fields held danger in every lump of dirt. Most of the land away from the Euphrates and Tigris Rivers was barren dirt, but along the rivers and near the lakes like Tharthar to our north and Habbaniyah to our south, there are farms. They were all in our area of operations and they all had to be engaged. Some of the companies had to attend meetings of the Sheiks and some had to clear vast areas of fields and dry lands for any sign of insurgent activity or weapons caches. It all culminated in our gathering of "atmospherics" to report to the regimental headquarters and on to General Petraeus in Iraq and the powers to be in Washington, DC.

We had discovered a tremendous amount of buried weapons caches. The rifle companies used a combination of techniques to find them, but the best technique was always to converse with the local nationals who wanted them out of their area.

I'll never forget an example early in our tour. A young girl playing in a rural area discovered IED making material in the dirt near her family's house. She came and told her father, and a few days later when our Marines were patrolling nearby, the father came and led our Marines to the IED cache. Our patrol called Explosive Ordinance Disposal (EOD) out, and detonated it. They were about 300 yards from the family's home, but the concussion blew out every window in their house!

Bad news! Definitely not the way to win the hearts and minds of the people, so we made sure they were taken care of as fast as possible. But, it really brought home what it's like to live in a land where warring factions in some way affect every family in every corner of the land. Less than a year before, that same family would have paid the ultimate price for even talking to us!

In the cities the danger was the same, but the duty was different. I sent pictures home of our Marines interacting with Iraqi children. You could superimpose a picture of a WWII soldier giving French or German children chocolate. Our new breed of young Marines reaching out to the youth of the country we hoped would ultimately yield a better life for them. But even this was dangerous. Many of our battalion's Marine reservists were college students and started learning Arabic when they first learned of our impending deployment to Iraq. We still used interpreters, aka "terps," like the active duty battalions, but needed fewer because we had many of our own.

Break 'em in Young!
In all my years of service, there was one constant in my observations of how the Marine Corps operates. Whether it is combat on foreign shores, or peacetime duty at home, you got a lot of responsibility at a

very young age in the Corps! I have always said that the typical
eighteen-year-old Lance Corporal Fire Team leader has only a
fraction of a second to make life or death decisions, whereas
corporate giants have at least six months to screw up before anyone
notices. Even when they do, a bank account goes dry, and at worst,
jobs are lost.

The Fire Team leader's decision will undergo intensive scrutiny,
more than likely by lawyers that have never seen a day of combat and
took six months to go over the actions that took a second in time. The
corporate giant is given a golden parachute and lives happily ever
after. No matter how it works out for that young Lance Corporal,
they'll live with their decision for life. In Iraq and in those MRAPs, I
realized how much I'd rather be with that Lance Corporal any day of
the week!

Father's Day in Iraq
And so our tour in Iraq continued with mission focus, continual
training, and early planning for our trip back home. Father's Day was
upon us, and I looked forward to my free time after leaving the
combat operations center around nine or ten every night, provided
nothing was going on. My room was an escape from it all. I received
Father's Day cards from Terri, Kurt, and Kristin. Kurt sent a box of
my favorite peanut butter crackers! I was lucky enough to catch Kurt,
Kristin, and my parents on a single SATCOM call to my house in
Sauk City! Dad's birthday fell on Father's Day, so it was a special
treat to talk to him! Terri was in Branson for our nephew's wedding,
but we still had our daily call.

I thought back to the Vietnam era when I was overseas and there
were no cell phones, no SATCOM available for use, and no email.
Only snail mail was available, and it often took ten days to
communicate. Balancing my love of family and sense of duty was
much easier when I could utilize modern technology!

Keeping the Focus
On 26 June, our sister battalion, 2nd Battalion, 3rd Marines, in the area
of operations next to ours, were attacked with a Suicide Vest
Improvised Explosive Device (SVIED). Their battalion commander
and driver were killed along with two "terps" and nineteen civilians.

Over forty civilians were wounded. The battalion commander was another close friend of Major Strey. Jeff took it like a professional, but it was easy to see the strain and the reason behind his readiness to retire and get on with a "normal" life.

In the meanwhile, our Marines continued mounted and dismounted patrols, IED and Cache Sweeps, local populace engagements, and Al Qaeda (Iraq) interdiction missions, and all the logistics it took to support these. As we learned that day, a lot can happen in the forty-some days we still had left, and we would be hard at work right up to the last day when our replacement battalion formally took the reins. As our days wound down, we planned new operations. Our Marines would be very active until the day the coveted Relief in Place/Transfer of Authority (RIP/TOA) took place with our replacement battalion.

Staying Connected

Terri was never far from my heart. I felt her presence. Her love, devotion, and loyalty not only to me, but to the Corps was unfailing, and I was starting to think a great deal about what it would be like to be together again! I was able to get on the internet one day and sent her a flower bouquet in a University of Wisconsin Band Bucky Wagon with Cheerleaders from Felly's in Madison. Terri is a PhD graduate from the UW and proud alumna. She hadn't missed a football game in fifteen years, and we still had season hockey tickets. The catch of a lifetime! Am I a genius or what?!!

A friend had sent me an email about booze being smuggled into Iraq disguised as Scope and other similar items. That would violate General Order #1 as was made clear the minute you hit Kuwait on your way to Iraq. My age, treachery, and common sense surged against such foolishness. The younger Marines may have partaken, but the last thing this fifty-five year old Marine needed in 100+ degree temperatures with ninety pounds of armor and ammo was a hangover!

It sounded to me like America's finest Remington Raiders and cooks, bakers, and candlestick makers in Baghdad were the primary recipients. They had it much easier and it may have happened, but regardless, it was dangerous. Radical Muslim fundamentalists in principle don't react well to even the sight or smell of alcohol, and I wasn't going to be the one to get my commander in trouble with the highest levels. Hell of a price to pay for a drink in my book!

Eyes Forward!
We continued our mission focus. The operations were executed with precision, professionalism, and a touch of American hospitality only American foot Marines and soldiers could offer. As a part of our humanitarian operations, or perhaps a combined medical or veterinary event, we partnered patrols with our Iraqi counterparts, and took every opportunity to hand out school supplies to the kids wherever we went. According to our standards, the schools still had a long way to go. Factoring in this country's infrastructure and resources, they did pretty darn well. The children welcomed us. Our Marines and sailors brought soccer balls and treats and joined the kids in play and friendly conversation.

Along with our battalion's tour winding down, the Status of Forces Agreement (SOFA) was set to expire soon. This agreement provides the legal basis for our presence and governs our roles, responsibility and authority boundaries and is critical to maintain our presence in Iraq. It was looking like an agreement between Iraq and the US wouldn't be reached on time and an extension from the UN may become necessary.

Things were working in Iraq first and foremost because of Al-Qaeda's own mistakes with their brutality and lack of respect for life. The surge helped too, but the real key was to bolster the ISF (all Iraqi Security Forces, including the Iraqi Army, Police, Provincial Security Forces, etc.) long enough for them to keep radicals out of the mix. They had enough of their own tribal and ethnic problems internally. That was important to us, Europe, and free countries everywhere. We had disrupted them sufficiently to stem their recruiting, training, and deployment of small cells to conduct terrorist acts because we were here in the middle of their operating area. If we left too soon, things could be reversed quickly. That would have been bad for Iraq, but worse for us not wanting to bring the radical fight to America and Europe.

For the Marines of 2nd battalion, 24th Marines, it was still a matter of mission focus and getting through the days and nights. Sand storms persisted on a regular basis. Our enemy actually liked sand storms as they could move more freely without our aerial surveillance or our many other forms of observation. Sometimes you can't replace good ol' boots on the ground, and we knew where to watch for them!

Surprise from Headquarters Marine Corps (HQMC)

As we approached our last month in country, I was somewhat surprised to be contacted by a personnel officer in HQMC. He came there from the US Central Command (CENTCOM) where he served as the Executive Officer for the J6 Operations division. He was looking for a replacement for the CENTCOM billet he had just left. He highly respected the Marine Colonel he worked for and wanted to make sure he found a good replacement. He was going through his Marine Corps records and noticed that I had been in the Marine Central Command (MARCENT) and served quite extensively with CENTCOM in 2001 and 2002 up to my retirement, and asked if I'd be interested in returning.

I loved my time at Tampa, MARCENT, and CENTCOM back in 2001 and 2002! Jokingly, I said, "Sure! If you can get me orders, I'm all over it!" I figured my being on active duty as a retired recall would end his creative plan to get someone to Tampa where nobody wants to go. Everyone assigned to CENTCOM in all likelihood had already served one or more tours in the sand box with their home branch of service. Going to a joint command meant certain additional trips, and they weren't scheduled in advance!

Thoughts of staying on active duty to serve under General Petraeus in Tampa, and potentially more Middle East duty were consuming my mind. I worried more about what I would tell Terri and Tony (my boss at WPS) if it were to actually happen. They were already doing more than required by allowing me to come off retirement and serve this current tour of duty. Terri believed in me, and knew how important being a Marine was to me. Through our marriage, she supported me no matter the cost. Over and over! Certainly losing my position at WPS was a calculated risk. What if these new orders actually come through? Convincing myself it would never happen, there was no need to mention it to them. In the meanwhile, I made sure to keep up my gym workout schedule and behave in the chow hall.

Dukes of Hazzard in Iraq

Through it all, home never leaves your mind. I would watch the "Dukes of Hazzard" playing on Arab networks whenever I stopped in Al Taqaddum's and Camp Habbaniyah's "Haji Shops" and barber shops. Having grown up in Lodi with the Wopat family as friends and business associates, I came to know Tom Wopat who was one year older than me. He would go on to gain fame as Luke Duke in the "Dukes of Hazzard." His father Al was instrumental in getting me a big mowing contract for the Lodi High School at the tender age of thirteen (or so). Tom and I were both on the Lodi Blue Devil football team. It's a small world after all!

Balancing War with Culture

As we got closer to the end of our tour, the op tempo on redeployment tasks, in addition to regular enduring duties increased, but I kept up with my reading. I had just finished "Kite Runner" by Khaled Hosseini about a couple of young boys that grew up in Afghanistan in the mid-late seventies and how the Taliban, Russians, and now the Coalition Forces affected their lives. I found a dog eared copy of Herman Wouk's "The Hope" and decided to read it again. I read it years ago and liked it. It's a good fiction book that also has history of Israel in the background with a realistic story line. It was followed by "The Glory" which I also read and loved. Shortly after marrying Terri I took notice of world current events, and decided to read them. I had a sixth sense that the struggle between Islam and Christianity would ultimately impact my life in a big way. Hmmm…

The struggle goes back to the biblical days of Abraham when his wife Sarah was too old to bear children. She encouraged him to choose an Egyptian slave woman to beget a son to carry on his name as was the pagan custom of the time. He chose Hagar, and Ishmael was conceived and would be their son. Some thirteen years later, Sarah was shocked by a visit from an angel to hear she would bear a son and should name him Isaac.

To ensure the true son of Abraham would become king, Hagar and Ishmael would be banished to the desert where survival would be impossible. But they survived, igniting the argument that would influence the history and future of mankind forever. Jews will say Isaac is the true son of Abraham, but Arabs will say that they survived by God's intervention. Hagar went on to find an Egyptian wife for Ishmael and he fathered twelve sons, just as Isaac's son Jacob would, leading to the argument still raging today.

Were the Jews or Arabs the true inheritors of God's rule? And was this why I was away from Terri, Kurt and Kristin in old Mesopotamia, the cradle of civilization?

Dangers of "Being Short"

The last days of a combat tour are very dangerous. I remembered the Vietnam era days where so many lives were lost in the last weeks and days of individual tours of duty. In those days, it was your individual Rotation Tour Date (RTD) that drove everything. It even established your social status in your unit. The "shorter" you were, the more respect you got. Until some poor new guy came in, you were the "F'ing New Guy" (FNG). It was common for people to die because they were too careful in their first days and too careless in their last days.

We changed to unit rotation as a lesson learned, and now we do things at the battalion level. We all come the same day and leave the same day. We all worked hard to keep our edge and to stay sharp even though things were relatively quiet. As if to help us in this endeavor, an explosive device was found near the base, reinforcing the importance of vigilance and affirming the will of our young Marines to get us all home soon.

The War Goes On

In the meanwhile, we were still very aggressively conducting combat operations. Fox Company (Milwaukee) and Golf Company (Madison) were very busy with their normal counter insurgency work in the more local areas of operations, and had become quite involved in local tribal and political processes. Additionally, they still had their share of raids on suspected insurgents. While the people waited for the Iraqi government to be elected in Anbar Province, life was still pretty much driven by the most influential political party or tribal leaders. In the absence of any sort of civil leadership, the tribal laws tended to supersede any attempt at establishing and enforcing the Rule of Law. Echo Company (Des Moines) and Weapons Company (Waukegan) were operating further north in more open, desolate areas and were more focused on interdicting remnant insurgent activity. Such patrols earlier in our tour would have turned up something, but most of them were pushed north to the Mosul area, which would be addressed after our departure.

One of our outposts was where a canal flows out of the south shore of Lake Tharthar, and was on the site of one of Saddam's exclusive palaces for his wife. They had extensive irrigation and canal systems that were now broken. The new government had plans to fix them, but things weren't stable enough for it to become a priority. If the country would settle into an effective structure, they could fix the canals and restore the Euphrates and Tigris to a point where there would easily be enough food to feed the entire Middle-East! That, along with their oil, gave Iraq great promise to become part of the world economy instead of proving a safe environment for terrorists wanting to use the land for recruiting, training and deploying to America and Europe. It wouldn't happen overnight, but the potential was there if the politicians didn't screw it up. That would prove to not be possible in the years to come.

Sand storms hindered my travels, but I eventually got to all of our SWA huts on combat patrols. I did my best to spot any electrical fire hazards and make sure upgrades were made to help ensure we didn't suffer any unnecessary casualties in the last twenty days of our deployment!

In another effort to provide some USO entertainment, Gary Sinese (Lieutenant Dan in the Forrest Gump movie) and his crew made a successful visit to our battalion. It would be the only one that wasn't cancelled by sand storms through the entire tour! I had been outside the wire on a mission, but he sat in my chair! My fellow FOBBITs took a picture for me, so it would become a prized part of my Iraq picture album.

As the days drew down to our tour's end, our replacement battalion was at the ready and we were ready to leave.

Things Back in Wisconsin

Thoughts of going home continued to become more and more like it was actually going to happen! But getting back home wouldn't be all fun and games. My youngest sister Cherie had another surgery on her brain tumor. This time, it resulted in limited movement in her left side. The doctors warned us of this with each tumor removal. The good fight had gone well until this surgery. The next six months would bring pain, uncertainty, and much family trauma.

Chapter Twelve
Relief in Place-Transfer of Authority/Redeployment: Aug 2008
Camp Habbaniyah, Iraq

End of Combat Operations

The 1st Battalion/2nd Marine Regiment had obviously done this before! They only had a year break from their last deployment. It was hard for everyone during the Relief in Place/Transfer of Authority (RIP/TOA) process. We wanted out, and they wanted in, and it was crowded. I would be staying at my post until midnight of the night of the transfer of authority as I was the one who did the formal reporting to the regimental headquarters for Lieutenant Colonel Charlonis, and of course, he wanted his own team doing that.

Things went smoothly as we all worked with our incoming counterparts to turn over inventories, orient them to the various company area of operations, and meet the local Sheiks, Mukhtars, Mayors, and Iraqi Security Force leaders.

We had one of those memorable moments on one of our last days in the combat operations center when one of our Marines reenlisted. He had received a well deserved promotion to Sergeant a couple weeks prior. I always enjoyed being around when young Marines who give so much take on another hitch or get recognized or promoted. It did my heart good. When anybody asked me about the "New Corps," my response was always that there is no such thing as the "New Corps." These Marines were smart, and they all volunteered.

I always thought it would be interesting to get an average Lance Corporal from the Vietnam era together with today's average Lance Corporal. There would be culture shock, but the best of the "Old Corps" was bred into the "New Corps," and I felt so proud to see it in person. I had no problem returning to retired status knowing these Marines were on the job. After getting home and getting the sand out of their ears and underwear, they'd be ready to go again to "any clime or place" as our famous Marine Corps Hymn says of them.

Our flights were all scheduled by now and we would start flowing out of Camp Habbaniyah in just a few days. I couldn't help but think of my Vietnam era days. My Lodi classmates would remember several of our friends and family members that survived Vietnam only to be killed within a year back home by a car or motorcycle accident. This was also a big concern for us now, as RIP/TOA time is also more dangerous on the convoys and patrols. The few insurgents left targeting Coalition Forces instead of Iraqi Police pretty much have our replacement cycle figured out and know our convoys increase. We were careful to spread out the movements and use alternate routes, but most importantly, we became very good at spotting and defeating IEDs. We hoped and prayed our skill and alertness held up for another week.

It didn't take long for our replacements to get into the fight. On 6 August, on one of their first mounted patrols, they sighted a possible IED on the road directly in front of them. They swerved to get off the road and set up a cordon, but one of the Humvees rolled over and three Marines were seriously injured.

The Tug of War Persists

In the last days my thoughts drifted back to why I was here. I didn't have to be. It was so important for me to do my part after fighting so hard to come from retired status to join my old battalion. I knew how important it would be for Iraq to be a potent force in the Middle East, in order to fight radical Islamic fundamentalists, seeking to spread their version of the otherwise peaceful religion of Islam around the entire world. So goes Iraq, so goes the safety of our streets, roads, elementary schools, county fair beer tents, and skyscrapers in the United States, Europe, Australia, Indonesia, and everywhere.

So, I was leaving with the thought that a ray of light I saw shining down on Habbaniyah through the sand filled air would bring continued hope to Iraq. Politics would drain the hope out of those thoughts in the years to follow.

Leaving Camp Habbaniyah

On 10 August, the formal transfer of Authority was executed exactly at midnight. At this time, all coordinating commands in the regimental headquarters area of operations would be communicating, coordinating, and conducting operations lead by the 1st Battalion, 2nd Marines. The 2nd Battalion, 24th Marines would pack, clean our weapons, and take care of every last detail. We would meet at the compound's flagpole in the morning to load seven ton trucks for one last trip over the Euphrates Bridge to Al Taqaddum (TQ). There we would await our Freedom Bird that would take us to back to the Marine Corps Air/Ground Combat Center at Twentynine Palms, California for final processing and transportation back to Madison, Milwaukee, Des Moines, Waukegan, and Chicago.

On the morning of 11 August a Humvee and young Marine arrived at the Red Castle to assist me in carrying my bags to the flag pole. My mind was racing. In minutes I was on my way home to see Terri and my family and friends. The competition of who gets to see Mommy first, me or Grand Runt II (aka Little Beaner) was on!

Before we knew it, we were in some old, very hot tents at Al Taqaddum. The air conditioners weren't working, and it was some kind of hot! We all laid in dirty cots with one of those blue striped mattresses with no sheet or poncho liner. Hopefully we would only be there for a few hours. I was completely soaked in sweat with my boots on and feet resting on the bed's foot rail. All in all, it felt good to rest after lugging the bags in the heat.

At about 0300 we were ordered to move to a plywood SWA hut near our aircraft location. In a couple more hours we were lined up with full packs, weapons, and armor to board our C-130 that would fly us the 90 minute or so trip to Kuwait. I was near the end of the single file line with Lieutenant Colonels Charlonis and Mann. It was light by now, and very hot! The C-130's engines were running, and the engine heat blended with the Iraqi heat to blow right into our faces making the wait even more uncomfortable as we lined up behind the aircraft for boarding.

We were finally on the plane, but it was tight! We interlocked knees with Marines in the seats across from us. Bags were being passed around lap to lap, chest to chest, to get settled. Finally, we all found our seatbelts and were settling in. The last thing was simply to place our rifles barrel down between our legs, put our ear plugs in, and wait for takeoff. Having problems finding the aircraft floor with my rifle barrel, I did the only reasonable thing and used some force. A square peg will fit in a round hole given sufficient force, right? I soon learned from the look on Lieutenant Colonel Charlonis' face that it wasn't the floor I was pounding. It was his foot! I'm guessing that's why I never got a medal...

Kuwait
We arrived at Camp Virginia, Kuwait, got unloaded and settled into the large tents holding seventy cots just before the chow hall closed at 1330. We were super impressed to feel air conditioning in the huge tent! Chief Warrant Officer 2 Kenny and I bunked close to each other and made the long walk across the vast, flat desert sand to the chow hall, seeing nothing but tents for as far as the eye could see. We made it before they closed and I thought I was going to drink their entire supply of iced tea, juice and water dry! After a very welcome meal and re-hydration, we got back to the tent and began the wait for processing and aircraft scheduling.

The word spread that we would have to wait two days for the flight home. I relaxed and read Nelson Demille's "Spenserville" on my cot. It was quite comfortable with my poncho liner and sleeping bag. My bags were packed and ready for anything. I was rested and at peace.

The Freedom Bird Takes Us Home
On 15 August we were loaded on trucks and taken to the customs site at Ali Al Salem. We finally got through customs and loaded the buses to take us to Kuwait International Airport. There was a long wait on the bus, but we were happy and eventually boarded the plane. The quality and spaciousness of the aircraft was awesome! It was an OMNI Airlines flight and promised to be very comfortable. We even had plenty of room for our rifles, which any infantryman will tell you is very much appreciated!

It was in fact a good flight! I read when I wasn't sleeping. The route took us from Kuwait to Shannon, Ireland in six and a half hours, Shannon to Bangor in five and a half hours, and finally Bangor to March Air Force Base in six and a half hours. It would be 43 hours from the time we left Al Taqaddum. Just being in the USA was a very welcome feeling! Memories of past tours flashed through my mind. Here the people welcomed us as heroes. During the Vietnam era, we would have garbage thrown on us and would be called baby killers. I wished every Vietnam veteran could feel the feeling I had that day!

In Shannon we had our first drink of alcohol in over seven months. Not that I was a Killians fan, but I didn't know what the penalty was for being in Shannon, Ireland and not ordering it as my first drink and I didn't want to find out the hard way! Doing the only thing that felt right, I ordered two, our prescribed limit. The fact that it was 0500 was not a problem for the bar at the airport. Apparently we weren't the first flight of Americans being flown home from the land of General Order #1!

The beer brought out the creativeness in me! My only grandson at the time was Dylan so I decided it was time for him to learn about leprechauns! I bought him one and told him all about them when finally meeting him again. He was now three and very impressed!

We were met at March Air Force Base by Marine Colonel Mark Smith. He had assisted Lieutenant Colonel Charlonis and his staff in the mobilization process and was instrumental in getting me off retired status to join them. Major Jeff Strey, and the crew from our ADVON at Camp Habbaniyah were there to guide us as well. We transferred to one more set of buses that took us to Twentynine Palms, had a quick gear turn in drill, and got into our assigned rooms in the officers' quarters.

Uncertain Future

I was still in communication with the personnel officer at Headquarters Marine Corps (HQMC) who was interested in getting me orders to the US Central Command (CENTCOM) in order to backfill his previous job as Executive Officer of the J6 Operations Division, under Marine Colonel Steve Corcoran. He was very loyal to Colonel Corcoran whom he highly respected, but was torn between taking the HQMC assignment in order to keep his own Marine Corps Reserve career alive, and staying with Marine Colonel Steve Corcoran. As it turned out, I was the answer, and very willing! It was difficult to imagine it coming together, but at this point, I'd never had anything that I wanted more! I had learned much about Islam and the radical elements threat on the world and was interested in being a part of whatever it would take to ensure some sort of world peace. Isn't that the goal of every young idealist? Shouldn't it be the goal of an old Marine too?

In order to have a chance of it coming together, I would need to wait to be detached and submit a new request for retired recall duty. It is a 45 to 60 day process, but the skids were greased at HQMC. It took a lot of star power to get me back on active duty to join the battalion in Iraq. My contacts at HQMC were confident that my previous Marine Central Command (MARCENT) and CENTCOM experience, combined with my newly completed Iraq tour at the staff level would do the trick, and I was willing to try. First things first, I had to get processed back to retired status and get home to get it submitted! Terri and I had talked it over, and she reluctantly understood and supported me. Again!

Battalion Out-Processing at 29 Palms
Our processing at Twentynine Palms went quickly. We went through all the normal battalion out processing and conducted another memorial service for Corporal Nelson and Lance Corporal Opicka. After three days and an out-call with Lieutenant Colonel Charlonis, Chief Warrant Officer 2 Chuck Andrews and I were in a rental car and on our way back to Camp Pendleton for processing back to retired status. We wouldn't be able to join the Headquarters & Service Company's homecoming, and Terri wouldn't be able to share my homecoming with the friends that had grown to mean so much to her during the past year. But we were still excited to celebrate my own homecoming!

Processing Back to Retirement Status
On 21 August, Chuck and I arrived at Camp Pendleton to conduct our further processing off active duty and back to retired status. Along the way, Chief Warrant Officer 5 Jim Rousell returned to clear up a few administrative details as well. Colonel Mark Smith was also still serving in the area, so all four of us had a meal together.

Jim and Colonel Smith served together on the battalion's first Iraq tour in 2004. Colonel Smith was the battalion commander. During that tour, fifteen Marines were lost, five from Madison alone. Jim and Colonel Smith took the deaths personally and were still struggling. I'll never forget Colonel Smith's remarks to Jim who had just returned with us on this tour. Jim said he was going to visit their graves. Colonel Smith went silent after admitting he had already done so. His only words to Jim were, "Strap up, it won't be easy."

A Prelude to Home

Terri came to San Diego for a visit while we awaited our release. We stayed in the Gas Lamp district which was a favorite place for me during my six month IBM assignment after retiring from the Marine Corps. What a great feeling! Approaching the hotel, I saw her inside. I stood and gazed at her for a moment through the window before going in. Thoughts of her love, devotion, loyalty and pride in her role as a honorary Devil Doggette filled my mind as tears filled my eyes. It was a homecoming better than we could have ever imagined!

She returned home after the short weekend in San Diego. Chuck and I continued our daily regimen of daily trips to Camp Talega's out processing center, and other base business that two retired Marines liked to do. We finally had the required medical appointment, and what a joke it was. It lasted less than five minutes and included very complex questions like "Do you feel any different than you did when you left?"

Going Home at Last

On 11 September Chuck and I were ready to go home! It had been nearly a year since we met, but thinking back to the beginning, it sure seemed much longer! We enjoyed one last drink in the San Diego airport and went to our respective gates. We toasted our successful tour and the date of our return (9/11). Okay, so it was two drinks. How appropriate! It was with great happiness and pride that I learned Grand Runt II beat me in the race of who would meet Mommy first. They set the date for his arrival to be 9 September, and he stayed right on schedule! I would hold Gavin and congratulate him on his win as soon as humanly possible!

Back at Rocky Point

The memories of my Iraq tour were now three years old but it was as if it was yesterday. I thought about going back to Afghanistan, and searched my soul for an answer. Did I really want to go back again? The chances of staying in Tampa were nearly nonexistent if I were to be extended again. Yet, I had the rest of my life not to be a Marine. I put my fate in the hands of the Barbarians of Bureaucracy up in HQMC, and just put one foot in front of the other on the Rocky Point running path. My three mile run and 40 year mental journey continued...

Chapter Thirteen
A Short Homecoming: Sep-Dec 2008
Sauk City/DeForest, Wisconsin

Homecoming Surprise – 11 September, 2008

My thoughts were consumed with meeting Terri and perhaps a few family members at the airport and walking on that carpet that connected our master bedroom and bathroom in the middle of the night! Kristin and her husband wouldn't be there, as they and their first son Dylan were very busy welcoming little Gavin into the world and to their young family. Gavin and I would always have a special story of how he and his Grandpa raced to see who would meet Mommy first to tell when he was older. I couldn't wait to greet him, but it would need to wait until they were home from the hospital.

The long awaited flight home was finally at hand! Unlike the bigger body of the battalion's companies that already had flown into their hometown Training Centers in uniform and had crowds of families and well wishers to greet them, Chuck and I would arrive in civilian clothes and would only have our loved ones to greet us. It was actually better this way. Our tours would be a part of the rest of our lives whether we came home in a uniform or not!

At last, the special moment was upon me! We arrived in Madison and I couldn't wait to get down the escalator to meet Terri. I spotted Terri in an instant and couldn't wait to get to the bottom! Then I caught sight of much more behind her. Wow! There were my parents, Kurt, the Schumanns, and many other family members and friends. There was even a group of several high school classmates! In front of them was a huge welcome home sign stretched across the arms of several Marine Corps League friends I had known through the years.

And there was Javier Teniente playing the Scottish Bag Pipes! He was one of my old Delta Company infantry platoon Marines that went on to become a platoon sergeant in Desert Storm. He went on to build a fine Madison Fire Fighter career path and somewhere along the way he learned the bag pipes and was doing a fine job playing them! As if all that wasn't enough, he had also learned to fly and earned his pilot's license!

There were news cameras, and after only a brief hug with Terri, I was whisked aside for an interview with them. I was not prepared for this! Anybody that knows me understands that I'm not known to think on my feet. I was in shock and only God knows what was said! I never saw the newscast, but was told by those who saw it, that it stayed on the air for weeks as part of the beginning of that channel's newscasts throughout the day. I was told it was also a part of the local media's September 11th special coverage.

Finally Home!

I finally met my second grandson Gavin. Oh what a cutie! It was only due to a flight schedule change that he beat me to see his beautiful mother first, but I was so glad it worked out this way. This way I could see them both together at the same time! He won the race and it was truly God's way. Big brother Dylan wasn't quite as sure as the rest of us of how great of an idea it was to bring Gavin into the fold. He soon was won over as well, and it was a special joy watching Kristin, Mark, Dylan, and now Gavin come together as a family to make a home.

I thought of what I saw in Iraq compared to their wonderful life. The dilapidated buildings, sand, dirty streets, every mix of traditional Arab cloth and neatly cropped beards of pride, to torn blue jeans and scraggly beards of defiance. Everything from modern SUV's to mule carts with locally grown crops traversing the streets of major cities. I thought of their lives in Sauk City and knew everything I had done since my decision to join the Marine Corps in 1971, to coming back off retired status to do my small part to make a better life for my family, was so worthwhile.

If it weren't for those who know what it takes to keep our freedoms and seek our chosen way of life, and were willing to fight to keep it, my daughter's beautiful family could be living in the rubble and dirt like so many countries I visited. In those countries, dilapidation wasn't all a result of war; it was a result of lifestyles dictated by those few that the many put in power.

If I knew this was the end of my service, I would just have to suck it up and make the civilian job work for me, and just be happy with it. But the prospect of going back to serve my country was alive and well, and I desperately wanted to do just that! How could I enjoy such a heartfelt homecoming, love being together with Terri again, have a new grandchild, and have a chance to enjoy the comforts of home, and still long to stay "in the game?" Maybe this PTSD thing was real?

I started visiting my sister Cherie in the nursing home every chance I got. Judy and Tammy, my other sisters, lived in the area and were very involved in Cherie's life. By now she was in the local nursing home, but we were all still hopeful that while we knew the brain tumor was a serious aliment, the immediate problems keeping her in the nursing home after her last operation were temporary, and she would get back home after some recuperation.

We just didn't know, or weren't ready to accept the truth yet. I was very proud of myself for sneaking her in some onion rings. She loved them! I really don't think anyone would have cared at this point, but it was our secret and we only let Tammy and Judy know. It hurt to see Cherie in so much pain! Terri once massaged her arms and legs and Cherie certified her as a professional massage therapist. She hired her on the spot! My little sister in so much pain was nearly unbearable!

Hawaii, Terri & Kurt

The dates we set for a Hawaiian vacation and some rest and relaxation would work out. After over five years of reserve duty at the Marine Forces Pacific Command (MARFORPAC) headquarters at Camp Smith, I had established my regular liberty stops in Waikiki and had quite a few people that knew me. Terri joined me for at least one of those visits every year, so she was also well established in the community.

I was ready to enjoy my time under the Banyan Tree at Waikiki's Moana Surf Rider hotel. It was perfect for me! Close to the sand and water, and plenty of shade to roost, read, and relax, the three R's that at this point were Nirvana to me!

On this trip, we were honored to have Kurt as our guest. With two houses back home to take care of, an active duty tour would have generated a great deal of stress, but with Terri in her DeForest house, and Kurt running his business out of our Sauk house, I never had to give either a thought. He more than earned his Hawaii trip with us!

He loved the trip, and took in as much as he could. Kristin had joined us during one of our previous trips during my MARFORPAC duty. I remember taking her and Terri to Kaena Point, a place unfamiliar to most tourists. You had to walk three miles over very rugged terrain with mountains on one side and the ocean on the other. It takes a while to walk three miles.

It was pretty quiet between the three of us until one of the girls (Terri or Kristin) let out a scream of discovery worthy of great praise, if only one of them would admit to it! The screamer in question noticed a huge whale not far out in the ocean jumping and providing a free whale watching tour for most of the remaining walk back to the car! Who did the screaming has not been agreed upon to this day. Kurt enjoyed almost everything there is to enjoy in Waikiki, but loved the shooting ranges the best. We had a great, memorable vacation. What a great team! The keepers of the forts and their wayward Marine!

Back to the World of Work and Home

Our return to Wisconsin meant the return to all that was, before fighting so hard to be called back to active duty and pursue my desire to participate in world affairs. I knew this would become a permanent part of all our lives. I enjoyed working on the house and the yard, and worked hard to catch up on things. Terri and Kurt did a great job, so it was just a matter of blending back into the process.

The time finally came to face the music and go back to my civilian job at Wisconsin Physicians Service (WPS). My job as the Technical Support Manager was to supervise the technicians that maintained the large scale IBM mainframe computer complex. It was the centerpiece of many layers of distributed server technologies, providing access to our many insurance systems. All the while I was gone, my boss Tony and I stayed in touch. He basically covered my job duties, so I could come back to the same job, desk, and responsibilities. WPS had received the Employer Support of the Guard and Reserve (ESGR) award I had requested for supporting me during my service, and I was warmly welcomed back. Unbelievable!

I was getting resettled in my job, but knew that we could be hearing from Headquarters Marine Corps (HQMC) anytime. The normal process for requests for retire recalls took approximately 45 to 60 days, which was nearing since my homecoming. Much of the unnecessary intensity and pressure that existed before my request to leave WPS and go to war was gone. The senior vice president driving most of the intensity and oppressive atmosphere was no longer at WPS. My team had worked through many issues to achieve a smooth operation to process over five million TRICARE claims per month for military members.

As life at WPS was settling in, I was getting word from HQMC about the possibility of going back to the US Central Command (CENTCOM) to replace the Major that left his Executive Officer billet under Colonel Corcoran in the J6 Operations Division. It was looking highly likely that I would be recalled. The combination of my civilian and Marine Corps experience, bolstered by my recent combat tour in Iraq as an infantry staff officer and previous CENTCOM experience, was likely to end up in another set of orders.

Torn Again
So, things were very good at home. I had everything! Terri and I loved our time together and both kids were still in the area and doing great! I kept a job with a team I worked hard to build into a well oiled machine that stayed together during my absence. Once again, family and duty were tugging at my heartstrings, but Terri was right there by my side every step of the way! Her unconditional love, unfailing friendship, and companionship gave me much needed strength and courage.

Chapter Fourteen
Family Sadness: Dec 2008
Sauk City/Mazomanie, Wisconsin

A Family Comes Together

Our family was always close, and my love for family and my sense of duty to the country had been on a collision course before. Growing up with my parents in the JI Case business in Lodi was a unique blend of getting a real business education from them while still enjoying family life. I had a great love and respect for Mom and Dad, and felt close to my brother Ron and three sisters. For so many years we seemed to be spared of any sort of major family illness or disaster of any kind. It was all fun and games, and we had our fun!

But then Dad's cancer hit in 2002. By all rights, he should not have survived the complications from the original surgery several years prior, but we were blessed with the best doctors and nursing staff anyone could ask for at Theda Clark Hospital in Neenah, Wisconsin. They literally pulled him out of the grave three times before his recovery allowed him to keep building oak furniture in his Wild Rose craft shop. We would have more to deal with in his battle with cancer later, but for now, the saw dust was flying! My houses were both full of oak furniture he built after we thought we were going to lose him. It made our time together even more special.

But fate wouldn't leave our family in peace. Cherie's brain cancer diagnosed at age 40 hit us all hard. I never would forget her support and kindness when going through my divorce. As time passed, we would get to know each other more on a spiritual level as well.

By the time I returned from Iraq, her condition was getting worse. Nursing home visits were getting grim. She desperately clung to what the brain surgeon had said weeks prior about having hope for a good six months or more, but the last operation left her with a paralyzed left side. Yet she was still expecting to be released and wanted home modifications for her wheelchair to enjoy her last months. It was so hard for Chris to say no, but it was clear she wasn't going to be able to go home, as nursing home care was being arranged. Her constant pain was unbearable and at night Judy and Tammy would see her tear off her clothes and thrash around in bed screaming. Hospice care was now involved and had prescribed morphine to make her comfortable.

My sister Judy couldn't take it anymore. She made a decision to bring Cherie to her home. Cherie agreed that Judy's home would be better until she was able to get back to her own home with the kids. She was still able to enjoy our company. Her kids and all of us were by her side at all times for the next weeks. I'll always remember Katie, her oldest, so lovingly and gently squeezing her medicine into her cheeks and rubbing them to circulate it. The love she had for her kids, and the love they had for her was something out of a book!

The family clung together. Every one of us was there when our work schedules allowed. Mom and Dad moved down from Wild Rose and, as promised, never left her side. Chris's parents certainly carried a heavy share of the support load as well. When Judy's husband Ken and Dad came home from an errand one night, they noticed two very bright lights just above the house. They looked like airplanes or tower lights, but Ken said that there were no antennas nearby. They realized they were extraordinarily bright stars, or as it would turn out, the two brightest planets, Jupiter and Venus, which converge every 30 November. But, Mom's face went white!

She suddenly remembered a conversation with Cherie that she didn't understand right after Cherie's last operation several months earlier. They were alone in the hospital and Cherie told Mom not to worry about her. Two stars would come to get her when it was her time. Cherie was no scientist or astronomer, believe me, but somehow she knew six months prior that when it was her time, she would be met by two bright stars. She obviously had access to a flight schedule nobody else on earth had...

Years later I would be reunited with Father Tom Sosinski through Terri's friend Kathy. He converted both Cheri and I to Catholicism and Cherie really took it serious. It turned out that Father Tom was living upstairs from her apartment in Madison. She took him meals and spent time with him. She spoke of him frequently, and I finally put it together. It was him! After way more than twenty years!

Kathy and Father Tom invited Terri and me for dinners at his apartment. At one dinner, Father Tom said what would stick with me forever about Cherie. As we talked about my conversion compared to hers, he simply and quite quietly said, "Cherie is an old soul." It got my attention. Big time! Even though I was oldest of five, and Mom and Dad were her parents, we all knew she had wisdom beyond this world. She truly had something more than age and parental authority about her…

Cherie's Call Home

By late November, every night was to be the last for Cherie. The family understood that this was truly the end. Each night, hospice would check her vital signs and didn't think she could last until morning. But her heart was young and strong. It was being driven by her will to live and care for her children. Even God would have to wait!

Finally, on 3 December 2008 at 2AM, the angels took her home and eased her bodily pain. We had a routine by now. Mom, Dad and my sisters were pretty much day on/stay on. Kurt and I decided to drive the fifteen minutes back to Sauk City to sleep at home. Ron lived in Lodi and decided to stay with the family in Mazomanie. He had already experienced his father-in-law's death and knew it was time to be close.

He was awake when Chris checked Cherie's ever weakening pulse and finally looked up and said she was gone. Kurt and I returned immediately. Nobody wanted this to happen, but at the same time, there was a great sense of relief. We all knew we had no choice. We knew she was now a part of something far bigger than we could imagine.

We waited for Hospice and the funeral home to come. Her kids were all up and the family was interacting as normal as could be expected. Her only son Justin and I played Sequence. Her husband Chris who was a pillar of strength every step of the way for over three years, cried at her side. When the funeral home arrived to take her, the kids all went downstairs. The rest of us said tear-filled goodbyes and prayers as she was wheeled out to the waiting hearse.

The Funeral

By now the entire city of Sauk City and all the members of our church knew about Cherie's illness and the courageous battle she was fighting. The line was long, and the love was strong. She had the very best family and friends anybody could ever ask for. Mom and Dad were extremely well respected and many of their long-time friends came to the service to pay their respects.

It was a typical Wisconsin cold, blustery winter day for the service and burial. Chris and the kids would have made her proud. The youngest girl Natalie and Emily had dresses on and didn't have coats. Chris picked up Natalie and held her close to his chest and Terri put her arm around Emily and held her close. The harsh, cold winter wind and snow blew hard as the priest said prayers over the casket on the gravesite.

We all walked tearfully back to our cars through the footpaths in the snow, against the harsh winter winds. I was doing okay. I was a Marine. I could handle this. But, as I got into our car, I looked back to the gravesite just in time to see the release of a large number of white balloons, immediately losing total control of my emotions. My tears blinded me and totally severed my ability to see or say anything.

To know Cherie and to have but a slight understanding of the depth of her commitment to her faith, I knew those balloons were truly the very flight of her soul back to God for further instructions of her new assignment in His Kingdom. As premature as it may have seemed to the rest of us, her work here was done.

Back at Rocky Point and the Bay

As my mental journey led me back to Cherie's death, it was very difficult to see the beautiful bay and scenery through my tears as I continued my run. The misfortune was only three years earlier, but so much had happened since! My thoughts continued to drift as I pondered my own near future…

Chapter Fifteen
Back to Active Duty: Jan-Feb 2009
Rocky Point Area, Tampa, Fl

New Orders/New Challenges

Two weeks after Cherie's death, new orders arrived instructing me to report to the US Central Command (CENTCOM) in early January, 2009. We were all readjusting to normal after months of our center of attention being on Cherie's family. There comes a time when the bittersweet realities bring relief. Cherie's pain was a thing of the past. She was now in a place where she was needed more. Chris and the family could now focus on their future.

The waiting ended and new orders arrived. Once again we would have to make plans to share our lives separately. At least Terri liked Tampa, and was all right with things as long as I stayed there and she could visit. She had gotten to know the Hyatt folks that treated us like family back in 2001/2. She looked forward to rekindling those friendships. It occurred to us both how ironic it was that we met at a seminar on the book called "The Road Less Traveled" by M. Scott Peck. The theme was basically "how to be together separately." We would be reminded often of how important those skills would be to our relationship years later.

A Return to Duty

On 5 January, we would say goodbye once again. She drove me to the airport. It killed me to leave her in the cold and snow. Was I doing the right thing? Did I really have a choice? Was it time to give her priority over the Corps, duty, and honor? She stood and watched me at the top of the same escalator where we so recently jubilantly enjoyed my return from Iraq. Tears clouded my vision as she turned to leave to begin her new routine of being alone once again. My love for her was so strong! At that moment I wanted to run back down, take her into my arms and tell her I'm staying home!

I went on to the Marine Corps Base, Quantico, Virginia to process back on active duty, and she continued on to work. The flight to Dulles arrived on schedule despite the challenging weather conditions. Aside from the narrow doors leading to transport vehicles and poor signage, the trip was uneventful. I checked in to the Liversedge Bachelors' Officer Quarters (BOQ) and settled into my room. The old quarters were made of cinder block brick so it was hot inside, but clean and actually quite nice. It brought back memories of being in Quantico over the years.

A large sign over the front gate welcomes you to "The Crossroads of the Marine Corps." It is the home of Officer Candidate School and many others. Every officer that made it to mid or senior career level would come here for advanced training. I attended COBOL Programming training there in the seventies as well as Amphibious Warfare School and several Communications and Staff Planning courses through the eighties and nineties.

The early morning wooden and hilly drive to Camp Upshire was beautiful. I always loved my runs through Prince William Forest during my many Quantico tours. It was much like Wisconsin, only the hills were more pronounced and the woods were much more vast. It was a cold, rainy morning that matched my mood. I knew I would be happy getting back into the groove at CENTCOM, but at that moment, Terri was on my mind.

Not much was accomplished the first morning. Camp Upshire still had Quonset huts, and my check-in station was in one of them. Being the only one checking in, I got my check-in sheet and headed back to mainside, to start bouncing around gathering signatures and endorsements.

The physical exam I had done at the 5th Marines headquarters back at Camp Pendleton expedited my medical processing. I quickly cleared the administrative gauntlet and was ready to proceed to MacDill Air Force Base to check in with the Marine Central Command (MARCENT) and be assigned for duty at CENTCOM.

I arrived in Tampa on schedule and drove straight to the MARCENT HQ, signed the log entry, and headed out to get settled and enjoy the weekend. When I last worked there as the Assistant G6 in 2002, we were in one small building in the CENTCOM complex. The Navy Central Command (NAVCENT) had the other adjacent buildings. By now they moved to Bahrain and MARCENT spread out to occupy the buildings left vacant. I had helped plan the expansion of MARCENT, so it was neat to see the plan come to fruition.

SNAFU in Processing

Any Marine knows what a SNAFU is. Situational Normal, All F'd Up. On 12 January I started checking into the MARCENT headquarters in earnest and looked forward to getting started at CENTCOM. The buildings were very close, so that helped. We hit a snag right out of the gate. My security clearance was not showing up! What a sinking feeling! I would need a Top Secret/Sensitive Compartmentalized Information (TS/SCI) clearance to work at CENTCOM in the communications field. I started contacting everyone I knew down there and everyone helped where they could. The G2 (Intel) Officer from my original tour was still in the area and had made Colonel. I also found "Gramps," the Marine Corps Lieutenant Colonel that presided over my retirement ceremony. Everybody was at the ready to help where they could to bring things together!

I returned to my room with a very bad feeling. Maybe this was an omen. Was I supposed to be home with Terri? Maybe Cherie was protecting me from above? Was there danger ahead that somewhere, someone was protecting me from? It turned out that my old battalion still had ownership of my security clearance and would have to release it so MARCENT could take ownership. I was able to contact the Inspector & Instructor, Lieutenant Colonel Robison, back in Chicago, who was a tremendous help.

He made it happen and we were making progress. I was told to hang on and they would get things untangled as soon as possible. The bad news was we had to start all over. The good news was that we could go directly for the TS/SCI clearance. I just had to wait for the SECRET part of the application to clear the initial investigation and could then start at CENTCOM at that level until the TS/SCI came through.

I started a daily regimen of Pilates exercises and reviewing technical and staff planning manuals I had picked up while processing at Quantico to get up to date. I read every chance I got and was becoming learning more and more about the Middle East. It had been a long time since my original premonition that the Middle East would one day have a significant impact on my life, and by now I had read many books on the subject. There was so much to consume my thoughts. I was missing Terri and home, and was thinking about Cherie and her family. I branched out on my weekend liberty time and would add the Don Cesar hotel in St Petersburg and the Tiki Hut in Clearwater Beach to my reading venues.

Getting Ready for Duty/Enjoying Some Terri Time

The CENTCOM area of responsibility basically extends from the eastern European area to the western Pacific area, including Iraq, Afghanistan, Saudi Arabia, Iran, Qatar, etc. Needless to say, there were plenty of materials for me to get up-to-date while waiting for my security clearance!

On 10 February Terri arrived. Whether I would eventually report for duty, or come home, we decided to enjoy some time together with our old Tampa family! We did the rounds and hit all favorite places and saw all our friends.

A Welcome Call Back to Duty

On 27 February the watched pot finally boiled! Just when I was gearing up mentally for another week of waiting, Air Force Lieutenant Colonel Fontana from CENTCOM called me and said that an interim SECRET clearance was granted and I should come to work! After finishing some check-in, I finally got to meet with some of the CENTCOM staff. I was gratified to hear that they had definitely been waiting for me! My work location would be in the main CENTCOM building 540, which was very familiar from my recall after 9/11.

Chapter Sixteen
Learning the Ropes: Mar-May 2009
US Central Command, MacDill AFB, Tampa, Fl

Back in the Game

On 2 March I was finally "back in the game." I would be assigned to the J6 (Systems) Directorate, Operations Division as the Executive Officer of the Plans & Orders Division reporting to Marine Corps Colonel Steve Corcoran. He was a highly respected officer throughout the US Central Command (CENTCOM).

Now if I could only live up to the expectations! Those premonitions of getting involved in Middle East affairs many years ago were definitely taking shape! Feeling somewhat knowledgeable of Middle East history after a few years of reading, the intellectual learning would now start turning into practical application!

My head was spinning for the first week. The three-day Staff Indoctrination course was very good and got me versed in CENTCOM's battle rhythm and various procedures and communications flows.

Our division had basic responsibility for planning, installing, maintaining and operating all communications and data networks in CENTCOM's area of responsibility. This included all communications and data systems in support of US policy and operations. As you may imagine, we had a great deal of energy being directed to Operation Enduring Freedom (OEF) in Afghanistan, but there were also a great deal of operations to support in the other nineteen countries. Even though Somalia had been transferred to the new Africa Command (AFRICOM), they weren't up to speed, so we also covered that area. There was a lot going on everywhere!

There were 85 total members from all services in our division out of 3,000 staff members under General Petraeus' command. My duties included a combination of administrative and operational tasks. I focused on my administrative duties and made sure the members of our division were up-to-date on their evaluations and awards. This was an eye-opening experience for a Marine Corps Warrant Officer! In theory, Warrant Officers held equivalent rights, privileges, and responsibilities as "regular" officers, but would focus on their technical specialties, not to be distracted by command, staff, and other responsibilities. Right! Good theory, but it didn't work out in this Warrant Officer's case. Again.

Not knowing what else to do, I turned my mission oriented focus on administrative duties and started learning the other services' administrative procedures. Talk about culture shock! Every service had their unique, very specific, and very bureaucratic methods and procedures. The immortal words of Marine Corps Colonel Mark Smith uttered in frustration while blasting a hole in Marine Corps bureaucracies, to get me back on active duty, echoed in my ears! He didn't let the "Barbarians of Bureaucracy" slow him down, and neither would I! Early in my Marine Corps leadership training, I learned one of the most important leadership traits "take care of your people, and they will take care of you!"

I was learning more and more about the global combatant commands, how information flows, and how decisions are made by the President, Secretaries of Defense and State, National Security Advisor, Central Intelligence Agency (CIA), Defense Intelligence Agency (DIA), etc. It was very fascinating to see how things come together when information is requested by higher authorities and how we implement decisions and policies abroad.

The Human Side

I was finally able to start treatments to fix the tooth I broke in Iraq! The Expeditionary Field Dentistry crew did great in getting me through my Iraq tour, but I couldn't start permanent treatments until I was settled long enough. The VA would have started in Madison, but I didn't know for sure if more orders were coming. Now I was settled, and I was looking forward to getting a tooth back. The PLP400, or whatever compound they used in the sand filled dentist office, did not hold, and my tooth was falling out again! It would soon be back to normal. Thanks Navy!

Terri was scheduled to visit again too! She arrived after my fun filled suicide prevention training and follow-up dental appointment. She was sporting a walking boot cast after suffering a broken lower leg while personal training. She had been seeing a personal trainer and was really doing well and looking good! But the trainer went off on a Ninja binge and had our beautiful, loyal 55 year old fitness student doing things that didn't make sense any more. As much as I loved her dedication to keeping herself in good condition, he had obviously gone over the edge and we needed to fire him!

We enjoyed a wonderful weekend together. This was her second trip down, and we hoped to keep it going throughout my year tour here! We spent both days in St Pete Beach, and the weather was beautiful! We parted and I was torn again. It felt so good to see her again, and I missed her dearly! What drives this madness! Why couldn't I just have stayed home? I was retired! I had done enough!

Keeping Up with the Jones'

Along the way I passed a personal challenge in order to keep my deployment readiness status up-to-date. I dreaded the new Marine Corps Combat Fitness Test. When I was a young Marine, the Marines over 50 didn't have to perform up to the same expectations as the younger Marines. Not anymore! I would be required to pass not only the age old Physical Fitness Test (PFT), but also the new Combat Fitness Test!

The test started with a 880 meter run. Then we had to lift a 30 lb. ammo can from our chest over our heads a minimum of 45 times in two minutes. The last event was called Fire & Maneuver. In this event you started from the prone position, got up and ran 25 yards, crawled 25 yards on hands/knees, crawled 25 more yards on all fours, zig/zagged up to a casualty (another Marine taking the test) and dragged them 25 yards. Then you had to put them in a fireman's carry for 60 yards back to the start line.

You'd drop the casualty and grab two full ammo cans and had to carry them 60 yards back through the course, throw a grenade, do 3 pushups, and take the ammo cans back to the start line again. The time limit to complete the test, at my youthful age, was 4:28. I did it in 3:50. Even though I was probably the slowest one, it just felt damn good to not embarrass myself in front of all the young Marines cheering me on!

I also had to qualify with the M9 (9mm Beretta) pistol. Again, I was very nervous having not shot a formal qualification course for a score in many years. I shot plenty last year while training for Iraq, but it was mostly the M-16A2. The pistol shooting was issued just for familiarization firing, not formal qualification. The Air Force range was much more relaxed and quite a bit easier than Marine Corps pistol qualification. Even in losing much of the steadiness gained through the years of Marine Corps pistol qualification, I still shot expert. I was very happy!

Life at CENTCOM

By late March, Colonel Corcoran had his sights set on a new command. He aspired to take command of the Joint Communications Support Element (JSCE) and had been selected to do just that. It was an elite unit tasked with being perpetually ready to fly into any area of the world and set up an initial communications capability within 48 hours. The process to replace him started. What would this mean for me? I was handpicked to be his assistant!

By early April, things were in full swing for me. My schedule was brisk, and the days were passing quickly. I continued to serve in the capacity of the Executive Officer for the Plans & Operations Division in the J6 Directorate. My duties were very interesting, and very broad. One minute I was teeing up a request to the General to get an Army Lieutenant Colonel frocked to Colonel (early promotion for selected officers that require the horsepower when they are filling a billet normally held by higher rank), and the next minute I was in a video teleconference (VTC) with people in Iraq, Afghanistan, Pakistan, etc. supporting communications requirements between forces and countries.

I was becoming Joint! We all received an invitation for an Army Colonel's retirement ceremony. He was close to General Petraeus and both of them spent over 46 months of combat service in Iraq over three tours, and he had an amazing background. It was an honor to represent the Marine Corps at his retirement. After the ceremony, General Petraeus came up to shake my hand and we talked a bit. He knew a Wenger and wondered if we were related, but we weren't. That Wenger obviously impressed him, so I only could hope I wouldn't screw that up!

He surprised me by giving me his coin! Since my return to active duty, it became common for senior leaders to give personal coins as mementos of serving together. I was sure we'd be talking more throughout the year, and getting his coin was a great honor! I would put his coin in my small collection back home next to General Frank's coin I received in 2002 when he was the CENTCOM Commander.

There was plenty going on in CENTCOM's area of responsibility in the Middle East and the Pacific Command (PACOM's) area of responsibility in the Pacific to keep us all busy. The Korean War never really ended. North Koreans were waving their swords again. I spent my reserve duty from 1996-2001 at the Marine Forces Pacific Command (MARFORPAC) in Hawaii preparing and rehearsing for an attack of North Korea into the South.

My Dad served in Korea for six months before the truce was signed, and another seven months afterward, before he could come back home to his new little boy (me). What many people don't seem to realize is that the truce was between North Korea and the UN. It was never followed up with a treaty or formal end to the war. South Korea never entered into any further agreements. North Korea says they were considering the truce null and void and the war was officially back on! This would go on for years to come.

Our brethren in PACOM in Hawaii, and our forces in Korea and Japan were on high alert! It is noteworthy that the North Koreans had been so vocal about their threats so often, that it was unlikely they would actually attack this time. However, they were certainly capable of initiating an attack any time, even if they weren't so vocal about it. Just another way our freedom and way of life need to be protected!

The current Korea crisis was a result of the United Nation's (UN) handy work in 1953. It is the same UN that everybody thinks should be the ones to solve all world conflicts. I didn't think they did so well in Korea, and didn't think resolutions would do much to deter the current troublemakers in Korea, Iran, and several other areas. As diplomats, they just didn't have a concept of the impact of "time" in conflict, or of how time is the key factor in how many people die.

I happen to believe that if Truman would have listened to General Douglas McArthur regarding Korea, things would be much different today. If he had listened, it doesn't seem we'd be seeing complete blackness in the north and vast brightness of the neighbors like South Korea and Japan when you look at an evening satellite picture of Korea!

South Korea was doing very well while North Koreans were starving. We stopped the shooting in 1953, but who has been counting the people who have been dying in the North for over sixty years now? And who is taking responsibility for the nukes that the North sells to Iran? It boggled my mind to hear otherwise smart people say that we should go to the UN to solve our problems!

In our own CENTCOM area of responsibility, our forces continued to flow into Afghanistan. I had made arrangements for several members of our Operations and Plans Division flying over in advance of the units, to cover staffing requirements until their replacements were in place. Everyone at CENTCOM was liable to be sent over for 40 to 90 days in advance of the incoming units, but I hadn't been seriously considered for that duty yet. Colonel Corcoran wanted me to go to our CENTCOM Forward Headquarters (CFH) in Camp As Sayliyah, Qatar to support the high-level "Corporate Board" conference of communications/systems directorates. There would also be another conference in September that I may have to go over for as well.

At the same time as all this, Pakistan was taking charge in their hills and reclaiming territory from the Taliban. We were very much involved from an advisory and monitoring perspective, and we were in very close contact with our people in Islamabad. We still conducted regular conference calls between our Command, Control, Communications, Computers, Intelligence, Surveillance, Reconnaissance (C4ISR) Operations and Plans officers here and our contacts there. We usually set up a Crisis Action Team (CAT) for this type of thing that is manned around the clock.

Back to Rocky Point

My thoughts drifted back to the present on the Rocky Point run. Will there be one more year of mixed Tampa/Middle East duty or will my military service to the nation finally come to an end?

Chapter Seventeen
A Gathering of the Minds: Jun 2009
Camp As Sayliyah, Qatar

Qatar

I would soon be headed for our US Central Command (CENTCOM) Forward Headquarters (CFH) in Qatar. Qatar is located on a very small 4,400 square mile peninsula located along the Saudi coast on the Persian Gulf. It served as a good central location for the CENTCOM area of responsibility. We moved the CFH from Prince Sultan Air Base (PSAB) in Saudi Arabia to Camp As Sayliyah in Qatar in approximately 2002 or 2003 as the Saudi government became less comfortable with a significant US military presence on its soil.

The reason the main CENTCOM headquarters is in Tampa is because most of the countries in the area of responsibility are predominantly Islamic or strongly Arab nationalist, neither of which are conducive for supporting a two to three thousand member US military command staff and associated support structure. Qatar was an absolute monarchy with a king as the sole source of authority and a prime minister to run the daily business. Since the previous and very traditional Emir of Qatar was overthrown by his son in 1995, it has quickly gained economic prominence with the second largest gross domestic product in the world. Heavy construction was still in process, and Qatar's move to a free economy and capitalism made our partnership much more suitable than anywhere else in the Middle East. It enabled us to set up house with minimal impact on religious or nationalist cultures.

Off to the CFH and Corporate Board

On 8 June, Chief Luge and I met along with our small J6 Plans & Operations team that would provide the administrative and logistical support for the upcoming "Corporate Board", a gathering of the senior communication command staff officers in the area of responsibility.

Always loath to waste a minute of valuable time, I used the time at the Tampa airport to finish a tutorial for my Cardinal Stritch University Adjunct Professor position back in Wisconsin. I taught management, leadership, and project management courses for the graduate and undergraduate adult evening courses back in Madison. They had requirements for maintaining proficiency, and this course would keep me in good standing to teach upon my return, not knowing when that would be. If WPS threw me out while I was gone, at least I'd have a backup!

We landed in Doha on schedule at 1815 hours. The airport was truly a mix of traditional and new world travelers. There were many gowns, with each country and region easily discernible by the variances in styles. There were suits of all kinds, old and modern, wrinkled and highly pressed. I was somewhat nervous going through customs. The official at the desk was a female in a very heavy burka, complete with a black leather hood and very stern eyes. I felt lucky to be passed through. All we needed as US Military Officials were orders and an ID card. They didn't seem to like this, and she just seemed to not like us at all!

Once outside the Doha Airport, I could see the well lit and quite beautiful skyline of tall buildings, but the heat, humidity, and sand blowing in the air put me right back in Iraq again! How did I live in this day in and day out for so long? It was suddenly like I never left the desert! But the landscape soon changed as Harry Aiensworth (aka Rocky) swept us out of Doha across the flat sandy highway to Camp As Sayliyah. There was construction everywhere. Qatar was definitely in modernization mode. The highway was teeming with trucks in both directions. Those going away from Doha carried cement and construction materials. Those going towards Doha carried human waste. There were little or no waste processing sites where they were developing, so it all had to come back to the sea for processing.

Rocky and the Chief led the administrative support for the frequent conferences that were held at the CFH at Camp As Sayliyah. I was just along for the ride and would pitch in when possible. Rocky surfed the traffic like a pro. Traffic circles were common, so you had to know how to get to your destination. There was no room for procrastination, and the Chief would later instruct me to never look to the side or rear. The code of Qatari drivers was to always look forward. If those to the side and rear looked forward as well, life was good. Never be shy on the gas pedal!

Camp As Sayliyah

After the 45 minute lesson on Qatari highways, we arrived at Camp As Sayliyah. As expected, the security was very tight. Heavily armed civilian guards from Dyna Corp would guide us through three check points. First was an ID card and Defense Biometric Identification Data System (DBIDS) letter check. Everyone had to have the letters issued prior to arriving, and Rocky and the Chief had us all in good shape.

Then we would have to dismount, remove all bags, open doors, including the vehicle's gas cap, and go into a nearby air conditioned waiting area. Once cleared, we would proceed to the Provost Marshall Office (PMO) to have our DBIDS letters exchanged for DBIDS passes. Local Privilege Cards were issued to drivers that needed to regularly traverse between As Sayliyah and Al Udeid, the other American Base in Qatar.

We finally arrived at our quarters. It was a huge warehouse surrounded by barriers, bomb shelters, and sand bags that would easily consume a city block back home. It was constructed of two levels of shipping containers with a metal grate walkway accessing the second level. It could accommodate over 600 people, and provided clean heads, showers, and laundry facilities. For overflow, there was another warehouse with tents constructed inside with the same head, shower, and laundry facilities.

We had people deployed there for six to twelve months and they would be quite comfortable. The camp also served as a Rest & Relaxation center for our service members serving in Iraq and Afghanistan. They would come for a four-day break from the heat and anxiety of combat and combat support duty. It's much like Iraq and Afghanistan, but the big difference is that you can relax and "run slick" (no body armor), wear civvies, and enjoy a maximum of three drinks at the Top-Off or Oasis Clubs where movies, games, internet access, dancing, meals, etc. were available.

It was the Middle East, but it wasn't Iraq! It was hot, humid, flat, and sandy, but there was no armor, no weapons, and no Mine

Resistant Ambush Protected Vehicle (MRAP's). We traveled in air conditioned SUV's without armor! The Chief had done this gig so many times it made me feel like a puppet, but a happy puppet nonetheless. We quickly got settled and they took me to the Top Off Club. What? A club in the Middle East! What happened to General Order 1 that every American entering into a combat zone in the Middle East is hastily read and must adhere to? But this was Qatar, our friends. We had a special arrangement there. There were two places in As Sayliyah where you could get alcohol, with a three per night limit. The bartenders would ask for your ID card and swipe it for each drink. When it hit three, you were done and they would serve you no more. The two bars were connected, so no double dipping! Of course, if you didn't drink, you could give your ID to someone else. Non-drinkers could demand favors for this breach of orders. The bidding often got quite high!

On 10 June we were dug in and ready to go. It reached 121 degrees at mid-day and jet lag was setting in big time. Regardless, we established our battle rhythm immediately. The Chief and I were up at 0500 and headed out for his well practiced run and gym routine. I liked it. He could have been a decent Marine! After a quick shower, it was chow and then business.

Rocky had established our Tactical Command Tent inside another huge warehouse in advance of our arrival and it would be the center of activities to make the conference a success. Rocky and Chief Luge briefed us on the routine and the many conference tasks to be completed over the 10 day period. They had it all laid out, and it would mean one hell of a lot of trips to Doha and Al Udeid to pick up the various senior officers, get them safely to their quarters, and organize for the many meetings they would be attending. They had cleverly packed boxes from the last conference, so every item needed was immediately available and hastily put in place. They truly had a very well documented process.

Our first day seemed like a long one. Jet lag set in and I starting thinking of Terri and my family back home. Was this really necessary? What am I doing? I was retired from the Marine Corps! I could be home now instead of here, tired, hot, dusty, and stressed, but I knew this was where I wanted to be, and this was what I wanted to be doing. It was a once in a lifetime opportunity, so I did like I did as a young Marine climbing "Old Smokey" as all Marines had to do during our ITR training after boot camp, and just kept putting one foot in front of the other. The days would soon go faster and the duty would soon get more interesting.

Our orientation continued, as did the 0500 PT sessions with Chief Luge. Good stuff! It would commonly be above 120 degrees, so early morning PT was the best. The chow hall was quite good, just like Iraq, and things were quickly picking up. I took the Army's Traffic Course and got my license to drive in Qatar. Our first participants for the conference started arriving at Doha Airport. Our own CENTCOM reps, Army Lieutenant Colonel Shaw, and Navy Lieutenant Commander Jake Hill, were coming in, and we did our first run of many more to pick up conference members. Chief Luge, Air Force Staff Sergeant Garcia, and I were there to scoop them up and get them through the same gauntlet we went through upon our arrival. The traffic circles were wild and the two-way shuttle of cement out of Doha for the massive construction in process and human waste back to the sea was in full swing.

I enjoyed a few meals and conversation with General Petraeus' Personal Security Detail (PSD) that was permanently stationed there for his frequent visits. They were a mix of military and civilian agents, each with an interesting history and qualification. They had their own Navy cook who made plain hamburger taste like an expensive entrée! The chow hall was good, but these guys made eating in Camp As Sayliyah even better!

By 13-14 June, the conference attendees were coming in from all over the CENTCOM area of responsibility. We were making multiple runs to Doha's commercial airport and the US military's Al Udeid Air Base. We always had to travel in pairs, and I would travel with Chief Luge. We would eat where and when we could, taking advantage of the American dining facilities' "Grab n' Go's" for free food. They were like small food marts, and really hit the spot when you were hot, dirty, and dusty. And, as always, no charge! The civilian airport arrivals were required to go through the same security as us. The Al Udeid military air base arrivals would have to scan all their bags at customs, then again coming aboard As Sayliyah. The tired travelers would have to get all their bags out of our vehicles, carry them in to the security point, wait in line, and then return them to our vehicles. The Chief and I helped them, as did Rocky and the other drivers.

A Gathering of the Minds

By 15 June, the "Corporate Board" convened, safe and sound from their travels throughout the Middle East. Generals, Colonels, and their staff officers of all ranks came together to discuss issues of bandwidth scarcity, coordination, future operational plans, communications support requirements, etc. Colonel Corcoran told me that attending one of these meetings would give me the experience of many years' worth of what it takes to support US operations in the Middle East. He was right!

It's hard for the average citizen to know how much goes into moving large scale forces into an area of the world without an existing communications infrastructure. I was constantly amazed at the professionalism of our engineers and planners. The participants of this conference would coordinate large scale and rapidly changing command and control system requirements, as General Petraeus at CENTCOM and General McChrystal at the International Security Assistance Force (ISAF) changed the focus from Iraq to Afghanistan. We had to do this in addition to doing what was necessary in the other 19 countries in the area of responsibility.

These included Iraq, Pakistan, Syria, Iran and other high profile countries dealing with Islamic fundamentalist attempts to disrupt civil government and their attempts to gain footholds of influence. This would be especially challenging because of the lack of bandwidth in the Middle East. Commerce drives bandwidth availability, not military needs. If we had the bandwidth available in the European Command (EUCOM) with all the civilized nations and active economies, it would have been much easier, but that wasn't the case, and we had to coordinate, prioritize, and share.

The conference wrapped up and our team was extremely busy for a couple days getting all the conference attendees back to their points of departure. As it was upon our arrival, Rocky and the Chief had every detail planned and checked off as we wrapped the final details. Our shredding machines worked overtime to discard the large amount of classified materials that had been printed and couldn't be carried. It was an extremely stressful time, and the Chief took an opportunity to relieve some stress on the way back from an Al Udeid run.

The roads in Qatar were barely discernible when sand was blowing, and many Qataris didn't even bother with them if there were long lines at an intersection. They would just travel cross country as necessary to get where they were going. It wasn't unusual to see tracks to prove the point. We had been driving around a break in a fence that would have saved a great deal of time for several days now. But on this last trip, the Chief put it in low gear, drove through the break in the fence, did a couple of victory circles in the flat sand, and we continued on our merry way, saving a couple miles in the process.

Back to the States!

I was able to find a couple of singing camels in the base PX and sent them to my Grandsons in Sauk. I had no idea what the lyrics were, but I told Kristin to take the batteries out immediately if the boys started running around the house in their pajamas some night hollering "Allah Akbar!" Needless to say, Terri would be getting some trinkets as well.

We did our laundry, packed our trash, and straightened everything out with the billeting folks. Staff Sergeant Garcia drove Chief Luge and I to the airport in Doha for the long trip back to Tampa. It was hard to believe these guys did this so often. It wasn't unusual for the average CENTCOM staff officer to make at least ten trips to the Middle East in a year's time. It was a total of 24 hours door step to door step. As we flew over Iraq, and as I settled in to the 14 hour flight to Tampa across the Levant to Europe, and across the vast Atlantic, I watched the map of the area below us. I thought of the Marines that replaced us in Camp Habbaniyah, Iraq. They were right below me at that moment and they too would be ready to be replaced in just a couple months! It was a smooth flight, the service was outstanding as usual, and I slept through much of it.

We arrived in Tampa at 1030 on 18 June. Mission Complete! It was a short, but very intense Middle East trip. The hotel took care of all my belongings and had them ready upon my return. I left a lot of things in my car and they let me park it there. My decision to not deal with an apartment was again justified, and would be again and again in the near future.

In no time, my room was back in order. I was relaxed and feeling good after my participation in an important mission. I had no idea I would still be there over two years later wondering whether I'd still be there or if I would finally be home for good...

Chapter Eighteen
Life at CENTCOM: Jul-Sep 2009
MacDill AFB, Tampa, FL

The US Central Command

I was settled back in Tampa and getting back up to speed with my duties. It was difficult staying in touch with Terri and the family during my short Qatar trip, but we all caught up again upon my return.

I had received word in Camp As Sayliyah that my Top Secret/Sensitive Compartmentalized Information security clearance had come through, so I finally felt more a part of the crew. Colonel Corcoran would be taking command of the Joint Communications Support Element (JCSE) on 1 July, and I was pushing through General Bowman's recommendation for him to receive the Defense Superior Service Medal for his outstanding contributions to the US Central Command (CENTCOM) during his tour. We had a farewell lunch for him on 25 June. Immediately after that Terri would arrive for another Tampa visit.

After what was becoming our standard Tampa weekend schedule during Terri's visits, she returned to our Wisconsin homes and work. For me it was back to the interesting and sometimes frustrating combination of real world operational business and meaningless administrivia of CENTOM's daily routine. Hurricane season was coming and the CENTCOM took it very seriously.

With the move of the CENTCOM Forward Headquarters (CFH) from the US Army's Camp As Sayliyah in Qatar to the Air Force's Camp Al Udeid also in Qatar, we had to be sure it would work if we had to suddenly shift our command structure there should a hurricane hit Tampa hard enough to endanger our operations. For now, the preparation was paper driven, and I had to ensure our Standard Operating Procedures (SOP) were up to date. If we started getting wet and blown around, we could open them up and know what to do. I hated it, but it was something I was good at, and once again, the only reward for good work was more of it. Oh well, I was planning a trip back to Wisconsin soon.

Afghanistan/NATO

The op tempo remained intense with the assignment of US Army General McChrystal as the International Security Assistance Force (ISAF) Commander as part of the NATO's Supreme Headquarter Allied Powers Europe (SHAPE). NATO had 49 countries involved in Afghanistan by then. The ISAF would act in partnership with Afghan national security forces to create conditions for the governance, reconstruction and development of Afghanistan. I would expect us to be there for a very long time yet.

We now had 70 countries with military representatives here and they were now in their own new building. The new Joint Intelligence Center (JIC) went up fast and was quickly put to heavy use. I figured it would be a couple of years before the new CENTCOM building would be done, so I would likely finish my tour in the old one. One thing was for sure, "The War on Terror" would be going on for a long time afterward, regardless of what we want to call it.

Change of Command

Marine Corps Colonel Murray was aboard and went right to work. I helped him get settled in and organized. He held two briefs per day for awhile. In the perfect world, commanders of major units are allowed significant time for turnover. Colonel Corcoran's last day was Colonel Murray's first day. Lieutenant Colonel Beck and our very good section chiefs got them through it. Colonel Murray was off and running as Colonel Corcoran officially took over the JCSE. I would keep acting as the Executive Officer for Colonel Murray for the time being.

I would focus on routine administrative duties such as performance evaluations, awards, etc. The Disaster Recovery Plan remained a top priority as the construction of the new CFH was wrapping up right about the time hurricane season began.

More Marine Corps Training

Retirees on active duty get no break, not that I was looking for one. Another basic requirement of every Marine is to complete the first

step of the Marine Corps Martial Arts Program (MCMAP). When I
retired, it was still more common for Marines to be wearing the time
honored web belt with brass buckle, highly polished at all times of
course! But after five years of retirement and reentry on active duty, it
seemed everyone had, at a minimum, the green belt, signifying basic
MCMAP training. Even in Iraq, many of the Marines in the battalion
took time out of their hectic schedules to qualify for the next level
belt.

I had the opportunity to get my first level Green Belt then, but was
still nursing a shoulder injury, and knew attempting it would have put
me back at ground zero. The opportunity presented itself at
CENTCOM and I decided to go for it. The training immediately
reminded me of what we did in our Close Combat Training in boot
camp. No problem, after over 38 years, I may benefit from a tune up!

The hot, smothering sun and humidity added to the intensity of the
training. Every day was designed for a specific purpose. The one that
still stands out for me was the day that was meant to wear us down
with a series of heavy duty aerobic and strength stations. After that we
were matched up with an opponent to apply moves we had been
learning. The time for the most important test I've ever had in my life
came. I was as nervous as ever, but accomplished it. You can miss ten
checks, and I only missed two. I'll never forget how good I felt in the
shower room afterward! I put that belt on with the greatest pride, and
was no longer the last web-belt qualified Marine in the Marine Corps!

Dog Days of a CENTCOM Summer
By mid-July we had completed almost all of our key leader
transitions, with only Army Brigadier General Bowman, currently in
charge of the J6 Directorate, remaining to be replaced by Army
Brigadier General Donohue. That would happen in September and is
one of the reasons we were gathering the general officers in Qatar
next month. Our engineers and planners were heavily engaged in
standing up two major command headquarters in Afghanistan.

One was the new four-star ISAF headquarters in Kabul for
General McChrystal as the overall commander of NATO and
American forces in Afghanistan. It was being established to maintain
Middle East and neighboring country high level relationships. The
other was a three-star headquarters for Army Lieutenant General

Rodriquez also in Kabul to run day-to-day operations in country. Both would be in Kabul, Afghanistan. These were mammoth efforts, designed for the long term, and warranted a high level gathering at our CFH in Qatar to ensure proper preparation.

Fall and More Middle East Travel Approach

It was starting to look like I'd be spending much of the next three months in Qatar. The move of the CFH from Camp As Sayliyah to Camp Al Udeid about twelve miles away was nearing completion. The new CFH would be a permanent compound, whereas Camp As Sayliyah with living and working quarters housed in shipping containers in very large warehouses, was temporary. I'd be going over to support another gathering of six very senior officers in the area of responsibility. I would come back for under two weeks, and would go back with the new boss, Colonel Murray, for the "fall deployment."

As a test of the new systems in Al Udeid, we would conduct our annual exercise to transfer command and control operations from Tampa to the CFH as we did when hurricanes threaten Tampa. Our teams would go in three shifts. Colonel Murray and I were to be on the third shift during October and most of November. I was looking forward to the nicer facilities at Al Udeid as it was an Air Force Base. They were always much nicer than anything the Army or Marine Corps had.

The fall mission would be conducted during the Muslim celebration of Ramadan. The name "Ramadan" was the name of the ninth month in the Arab world long before the arrival of Islam. Muslims believe the Qur'an was revealed to Muhammad during the last ten days of Ramadan, and so they fast during the entire month. American servicemen and women were becoming quite familiar with this and many other Islamic customs. We were careful to show respect for their religious practices to maintain good relations and have a place to base our forces in the Middle East. At a minimum, this meant wearing long sleeves and not eating in front of them during the daylight hours.

Some Pre-Deployment Terri Time

Terri was coming in for another long weekend. After this visit, it would be almost three months until we would see each other again. If that held true, my orders would expire and I'd be going back home in mid-December already! The week before her visit was consumed with preparing for a couple of distinguished visitors. The Senior Communications Systems Officer of the Navy Central Command (NAVCENT) in Bahrain and the new Multi-National Forces, Iraq in Baghdad were coming. I arranged a day of meetings for each of them to meet all the senior people they would be dealing with for the next year, and to make sure they received a good overview of current operations and systems issues in the CENTCOM area of responsibility.

Terri arrived on 27 August, and together we met Colonel Murray at Armani's. It was a nice chance for the Colonel to meet her and for him and me to share a little of our past. My Hyatt friends there were excited to meet my boss! While he came to us from the War College in Rhode Island, his previous assignment was Commanding Officer of the Marine's providing security for nuclear submarines. Terri also got out to MacDill's beach area to meet the outgoing CENTCOM J6 Director, Brigadier General Bowman. In doing so, she got to meet some of the key players I'd been working with, including Army Lieutenant Colonel Shaw, Army Lieutenant Colonel Durham, Air Force Lieutenant Colonel Harbison, Marine Colonel Turner, Air Force Staff Sergeant Keaton, and Air Force Chief Master Sergeant Scott.

On 30 August I took Terri to the base for a CENTCOM tour. It was all quite familiar to her. She had been there in 2002 and it was all the same except for the nearby construction of the new headquarters. It was a quiet day, and while I couldn't get her inside the restricted areas, she still loved the hallway pictures. The new JIC was done so we toured that as well. It was named after Lieutenant Commander Otis Vincent Tolbert, who was assigned to CENTCOM from 1996 to 2000 and was killed during the attack on the Pentagon on 11 September, 2001. I didn't know it at the time, but I would soon be spending a great deal of time attending meetings there, well after what my current orders supported.

Terri left for home and my life would once again pick up speed. We probably wouldn't see each other again until November, so we made the best of our time together be her departure! I continued plans for my upcoming deployment to Qatar. The Hyatt, in typical accommodating fashion, allowed me to keep my car there during the three-month deployment in the very spot they set aside as my own. I knew I had made the right decision about staying there instead of taking an apartment!

New Orders Taking shape

I wasn't looking forward to traveling to Qatar for two weeks, coming back for only one, and then returning. Colonel Murray fixed that when he asked me to stay back and assist our incoming Deputy Commander, Army Lieutenant Colonel Jim Enicks, instead of worrying about the first meeting. Coming into CENTCOM with such a responsibility could be somewhat nerve racking for the uninitiated. I liked the idea! One trip to Qatar instead of two! Colonel Murray paid me high praise saying I'd done a good job coordinating the division through the summer transition of every key leader, and that he would feel more comfortable if I was the one who helped our deputy get started. I would then join Phase 2 of the CENTCOM fall deployment to transfer command and control to our CFH in Camp Al Udeid, Qatar.

Upon meeting Lieutenant Colonel Jim Enicks, I knew I had drawn a full house! I'm guessing Colonel Murray knew this already. He would need no babysitting! Jim was a very experienced communications officer with over 36 months of steady deployments. He was General Petraeus' Assistant Chief of Staff, G6 and the General knew him quite well.

My time was then consumed with our normal battle rhythm and pre-deployment preparation. Anytime we "go forward" for more than fifteen days, we needed to be fully deployment ready, which means medical, dental, weapons qualification, physical fitness tests up to date, etc. The hardest to get done was always the medical portion, as the Air Force hospital on MacDill was overwhelmed dealing with a large mix of active duty personnel and retirees. Somehow I broke the code and got my necessary appointments and was ready to go in just a few days.

Life Back Home

Terri was with her family up in Birchwood, Wisconsin at her Brother Bruce's "cabin." It's actually a beautiful tri-level log home overlooking Birch Lake. She had been in Hawaii for two weeks, and her sister and brother-in-law Kay and Tom Lettau from Larsen were with her for one of the weeks. We usually gathered at Bruce's cabin for a fall color weekend and I was thinking of them. Tampa was a good second choice of course, but I missed the company and companionship of my best friend and wife, and the cabin.

Back to Rocky Point
As my mental journey progressed to more recent memories, the pros and cons of staying another year were very real. I now knew what to expect, but just couldn't be sure of where I'd be sent and when. The memories of the uncertainty and interpretation came back with great clarity. I drifted right back to the flight to Al Udeid and what was to become an extremely intense mission.

The Citizen Marine
Living the Dream – In Every Clime and Place

Chapter Nineteen
Another Middle East Journey: Oct-Nov 2009
Al Udeid Air Base, Qatar

Running the War from Afar

Chief Luge picked me up and took me to the US Central Command (CENTCOM) office to get a few items squared away, before he took me to the Military Air (MILAIR) terminal to check in for the military charter flight. It wasn't like my Marine Corps experience with military flights over the years. The passenger terminal was quite nice!

I settled in early and read a book as the others checked in. The plane had capacity for 190, but only 40 of us would load at MacDill. We would pick up 55 more staff members in Norfolk. And, get this - all seats were first class! Now I can't say that I have never flown first class anymore. I couldn't believe it! Could it be I should have joined the Air Force? No, I can't think that way!

We flew on 6 October right on schedule. After our Norfolk stop, we flew straight to Germany. We avoided the usual stop in Gander, Newfoundland, saving several hours, but made up for it by having to wait for the Qataris to open up a landing window at our Leipzig, Germany stop. We arrived in Leipzig and made the best of the unexpected delay. I took time to harvest my face and brush my molars, a very pleasant experience by that time! They had internet, so I shot a few messages back home. It occurred to me once more how different it was being in the military overseas now than it was in my early Vietnam era years. The instant connections with loved ones made it so much better!

There were also Marines of the 3rd Battalion, 4th Marines on their way to Afghanistan in the Leipzig terminal. Their plane had broken down and they were having an extended layover as well. Everyone who knows what it's like leaving your family at the tarmac back home knows you just want to get the deployment underway. You want to get to the operating area, get settled in your new "quarters," usually a tent or plywood hut, before heading to the field for extended operations. You can't finish it if you can't start it!

Thinking of my own early years and my own family and friends back home, I watched them clutter around electric outlets with their PCs and games. It was a new world and a new war with new Marines, but yet the rosters were full of familiar names. They all had the same Marine Corps spirit of those of the Greatest Generation, the days of Korea and Vietnam, and everything in between.

They would very soon be locked in deadly combat in Afghanistan. I always cherish my association with young Marines, whether it is in uniform as I had the honor of then, or as a retired Marine shooting the breeze wherever we meet by chance. As I talked to them, I knew there was a good chance some of them wouldn't come back alive. That was always an unspoken reality among warriors.

Arrival at Al Udeid

We arrived at Al Udeid Air Base at 0335 on 8 October and were bused to the Customs/Immigrations area. Even though we were a military charter flight, we still had to clear customs. After an hour and half delay, we figured out what was clogging the line. The first one off the plane was an Australian general whose paperwork was not in order. The Qataris had one agent working and the rest of us sat while they haggled. He wouldn't take the next in line until he settled the general's situation. I guess he had not been to the Wharton School of Business…

Our bags were shuttled straight through by another Qatari that apparently had been to Wharton School of Business. We made up some lost time and were at the Air Force "dorm" by 0630. The Air Force came through with a barracks room! No tent! I dropped my bags in my much appreciated room, showered, put a fresh uniform on, and checked into the CENTCOM Forward Headquarters (CFH) by 0815. What an amazing facility in the middle of the desert!

The move from Camp As Sayliyah was complete, and this new facility was nothing short of an engineer's dream. It sprawled lowly and quietly in the sand and could withstand any rockets, missiles, or chemicals that broke through the Patriot batteries, and many other security operations that protected it. The halls were wide and the rooms were spacious. At the doorway was a trophy case with a huge gold key. Real gold! It was a gift from the Qatari Emir as a gesture of friendship. He would later come to formally turn the facility over to the US. Prior to his visit, I would witness his tents being set up with plush carpet over the sand where it stood just outside the new facility.

I darkened the door step of the Operations and Plans office and was greeted by Marine Lieutenant Colonel Gomez, Army Lieutenant Colonel Durham, and retired Air Force guy and civilian engineer Frank Marciniak. Much of the next 45 days would be spent eating and working with these guys. I never knew eating and working could be so much fun! They had all done this so often.

The Chow Hall, or as the modern military insisted on calling it, Dining Facility (DFAC), was about a half-mile walk on a wide cement walkway. What these guys couldn't come up with in a half-mile walk would be addressed at the table three times a day. They were so hard on each other that they had to declare "Civility Sunday." No inter-service slams, personal attacks, or profanity. No adverse comments about each other, no negative complaints, only civil discussion on Sunday. It never held up…

Another member of the CENTCOM contingent was Air Force Major Ray Estelle. He fit right in and was well liked and respected. He was a big man, quiet, very respectful, and worked out regularly in the gym. His regular duty station was in Washington, DC back home, but CENTCOM required each service to provide staff members to maintain their ranks with temporary augmentees. Most branches sent augmentees for a year, but the Air Force only sent them for six months or less. Ray was on the short tour and spent much of it with us at Al Udeid. After our return from this deployment, he would return to his base in Washington, DC and I would be sent to Afghanistan. I would later be very saddened to hear he also had been sent to Afghanistan and was killed. He was one of the eight US service members shot by an irate Afghan Lieutenant Colonel on his second day in the country.

Life at CFH Al Udeid

Living and working at the CFH was good by Marine Corps standards. As expected, the Air Force barracks were a taste of college blended with a taste of prison. Nice rooms, nice facilities, but under very strict control. Upon my arrival, I was in a room that could accommodate four men, but would only accommodate two of us this time. I was expecting an Air Force Colonel to join me in a week or so. They even had Wi-Fi! I tuned in to my favorite Tampa and Hawaiian radio stations on my personal computer, while emailing friends and family back home. Where was all this during my Vietnam era overseas experiences!

I was advised wisely by those who do these deployments multiple times every year to quickly adjust my body clock to the daily battle rhythm of the operations center. On the flight I dutifully slept or stayed awake on the Al Udeid schedule. Good advice! It really helped me hit the ground running.

Al Udeid was a very flat, sandy US Air Base in Qatar, bordering Saudi Arabia's east boundary on the Persian Gulf, south of Bahrain and north of the Strait of Hormuz. As Tampa's MacDill Air Base is the host base to CENTCOM as a tenant, so is Qatar's Al Udeid the host base for CENTCOM's forward headquarters. The temperature here was quite pleasant this time of year. When I was here in June, it was 120 degrees by 0600. It was still plenty hot, but not quite that bad. The sand is normally heavy in the air. The buildings were designed to blend into the desert. I wanted to take pictures, but it was prohibited of course.

My first week there was fairly relaxing. I was part of the advance party and the main body would arrive in a week or so. My days would typically start with a run around the sprawling compound while it was not cool, but cooler. Army Brigadier General Donahue was the senior officer of the CENTCOM J6 Directorate reporting to General Petraeus. He was there and I felt privileged to participate in occasional meals with him and my regular crew. They didn't stop their tom foolery just because the general was at the table though. I was glad I was still the adult at the table. Pretty much anyway…

When you're somewhere in the 20 countries of the CENTCOM area of responsibility, you feel justified in referring to the Tampa headquarters as "Tampastan." Most of the countries names ended with "stan," so why not Tampa? They had regular hours, and took holidays back there. What the hell! There is a war on! In reality, everyone who served at CENTCOM understood. By the time you get back to Tampa, you've put in a lot of sand time. But, there were those who somehow avoided deployments and earned the title of shirker.

Anybody with significant deployment had no time for them. They were the "Garret Troopers" of the Vietnam era, which I had to explain to a lot of the guys. I sometimes forgot my date of rank as Chief Warrant Officer 4 alone was longer than most of them had been in the service of their great nation!

Conference Business

By 19 October, the CENTCOM area of responsibility Commanders Conference was well underway. Our advance party made many trips to the terminals of Al Udeid, Camp As Sayliyah, and Doha to provide transport for the regional commanders. One day I was doing my normal gym workout after my early morning run. General Petraeus entered the gym with a good sized entourage, including the well known team of football commentators, including Howie Long and Terry Bradshaw, on their way to Afghanistan to broadcast a game for the troops.

It was especially memorable because General Petraeus saw me on my machine and went out of his way to come over and greet me. This caused concern with the Colonel in charge of the entourage and he stopped and asked who I was. I said that the General and I were the same age and had a few talks along the way and he just recognized me. He became less concerned when I asked him if he knew the difference between a "brown noser" and a "kiss ass." His quizzical look encouraged me to respond for him. When I said "depth perception," he knew I was a good guy and proceeded to catch up with his guests. Howie came over and worked out on the machine next to me. We nodded. Big day for me in a land called Al Udeid!

Our regional commanders throughout CENTCOM had plenty on their plates. Back home it was common to hear of Al-Qaeda, but the radical elements claiming to conduct jihad against the west included many more groups and individuals. Al-Qaeda had gained international fame, as would a spin-off group called ISIS (Islamic State Iraq and Syria) or ISIL (Islamic State of Iraq and the Levant).

US Army General McChrystal, the International Security Assistance Force (ISAF) Commander under NATO's control had submitted a request for a significant number of additional troops to deal with the situation. This would come from the 49 countries participating in the Afghanistan campaign.

For CENTCOM to be in a position to support any one of General McChrystal's options, or any sort of variation of them, there was a great deal of staffing actions and coordination necessary across joint and service staffs. We couldn't even start the crucial communications and coordination across joint or service staffs until the request became official. This was due to the political sensitivities and the potential for leaks with so many large military and civilian staffs handling highly delicate planning information. Many plans had to be built making many assumptions, and several of them would never get near execution. If the press got a hold of the planning information, it would turn into a nut roll for everyone. Now that the request was official, and we were authorized to work with the various agencies, staff, and organizations to conduct actual planning activity, we were in high gear!

Unexpected Help

Much of the power and might of our military comes from technology. As technologies developed, our capabilities expanded exponentially. Brilliance in action for sure! But there was a problem. All the highest intelligence capabilities derived from the exploding technologies, required the capacity to move the mountains of data needed to the people that analyzed it. Either we had to move the people to the source of the data, or we had to find a way to get the data to the large population of analysts around the world to leverage its value.

Most of us with personal computers and cell phones knew that we needed a good networking signal with high capacity to enjoy the offerings of the internet. This comes from the networking capacity called bandwidth, the ability to move large amounts of data across digital infrastructure. To move it around the world requires satellites. Satellite capacity worldwide is determined by market demand. In highly industrialized nations, satellites with huge capacities of bandwidth are readily available to move massive amounts of data to support initiatives. The eventual promise of economic profits and tax revenue justified the investment. The skies above the Middle East were not highly populated with satellites ready to move information for profit and taxation, because there wasn't sufficient commerce.

At the conference the problem of limited bandwidth was discussed. In addition, various military options were identified and priorities were set to deliver the highest bandwidths available to the military missions deemed of the highest value. It wasn't near enough. Intelligence agencies and command and control requirements that had come to rely on digital information required much more than was available in the Middle East, as economic development was nowhere near the highly industrialized nations.

Unexpected help came when a satellite intended to support other missions didn't function properly for its original missions. There was nothing wrong with its transmission capabilities, and it was reachable from the Middle Eastern regions of the world.

Teams of engineers were tasked to work with the appropriate government agencies to determine if this satellite could be pressed into service to support our missions in Afghanistan and other CENTCOM area of responsibility regions. A consensus was reached. It could be done! Because of its difference in intended mission support, special earth terminals would be required, but it could bring much needed bandwidth to the cause.

I was tasked with organizing an impromptu conference to pursue plans to put this errant satellite to use. Why me? I couldn't even spell satellite right eight out of ten times! Organizing a CENTCOM conference in the forward headquarters was not easy. Guys like Chief Luge and Rocky Aiensworth had made a life science out of it, and I was a neophyte under their tutelage just a few months before on my first Qatar trip.

I wasn't ready for this! But, I was a Marine and grew up with some true can-do kind of parents and uncles. And, I had Colonel Murray and Lieutenant Colonel Harbison to support me. Colonel Murray was our division chief and a Marine. Air Force Lieutenant Colonel Harbison was my direct supervisor and spoke Air Force fluently. He would guide me through the gauntlets that lay before me without the knowing hands of Chief Luge and Rocky. Enough said. I was on the case!

It was 2 November. My orders were to get it done by 13 November. I had to fight for coveted conference and working rooms. In a highly classified facility such as the forward headquarters, there were security procedures to meet along with billeting, transportation, and of the highest importance, coffee and chow! I found help in the J2 Intelligence Directorate in Army Master Sergeant Liberta. Between us, we put together the gathering of eagles that would pave the way to expand our communications capabilities in the Middle East, and aid our intelligence agencies and commanders significantly!

A New Direction in the Middle East

The once short, quiet deployment had spun about and we were extremely busy. With General McChrystal's request for troops and resources getting official status, all the various staff agencies had moved into high gear to make up for time lost to the politics. Within two days of finally being authorized to begin the formal staff planning actions, we had key planners from all directorates, across all subordinate service components, and joint task force flown into our Forward Headquarters. We conducted planning sessions to produce products to be sent to the Secretary of Defense (SECDEF) and Joint Chiefs of Staff (JCS). The goal was to provide summaries for the President (POTUS) so he could base his decisions not only on Afghanistan, but several neighboring countries.

During all this, we conducted our original mission. We ran CENTCOM from Al Udeid with the pretense of a hurricane in Tampa. The few "Tampastan" staff members that didn't deploy with us got some well deserved rest.

Terri and I stayed in close communications as always throughout the short but intense deployment. We talked on the phone periodically. My roommate was an honest to goodness J2 (Intel Guy) "Secret Squirrel" and an all-around good roommate. We both respected our private phone time with our wives. With the time and work schedule differences, it was difficult, but we worked it out. Life was good!

The flight back was a commercial flight. Colonel Murray, Lieutenant Colonel Harbison, and I were pulled off the MILAIR charter so we would have time to wrap up the loose ends after the impromptu satellite conference. It was a Qatar Air flight with all the amenities, none of which I enjoyed awake!

Terri and the Marine Corps Ball

I never missed celebrating the Marine Corps birthday in some way through all my years of serving, but this year I was pinned down in the operations center in Al Udeid during the cake ceremony. It was held for all of the Marines there. Lieutenant Colonel Gomez was supposed to bring me a piece of cake back so I could say I never missed celebrating it in the 38 years I'd been a Marine. He failed. Something about having a lot of shit on his mind. I think he ate it...

Not to be deterred by my deployment, my Devil Doggette went to Tampa on her own that year to attend the Marine Corps Birthday Ball. She was good that way. She wasn't going to let my deployment stop her from dressing up and getting to the Ball! She stayed at the Hyatt and was well taken care of by Joanie, John, Margot and the rest of our family there. The night of the ball she stayed right at the downtown Hyatt where the Ball was held.

She got a ride to the ball from our "retired" and very chivalrous CIA friend Jesse. She was greeted by friends we met during our first tour in Tampa with the Marine Central Command (MARCENT) in 2001/2, including now retired Colonel John Tempone who had presented her with her own Marine Corps Commendation Medal during one of her visits back in 2002.

Our friends at the Hyatt took good care of her, and the Ceremony was good for her as she was able to share the burden of separation with other Marines and guests going through the same thing. We hoped we would be together by Thanksgiving week and I was counting the days!

Back at Rocky Point
By now I was truly in the groove on my run. The memories of the Al Udeid mission were vivid. If I did stay for another, there would no doubt be several more of such missions in the coming year! But, that mission was only a small part of what was still to come...

Chapter Twenty
Joint Operations: Dec 2009-Mar 2010
US Central Command, MacDill AFB, Tampa, Fl

Thanksgiving in Tampa and a New Assignment

As we had hoped, Terri arrived back in Tampa to share Thanksgiving together after my return to Tampa. Even if we missed our traditional family Thanksgivings, we were very thankful to be together for our own and share it with our Tampa friends. We were especially honored to be invited to Massimo's family Thanksgiving meal at his restaurant in Palm Harbor! He had left the Hyatt shortly after my departure from my first tour in Tampa and started his own restaurant which was very successful. He was still making headlines in Tampa's Best magazines, and he still made his guests feel very special as only he could do.

He closed the restaurant to the public that day and set all the tables in a row for his family and special friends. What an honor and what an experience! A special meal by a "Tampa's Best" magazine chef and his wife Donna! It was reminiscent of when they invited me to their own family Easter meal in 2002. Great memories!

Our brief reunion was over and Terri departed for our Wisconsin home on 1 December. As I listened to news reports, I was reminded of why I volunteered to come off Marine Corps retirement and get back into the ranks in uniform. The president had delayed the decision to send additional troops to Afghanistan and was telling the public that his thoughtful delay would have no impact on the timeline. Anybody with a modicum of common sense knows you can't delay a decision to move people and equipment, equivalent to the size of a typical city of 30,000 inhabitants, and all their belongings, half way around the world, and have a place ready to put them!

We could have started the necessary staff coordination with the various commands around the country that would need to be involved without impact if we didn't have orders not to out of concern for a press leak. I swear that politicians live in a bubble and wouldn't know reality if they tripped over it!

I was reassigned from my role as division Executive Officer to the role of Operations Officer in our Current Operations branch, and would remain involved with the team working on satellite support. Contrary to the movies and spy novels that make it look like the world is completely covered by satellite signals, the US Central Command (CENTCOM) area of responsibility had less than one seventeenth of the bandwidth available in the European or Pacific areas of responsibility.

I was continually amazed at our engineers' creative approach and can-do mind sets, and can honestly say that while the satellite project was one of the hottest and most visible things going on and the pressure was significant, I was proud to be given the opportunity. In my new role I would be coordinating the activities of the Joint Chief of Staff Command, Control, Communications, Computers, Intelligence, Surveillance, Reconnaissance (C4ISR) Task Force, US Forces-Afghanistan (USFOR-A), and several other agencies. This seemed like an enjoyable way to finish up my retired recall duty that was now scheduled to end on 4 January, 2010.

Extension of Retired Recall Orders
Things were going well for me. I liked what I was doing, and the command seemed to appreciate the help. I was gearing down and preparing to leave for Quantico and process back to retired status when they asked if I would stay on if they could get it approved by Headquarters Marine Corps (HQMC). I said sure, never thinking they could pull it off. Well, they did! Shortly I received word that my orders were extended until 30 September, 2010. I frankly was surprised, but quite happy. The Marine Corps was still very stingy on retired recalls, and I was certainly pushing the envelope! Obviously a request endorsed by General Petraeus held significant weight, but I could just see the Barbarians of Bureaucracy in Quantico wringing their wrists. I kind of liked that picture!

Once again I had to think about what I was going to tell Terri and my employer. WPS had already held my job for nearly three years and it was putting great pressure on my boss and my friend Mike who volunteered to cover my duties. Terri and I stayed close as always and

she knew it was a possibility. She appreciated the way we kept her
involved and knew how much it meant to me. She once again proved
her love and friendship. But she did mention something like if she
knew I'd be gone three years, she may not have authorized my
original departure! At WPS, my boss Tony and friend Mike took it in
stride as well. What did I do in life to get this kind of support?

But any member of CENTCOM knew that all the pleasantries of
life in Tampa weren't ours to keep. Our duty was in the Middle East.
By staying on, I could be sure of yet more deployments, but would
they be shorter, or maybe even longer? Regular military organizations
had months to prepare for their deployments. At CENTCOM, we
traveled to the Middle East like civilian corporate executives on the
west coast fly to the east coast for meetings. By staying for nine more
months, there were plenty of opportunities for one or two more
Middle East jaunts.

Anybody with operations center experience at higher headquarters
knows that in addition to the many screens focusing on various
aspects of the mission at hand, there were also CNN, Fox, and other
cable news channels. Today's warfare is heavily information driven.
It was not unusual for the cable news companies to have reporters and
capabilities where the government didn't, as they weren't hamstrung
by regulations and politics. We had to know what they were saying at
all times so we could ensure our commanders weren't blindsided.

One particular story that got our attention was CNN's story on
how some of our drone intelligence feeds were being hacked by
opposing forces. It sounded like anybody with a Radio Shack account
could order equipment to intercept the drone's signals. I loved
Lieutenant Colonel Harbison's response when asked about it. First
and foremost, he mentioned that it was being fixed, not that it
mattered. He went on with the part I loved.

In essence, the only signal the Taliban or other unsavory
characters could intercept was the satellite downlink signal showing
what the drone operators could see. The signals to and from the
satellites from the drone were encrypted and were not being
intercepted. Therefore, the only thing the interceptor could see was a
picture of his own demise in real-time. He could see his every move
to escape the hellfire heading his way to no avail. My only question

was whether or not Radio Shack would give him his money back upon his arrival in Paradise.

Christmas at Home
On 18 December I headed home for the holidays. So far, in all my years, I never missed a family Christmas. Our traditional Christmas Eve gathering at our Sauk house was a great night of family warmth and togetherness, complete with a real Santa and continuous play of movies from Christmas Eves past. Terri and I were able to make her family tradition of oyster stew at the postcard-perfect winter scene of her childhood home in Larsen along with her brother and sister's family.

I once again enjoyed seeing my good friends Denny and Schumann and our road trips to our favorite country bars. I never tired of the beautiful, rolling hills, woods, and winding rivers. As my leave came to an end, I wondered whether I'd stay in Tampa or be sent back to Qatar or Afghanistan, or anywhere else in the vast CENTCOM area of responsibility.

The Gunny Lives
About 28 January I had read somewhere, online of course, that the famous "Full Metal Jacket" and "Mail Call" Gunnery Sergeant R Lee Ermey had died. I could have sworn I just heard from my old friend and fellow retired Marine Corps Chief Warrant Officer 3 Ray Schara that he had just shot a rifle match with him in my hometown of Lodi!

Ray confirmed that it was not true, so I immediately reported back to the source of the false claim of the good Gunny's death. If he is dead, someone should notify him, because he's still running around the countryside shooting rifle matches with old Marine Warrant Officers in Lodi!

Life Evolves at CENTCOM
As I spoke of earlier, we had 70 countries working with us in our counterterrorism efforts in the Middle East, most of which were focused in Afghanistan at this point. There were so many different types of uniforms and services and it was all interesting to me! I liked living and working in Tampa, but I never forgot why we were all there. Islamic terrorism was very much at the forefront of the minds

of the people and governments who were becoming more and more impacted by it. Most of the European countries had no real ability to counter what was becoming more and more a real threat felt by their populations. They had their "guns or butter" debates years ago and chose butter. They gladly became part of the coalition to counter the threat, but often needed to be provided with the equipment and weaponry to do so. Most Americans hadn't felt the terrorism threat as much as other parts of the world yet, but I was convinced if we didn't deal with it, we most certainly would be feeling.

For at least February and March, I was expecting to stay in Tampa. This would allow me to get in touch with the key people involved in getting additional capabilities in place to support the timeline and mission assignments. One of my counterparts would be the one to go "forward" and would leave in a few days. She was a highly experienced Air Force Lieutenant Colonel temporarily assigned to CENTCOM from one of three letter agencies in Washington, DC. She would drive things from that end, going from base to base to do what had to be done to get things in place, and would reach back to me for help on this end.

There was truly much to be done, and we all were doing whatever it took. To that end, I worked to ensure I was up to date on all my pre-deployment training and medical preparations required before being deployed for 30 days or more. If I get tapped again, the normal two to three weeks required to process wouldn't be available, so I had to be in a position to expedite and react. I assured my boss I'd be ready to go to the "sounds of the guns" on short notice. That was a must for any member of CENTCOM, especially then.

I felt very fortunate to have even a small role in continually improving our capabilities and capacity to support the dynamically increasing demand for getting more intelligence to more commanders in more places. It was a great feeling every time we got the opportunity to expedite another radical fundamentalist's burning desire to become a martyr!

Terri, Valentine's Day, and Skyping Grand Runts
I was looking forward to Terri's arrival for a Valentine's Day visit. She arrived on 11 February on time despite the snowstorms encountered along the way. I had every reason to expect to be

spending most of February and March in Qatar, along with a large number of CENTCOM staff members conducting a similar forward deployment like we did in October and November. I was excluded because of my role in the satellite project, so while it got me out of this deployment, there could be a trip to Afghanistan before being done in September. For now, I was in Tampa with Terri and we were looking forward to a restful, relaxing weekend.

It had been a record cold and windy winter in Tampa, so we didn't spend much time at our favorite beaches. Our Valentines weekend was short, but memorable. Terri once again headed back to our Wisconsin home and her work at the State.

The Pace Quickens

At CENTCOM, my duties were becoming more and more consumed by coordinating the efforts required to take advantage of the satellite that we inherited, and to increase our bandwidth in the area of responsibility. Everyone wanted their share of the additional capacity, but nobody would get any until we got terminals in place on the ground in Afghanistan. I was working with our engineers in Tampa and several agencies in Washington, DC, along with the logistics folks in the various bases in theater, where we wanted the terminals to be placed. Talk about herding cats!

I had every reason to believe I would not be pressured to stay on beyond my 30 September end-date this time, and was starting to allow myself to think of coming home to stay. It certainly felt as though I contributed my share the past two and a half years. Starting to tire a bit, it felt strange to be thinking about coming home in six months, while everything and everybody else at CENTCOM was bracing for the heavy lifting ahead.

I was sure the spring and summer would bring a vast increase in operational tempo there as our additional forces flew in. My employer had gone above and beyond its legal requirements to keep my job intact upon my return, and my family had been somewhere on the scale above fantastic with their love, support, and patience. My CENTCOM boss was aware of this and indicated he wouldn't push for another extension.

That said, six months was a long time. I was involved in the highly visible and extremely sensitive project to vastly increase the capacity of our ISR systems in the Afghanistan Theater of Operations. Always keeping my guard up, I'd remain alert and vigilant to the last day, and wouldn't be surprised to see one, or even two, deployments to the Middle East before being done. If you look at CENTCOM as a civilian company headquarters, it is common to travel to key business locations for short trips. That's what much of the staff members did, but the flights were hellacious, and the conditions grueling, for whatever short time we'd spend there.

The Afghanistan Surge
The surge (also known by certain politicians as the "Uplift") was going well, but we had organized chaos at many of our bases in country where people and equipment were flowing in. The president's delay was causing every command to scramble.

All inflowing forces had to go through processing centers like Qatar, Kuwait, Manas, etc. Once they airlifted from the processing areas to their assigned receiving airfield, they had to have ground transportation to their forward operating bases and other duty stations. The weather and terrain made that very difficult, and it was extremely hard for the various bases to construct billeting and messing facilities to support the folks as they arrived. Conditions were hairy over there. Soon the spring fighting season would kick in, which is where my project came in.

Life at CENTCOM Intensifies
My satellite project work was moving full speed forward. We were working feverishly to get satellite terminals installed at nine sites in Afghanistan and one in Qatar, but were competing for base support services with the massive flow of personnel and equipment involved in the "surge."

My counterpart in country was going from base to base to garner their support. Her access to our email and phone systems was spotty at best, so I was the one who had to do most of the communications and attend the many video teleconference meetings necessary to coordinate the activities between CENTCOM, concerned agencies, and the various points of contact in the theater. If all went well, we'd have some of the terminals operating at the bases before I left in September.

I hoped to come home with a great sense of satisfaction that I had a small role in increasing our C4ISR operations in not only Afghanistan, but the entire CENTCOM area of responsibility. It was looking bleak with the challenges of the delayed surge decision.

Afghanistan Orders

Things were moving quickly at CENTCOM and in Afghanistan as spring unfolded. Both of the higher headquarters we established in Kabul were in full operation by the previous fall.

Of particular concern to CENTCOM in support of the new four star International Security Assistance Force (ISAF) and three star ISAF Joint Command (IJC) in Kabul was the ability to support the forces flowing into the theater of operations. Of particular concern to my general, Army Brigadier General Brian Donahue, was the efficient and effective support of computer and communications capabilities in a part of the world where there are great scarcities of fiber, cable, and satellite availability.

He and Army Colonel Mike Allen understood the importance of the bandwidth capabilities of the satellite we were working on, and they needed somebody in country to take over for my counterpart who was scheduled to retrograde and return to her duties back in Washington, DC. Somebody was needed to be the ears and eyes for CENTCOM to ensure everything possible was being done to get the ground terminals in to take advantage of the bandwidth offered by the satellite. All heads suddenly turned to me....

I was given ten days to get through the pre-deployment process, get my personal affairs in order, and report for a 90-120 day tour of duty. I would assist Air Force Lieutenant Colonel Sam Arwood, the CENTCOM systems liaison to Army Lieutenant General Rodriquez's CJ-6 systems staff at the IJC.

Getting Ready

First things first, Terri and I had made our plans for her to come down for a week in early May so we could enjoy our 14 year anniversary on 11 May together. That wouldn't happen anymore, but she would come down to see me off. She would go home on 27 April and I would fly out on 28 April. We would have a nice four-day weekend together, and then I'd be gone for three or four months, or so we thought.

Alphabet Soup, Afghanistan and ISAF/IJC

I strove to understand how my Afghanistan duties would contribute to the big picture. It was difficult to keep things straight at first. US Army General David Petraeus, as the CENTCOM Commander, maintained US military responsibility for all the countries in CENTCOM's area of responsibility.

The ISAF Commander, US Army General McChrystal reported to the North Atlantic Treaty Organization (NATO) and was the overall commander for strategic political-military aspects of the ISAF mission in Afghanistan. He immediately assessed that he couldn't handle the combined requirements of dealing with the external strategic and political aspects of his command and give the day-to-day operations sufficient attention.

The day-to-day tactical operations throughout Afghanistan were then directed out of the IJC under US Army Lieutenant General Rodriquez. In addition to tactical military operations he handled the full spectrum of other activities including command responsibility over the Regional Commands (RC-North, RC-South, RC-West, and RC-East), the Provincial Reconstruction Teams and the theatre enablers, such as agricultural alternatives to the poppy fields, civil engineering, etc.

Think of it as four-Star General McChrystal at the ISAF headquarters in downtown Kabul facing outward to neighboring countries, and dealing with politics and strategic guidance. While three-star Lieutenant General Rodriguez, at the IJC in North Kabul Area International Airport (KAIA) facing inward, dealt with regional commands throughout the very large, mountainous country of Afghanistan.

My role in the three star IJC headquarters would be to assist Lieutenant Colonel Sam Arwood in representing Brigadier General Donahue and General Petraeus' CENTCOM interests. They needed bandwidth to support the delivery of real time command and control systems under Lieutenant General Rodriquez's command. In addition my role would be to support the transmission of ISR systems data to operations centers around the world.

This would include the project I'd already been working on. I'd also be coordinating with the regional command headquarters throughout Afghanistan to ensure maximum integration of systems to avoid a massive build-up of individual, "stove-pipe" systems that consume vast amounts of bandwidth, and drastically reduce the amount of voice and data we can move into and out of the country at one time.

With all the countries and the associated bureaucracies of each involved and all the territory to cover, coupled with constant pressure of the surge of personnel and equipment, we would have what I could only call an entanglement of cultures, customs, and politics. Something had to be done to break it up and get things done. We couldn't wait for the bureaucracies to get themselves untangled to get the gear in country, get the systems in place to find the bad guys we're tracking, and enable the vast increase of command and control systems needed for all the incoming major commands.

Brigadier General Donahue formed a special task force called Task Force 236 to get in country and find ways to work around the bottlenecks. Army Colonel Mike Allen was Brigadier General Donahue's point man to get the new task force off the ground in Tampa. Air Force Lieutenant Colonel Sam Arwood was in charge of forming Task Force 236 in Afghanistan. Marine Gunnery Sergeant Nate Powell was Lieutenant Colonel Arwood's Staff Non-Commissioned officer in charge. I was identified with other CENTCOM J6 division members from Tampa that they felt could be effective in making things happen in spite of the burdening bureaucracy. It was a compliment. I think...

Lieutenant Colonel Arwood worked with my predecessor over there and would be ready for me. Gunnery Sergeant Powell was already tracking me and would make sure I got there safely and that I stayed safe while there.

Sue Haack back at the Madison VFW 8483 Post gave me a guardian angel when I left for the Iraq tour in October 2007. It was time to get it back out and wear it every day. I pinned it between the middle buttons of my desert cammie blouse where it couldn't seen, but I knew it was there. It would once again be a source of comfort while I'm in a foreign land. It brought me good luck in Iraq, so I would press it back into service for this deployment.

Terri's love and dedication was unfailing and I couldn't do a day of this duty without it. Kurt and Jenny took away the worries of keeping my Sauk house clean and safe. Kristin, Mark and the boys would grow as a family and keep me supplied with food and artwork. Tony Konkol and Mike Endres at WPS were still going well out of their way to keep my position waiting for my return in October. This was a huge load off my mind!

I would need to be back in Tampa in early September in time to check out, drive to Quantico, VA for processing back to retired status, and be home by 1 October. I was getting very comfortable with the idea of supporting my satellite project from Tampa and come home with a good sense of accomplishment. These orders truly came out of the blue and while shocked, I was certainly honored to be entrusted with an assignment of this kind!

Another Tearful Departure

Terri came down for our impromptu pre-deployment visit. We had a lazy day in the hotel and went to a movie. We saw "How to Train Your Dragon" and went to the Bahama Breeze afterward. Terri even got to witness a Laundry Night at the Rusty Pelican! She was impressed and I would have clean clothes for the deployment! We got back to the room in time to see the current episode of "24." Terri wouldn't miss that for anything!

She left early on 27 April. It was especially hard this time. Even though I thought it would only be 90 or 120 days, it was Afghanistan. No matter how many times I told her I'm safer with Marines protecting me than her driving around on icy Wisconsin roads, she just would never buy it! I knew Marine Gunnery Sergeant Powell, Staff Sergeant Josh Sherwood, and a host of others would drive me around and protect me, but to her it was still Afghanistan where our military members were dying.

There were tears, a last hug, and I watched until I couldn't see her after she turned the corner to check in at the airport. I went to the Village Inn for breakfast and swallowed extra hard as I thought about being away from my best friend and wife in a foreign and unfriendly land. Again.

Rocky Point Tears

The heart tugs of our Afghanistan parting more than a year earlier involved vivid memories of how often we had done this. Tears clouded my vision and appreciation of my beautiful surroundings of Old Tampa Bay as I sensed a good chance to go home for good. If I stayed on active duty, I would surely be going back...

The Citizen Marine
Living the Dream – In Every Clime and Place

Chapter Twenty One
Going Forward: Apr-May 2010
Task Force 236, Kabul, Afghanistan

A Return to Al Udeid, Qatar

I left Tampa the next day on 28 April and arrived at Dulles airport with six hours to kill before my 14 hour flight to Doha, Qatar. I did the only reasonable thing and set up a perimeter in the Old Dominion bar in the A Terminal. Computers are great for killing time! I cleaned up my electronic junk yard, got caught up on my emails, and organized some notes. All this fun and they were paying me too!

I arrived in Doha, Qatar and the CENTCOM Forward Headquarters (CFH) at Al Udeid Air Base on schedule on 29 April. It was another smooth and comfortable flight on Qatar Airlines. It had become a familiar flight since it was my third one in less than a year. I had always been a sucker for maps and loved the flight map graphics. It was especially interesting to see Iraq and Kuwait as we flew over them. Bye suckers! Better not say that too loud! It was too easy to get sent back in this job. I slept or read for most of the flight. My strategy to beat the long hours was simple. I kept an open book on my lap at all times. If my eyes were open, I read. If they were closed, I slept. Maybe I should patent that!

My Air Force Lieutenant Colonel counterpart was coming out of Afghanistan to turn her weapon and gear in, so we got a chance to touch base. I would need to pick up where she left off. She probably forgot more about satellites and terminals than I would ever know. She debriefed me at "The Bra," the recreational spot for rest and relaxation in Al Udeid. It was comprised primarily of two large white tents that looked like a bra from a distance. We enjoyed our limit of three alcoholic drinks and she gave me lots of advice about how things work at each of the regions and bases where she had traveled in Afghanistan. It would prove to be an invaluable debrief! She would return to her duties at CENTCOM's MacDill Headquarters, and soon after would return to her home duty station in Washington, DC, and I would be on my own.

Mother's Day was fast approaching. I wasn't able to find a Mother's Day card in Afghanistan or in AUAB. I ended up just calling Terri to wish her a Happy Mother's Day and reminded her to send one to Mom.

On 2 May the desk manager at the barracks was kind enough to give me a ride to the passenger terminal on short notice. Gunnery Sergeant Powell hooked me up on a distinguished visitor flight with several colonels. When I got to the terminal, the Colonel in charge of the flight readily agreed to take me on. It was a Gulf Stream and had capacity for 20, but there were only five of us. The senior officer was a US Army Colonel leading a team of a US Army Lieutenant Colonel, a Canadian Colonel, and a Canadian Sergeant. They were pretty experienced flying around the area of responsibility and had no problem going to sleep. I was wound up and loved drinking the strong Hawaiian coffee the flight crew kept handing out. I was wide awake, even though it was the middle of the night. I got a good portion of Nelson Demille's "Gold Coast" read. Needless to say, I got absolutely no sleep on the three hour flight.

Arrival at Kabul, Afghanistan

We arrived on the military side of Kabul Area International Airport (KAIA) at 0030 on 3 May and were issued transient tent codes and temporary passes for base access. We were then assigned to a transient tent with wooden bunk beds.

Upon awakening and stepping out, the scenery would register memories never to be forgotten. We were truly at the foothills of the Hindu Kush mountain range. At 6,000 feet, and at the base of some snowcapped mountains, the temperature was great. The compound containing the International Joint Command (IJC) headquarters seemed surprisingly small to me. Cement and Hesco barriers were everywhere. There were a few brick buildings, but mostly tents. The IJC headquarters itself was a huge Quonset hut with extensive fencing and heavily guarded entrances that clearly stood out. Another strange setting in another strange place in another foreign land surrounded by people who would love to do me harm. Just like starting all over again in Iraq. Ain't this great! Oh well, it would only be for 90 or 120 days or so…

The North Kabul Area International Airport (KAIA) compound hosting the IJC headquarters was about a half mile long and only a few hundred yards wide. The Quonset style building had attached hard structures on both sides to give the space required for the entire three-star command staff. The living quarters were comprised of both tents and hard structures bounded by sand bags, Texas barriers (large cement walls) and fences. There were many troops from many European countries there, each with an assigned mission. Belgium and Bulgaria's mission for example was internal and perimeter compound security.

The compound was very small indeed, but had most everything we needed. There were two chow halls - I mean Dining Facilities, or DFACs, (my age is showing again). One was a tent a few hundred yards down the street from the IJC headquarters, and the other was a hard structure next to the IJC. They were run by the KBR government contracting firm, who did an excellent job in Iraq and Kuwait providing consistently outstanding organization, service, and pretty damn good chow given the conditions. This KBR was the British arm of the contract, however, and there was no comparison.

There was little or no internet availability on the entire compound, which was unusual for a higher headquarters. Sufficient bandwidth for personal use was being installed across the base for morale purposes, but it would be many months before getting it to the US barracks. The US footed the bill for all of it, of course, but the other nations didn't want to give the impression that just because we paid for it, we would get it first. They did the only reasonable thing and put us last on the list. Sufficient bandwidth for the US barracks would not happen during my 90 day tour. Isn't socialism great!

The Gunny and Lieutenant Colonel Sam Arwood brought me up to speed immediately on what was happening and made sure I was ready to hit the ground running. No plunderin' and wonderin' here! There was a lot to do, so every person and every day counted! I would be the Task Force 236 SATCOM Officer. I had never been trained and had no experience in satellite communications. My pucker factor was definitely up! I was sure I was blessed with this honor because of my involvement with the satellite project. I was immediately assigned to other problems that stood in the way of Task Force 236 progress as well. Great to feel part of a great team! I think...

Life at the IJC Headquarters
The IJC CENTCOM J6 (Systems) workspaces were adjacent to the large Quonset looking building that housed the operations center and other staff organizations. Our workstations were plywood desks and there was a lot of sand and dust. The office was very crowded with US, Canadians, British, Australians, and members from other countries making up the coalition in Afghanistan. Alaska tents were used by IJC Information Technology and logistic support functions.

Each regional command (RC) in Afghanistan was assigned to one of the countries in the coalition. On a regular basis, meetings would be conducted via video teleconference equipment between all the regional command communication and supporting staffs with the IJC Coalition J6. This would include the Southwest Asia Theater Network Operations and Security Center in Kuwait, the Joint Network Command Center, Afghanistan, the US Forces-Afghanistan, RC-East, RC-North, RC-Southwest, and RC-Capitol (Kabul).

Every military staff had a battle rhythm. On certain days, certain meetings were conducted with expected regularity and preparedness. Each of us on the Task Force 236 leadership team was expected to be ready to provide reports to the Weekly Activity Report, affectionately known as the WAR Report. Creative huh? It included all staff sections and went to the IJC Commander, Army Lieutenant General Rodriquez, and every subordinate and supporting commander in Afghanistan and back in Tampa. I kept diligent daily notes to make sure I could readily submit my portion of the WAR report on the appointed day at the appointed time.

Terri Goes Back to Tampa
Anybody that knows Terri knows she doesn't waste things. Her family taught her well. Her parents went through the depression and knew the value of every kernel of corn and every part of every meal. And, as a University of Wisconsin Badger football and hockey fan on a tight budget, she would never think of wasting part of a beer. Many a bartender had to learn that the hard way when they tried taking her last swallow of beer away for a fresh one! Well, she darn sure wasn't

going to waste a perfectly good airline ticket to Tampa for our
anniversary just because I wasn't there, nor just because she was there
for an impromptu visit to see me off a few weeks earlier! To Tampa
she went and enjoyed the company of our friends there.

First Casualties

On 8 May, 2010 a convoy of IJC personnel was hit by a Vehicle Born
Improvised Explosive (VBIED) attack. This had become an
unfortunate routine for those who were already there awhile, but for
me it was the first casualties I had encountered (in Afghanistan) and I
hadn't been there for even a week! Six Americans and one Canadian
Colonel were killed. As the reports came out, our hearts were in our
throats. Gunnery Sergeant Powell was scheduled to join the convoy
on one of their routine missions that day. It took a couple hours to sort
things out, but we learned that his plans had changed earlier in the day
and his vehicles were not in the attacked convoy.

Sadly, however, we did quickly learn that two of the dead were
from the IJC's security team. Another one of the dead was a US Army
Lieutenant Colonel from Waterloo, Wisconsin, not far from the
Madison area back home. It was especially sad as he was a reservist
on a Pre Deployment Site Survey (PDSS), where a small team from a
deploying unit makes an advanced trip to gather more detailed
planning information.

The memorial service for Army Staff Sergeant Richard Tieman
and Specialist Josh Tomlinson was held on 21 May in a tent large
enough to handle the large group on the IJC compound. It was
sincerely touching to watch the respect and reverence given them as
every member of this command from each country approached the
two sets of boots, rifles, helmets and dog tags. Each rendered the
distinctive salutes of their countries, and each provided their own
personal touches to the dog tags or helmets to offer their private
prayers. Many removed their country or unit patches from their
uniforms and laid them on the table as mementos to the families and
as reminders that their sacrifice was of a higher calling in the defense
and unity of civilized nations.

It had been a short time but I had gotten to know them. They were
the ones responsible for checking my credentials every time I entered
the IJC security gate, and they always had a smile on their face and

some sort of unique greeting. We all thought of the families they left behind, and we all knew any of us could easily be next.

An Anniversary from Afar

On 11 May I made an anniversary call to Terri from my work phone at the IJC, but we lost the connection several times. I was finally able to make a solid connection on a NATO Class A line with all the proper permissions. It was difficult to have to call her on our anniversary. I loved hearing her voice, but I loved seeing and being with her in person even more. We certainly had our share of anniversary separations and we both knew there couldn't be too many more as my retired recall couldn't last much longer. I swallowed hard as I thought of the losses we just suffered...

I got a bunch of pictures of Kristin and Mark's young family. It was always such a treat just to see all the color of the kids' world! Toys and playgrounds brought me so much pleasure when I had nothing but mountains, sand and sun all around me. Kurt and his friend Jenny continued to keep my Sauk house standing and well maintained inside and out. My family, the WPS team, and my many good friends made my service possible and I was very much looking forward to my return this fall.

In the ISAF Joint Command (IJC)

There were only 30 US Marines in the IJC, but wherever US Marines gather, the senior Marine will always seek other US Marines out and get us together. It's what we do. Our senior Marine was Major General Rengler. He insisted on meeting every Marine in the command. Just as we met and were making small talk, a casualty call came in and he had to tend to his pressing duties, but it felt good to make contact and I could count on him for anything.

Lieutenant Colonel Arwood and Gunnery Sergeant Powell had a tradition of a newcomer's brief which was very impressive. It took place in a warehouse tent that would become the place of many meetings to come. It was an Alaska tent with a big map of Afghanistan and quite impressive video teleconference capabilities. It was plenty hot inside, but Lieutenant Colonel Arwood was skilled in his leadership and motivational delivery and had people's attention. Immediately I sensed strong team building skills and a strong mutual respect among team members. I felt great sense of pride in being picked to be part of something good!

Task Force 236: A Special Mission with a Tight Deadline

So my first weeks at Kabul had been quite an adjustment in every way, but I was getting settled and accustomed to the camp, terrain, schedule and culture. My duties had my head spinning, but I was getting a grasp on what was expected of me. They were simple in concept, but daunting in practice.

Lieutenant Colonel Arwood and Gunnery Sergeant Powell had already been in Afghanistan since December with a small crew, many of which had rotated back to Tampa. These guys had done an absolutely amazing job of getting things done amidst the mind boggling confusion and collision of urgency and grid-lock. There were now 62 of us there, and it would swell to 80 or so in the coming days.

The Task Force 236 team was made up of all US military from CENTCOM and best of breed civilian contractors who were specifically recruited for this mission. We had a team lead and crew for each regional command with an objective to consolidate networks, achieve maximum efficiency, and get Command, Control, Communications, Computers, Intelligence, Surveillance, Reconnaissance (C4ISR) systems up fast. This part of the world had scarce communications capacity, so there were crews of six to ten at each of the regions. I'd stay in Kabul with Lieutenant Colonel Arwood and the Gunny, while most of the others would be spread throughout the regional commands.

In addition to working all satellite issues, my role was to coordinate all things related to my Operations and Plans division back in Tampa and help Lieutenant Colonel Arwood in any way he needed. I could do that!

Working in the Shadows of Heroes

I would never forget how on a daily basis I would meet someone who had already served so long and given so much. US Army Major Sayles was the Coalition J6 Operations Officer in the IJC. This tour was just another of many for her. In Iraq, her vehicle was hit by an IED and she still had pins in her back. I would meet her again less than a year later in Tampa getting ready for yet another Afghanistan tour!

Army Specialist Mitchell was a security driver and was shot in the chest once, but saved by his body armor. When his combat tour was finished, his supply officer tried to make him pay for the damaged armor, carrying on the reputation and traditions of all REMFs. That's one acronym I'll let you look up if need be.

Marine Staff Sergeant Josh Sherwood came back into the picture as well. Also a reservist, he had already served several combat tours and was once again here to get us around Afghanistan safely. His overseas longevity paved the way for certain quirks. He had a tattoo around his neck of a dotted line with "cut above dotted line" instructions as his last defiant act if captured. I pitied any bad guy that thought Josh could be captured. Definitely the guy you wanted next to you when things got sticky!

He drove our team around day in and day out, along with Gunnery Sergeant Powell, and a small security team. When we traveled, there was a driver and assistant driver with rifles in armored vehicles. In Kabul, it was often in bullet proof SUVs. We all were armed and wore full body armor while traveling, at all times of course. If we encountered any sort of incident, we were to stay in our vehicle unless otherwise compromised. If we left the vehicle, we were to seek higher ground, by force if necessary, and call the Quick Reaction Force (QRF) which was always at the ready.

Kabul was amazingly a very trashy, dirty city. I expected it to be much cleaner as the capital of Afghanistan. There were crumbled buildings that were not a result of war, but rather just plain dilapidated. There was trash everywhere with old shops and busy streets. The crowds of pedestrians wore every kind of clothing in the spectrum. There was a lot of traditional Afghan dress mixed in with western garb of all kinds.

We had some interesting requests for support as the days progressed. For example, we also helped the Independent Directorate of Local Governance (IDLC) to secure their computer networks. There was no truly functioning central government. Tribal factions didn't trust each other and the IDLC was becoming more and more a trusted source of bringing them together. But they were high on the Taliban target list, and members were being systematically executed because their networks weren't properly secured. The experts of Task Force 236 who were called to the rescue took great pride in what they did!

Terri and Home

Terri was back to her routine at home. She was introducing Chad, her new parakeet to replace the late Tweety, to his new cell mates. Butkus was the other parakeet and Daphne was the Senegal parrot. She loved her birds, and they had been instrumental in keeping her company during my recall to active service. She and Daphne were still bonding after several more blood lettings. The process took a big step forward with Daphne's newly acquired passion for Wisconsin cheese!

I was able to stay in touch with her and my family via phone and email, and received my first care package from Kristin's family. It was nice as the chow here was bad. They did a great job of sending things to nibble on that reminded me of home and the good ol' USA. She credited three-year old Dylan and one year old Gavin for the selections and sent pictures of the packing operation. When I saw the picture of Gavin's intense expression of ownership over the small package of M&M's, I was surprised it even made it to the box!

The War, the Threat, and Who's in the Game

There were 44 countries represented in Afghanistan which would grow to 49 during my tour. The US, of course, was the heaviest contributor with 50,000+ personnel and growing. Nine other countries had contributed over 1,000 personnel and all the rest were in the tens or hundreds. After the US, the United Kingdom (Great Britain) was next with over 10,000, then Germany, Canada, Italy, the Netherlands, France, Poland, Spain, Turkey each with two to four thousand. Regardless, the lack of reality that was common in politics and diplomacy amazed me. The constant plea by Americans for other countries to do more reflects a lack of some very basic knowledge of European society and the military's role in it.

The massive numbers and broad distribution of radical Islamic fundamentalists had grossly outstripped civilized nations' ability to comprehend and deal with them once they figured out the folks were not "I'm OK, you're OK" kinda guys. We had the only game in town, and that was the reality that folks back home couldn't seem to grasp.

It wasn't Afghanistan, it wasn't Iraq, and it wouldn't be Europe that we were abroad to build, protect, or help in general, although you wouldn't know that with the money the USAID people were spending! We were protecting the civil state government of the United States of America and our very way of life and freedom from becoming an Islamic Sharia Law led society! We were trying to accomplish this by joining our NATO allies to enable Afghans in establishing a way of life that rejects radicalism. This would allow them to be strong enough to protect their citizens against it; thereby allowing us to leave. We would then have confidence that they were protecting our own streets from afar. Politics would derail that effort in the years to come.

Recent Attacks

As expected, the spring brought renewed fighting throughout the country, as well as many NATO military and civil operations being put into play. There had been several attacks in Kabul and the Bagram Air Base areas. There was the attack that took the lives of our six NATO members along with twelve Afghan civilians with many more wounded. Another attack happened at Bagram Air Field, just northeast of Kabul. A group of around 30 insurgents stole US uniforms and attempted to infiltrate the perimeter. The security teams killed over half of them, while helicopter support took out their base of supporting mortar fire. None of the insurgents with bombs were able to detonate them and US casualties were either returned to duty or were in good condition. We did lose one civilian who drove a truck carrying the stolen uniforms.

On 26 May I experienced my first rocket attack in the compound. It was confusing more than scary. There was no explosion, no "Rocket Attack" on Big Voice, the compound's warning system and all clear notification. I often heard rockets or explosions twenty to thirty minutes before alarms, but none came. This one came in the middle of the night but went over us far enough that we didn't hear the impact. I didn't worry too much about rockets with the Hindu Kush Mountains so near. It was very difficult for the Taliban to get rocket trajectories high enough to launch and come down at steep enough angles to hit anything of value. It was the ground attacks that worried me. With 49 countries there, and all the different uniforms and body armor, you couldn't tell who an insurgent might be! Thankfully the Bulgarians and Belgians did a good job of internal and perimeter security. They stopped several ground assaults during my tour!

Memorial Day in the US and Peace Jirga in Afghanistan

As Memorial Day approached, I was close to finishing my first month in Afghanistan. I didn't know if I had another two or three months to go. I wasn't sure what would trigger my return to Tampa, but my guess was that I'd be there until at least mid-August. The senior IJC J6 (Systems) staff would rotate out in July. Our senior Task Force leaders, me included, would provide some continuity as the new IJC J6 staff was acclimated.

President Hamid Karzi announced the holding of a consultative grand council called the Afghanistan's National Consultative Peace Jirga (NCPJ), or for short, Peace Jirga, from 2-4 June. It would be held in a bad location, very vulnerable to attack. We knew the Taliban wanted to hit us and they would get the most press assistance if they could do it during the Jirga. They went on record to say they would kill any Tribal Leader who participates. So, we were taking no chances.

My roommate Uso was tasked along with a US Army Major from his team on the IJC staff to participate in the security process on the night shift. Imagine that. Uso would be hobnobbing with Karzi, Hillary Clinton and the whole gang! If only I could be there to watch Hillary's eyes go into mutually opposing spinning wheels when Uso tells her what needs to be done to end this war!

It would mean no highly charged, politically incorrect exchanges of 'intellectual giantry' in the room with me for awhile. I'd miss that, but Nelson Demille would entertain me with the "Gate House," a sequel to the "Gold Coast," which I had finished by then. That is, of course, if I'd won my game of solitaire in time to read, before Ralph the Rack Monster won our nightly battle. I'd been getting off duty late anyway, so there wasn't much time in the room either way.

The Taliban wasted no time. On the first day of the Jirga, I was actually worried about my buddy. Two rockets came in. Uso would say later that they heard them coming in, but they went just over head and exploded nearby with no casualties and little damage. Two insurgents were killed and only three friendly forces were wounded during the accompanying attack.

US Marine Major General Rengler and his aide were standing near a maintenance shed where side discussions were taking place. They had intelligence on a suicide bomber and were looking at maps where they may expect to find him. When the rockets came overhead they had a very low arch and were meant to hit the hotel. General Rengler said that just a small adjustment would have killed everyone.

The rocket attacks were complemented by small arms fire, rocket propelled grenade launchers, and IEDs of various sorts, but the Peace Jirga was not interrupted. I had to hand it to Karzi. He stood in the tent as the rockets hit not more than 200 yards away and kept everyone calm by all reports. He was clearly the target, and would remain so for the duration of the Jirga, but all would go more smoothly until it finished on 4 June.

It was notable that the Afghans did the heavy lifting, and our Turkish helicopters were kept quite busy protecting the Jirga, as well as their primary assignment of our IJC compound. Of course, the US and other countries not assigned specific security responsibilities, were in close over watch. We couldn't let our guard down. The Jirga definitely brought an additional layer of security concerns and I was very glad it was over.

The Taliban were also forcing local broadcasters to shut down for certain hours. If they didn't comply, they would blow up their towers. This worked against their cause, of course, but you can't tell that to a true, blue soldier of Allah who is itching for a chance to use an explosive device! In any case, we were looking at ways of moving the towers to places where we could protect them.

I had to travel to the US Forces-Afghanistan headquarters, also in Kabul, for some urgent business. Gunnery Sergeant Powell and Sergeant Williams would be taking extra precautions. It was a short trip, but we knew there were a lot of insurgents in the area who were most likely frustrated that they weren't more effective in disrupting the Jirga. There were several rocket attacks in the Kandahar area in which eight US Marines were wounded. Again, we took no chances. I had hoped the most intense concerns had passed, but the daily routine remained one of alertness and precaution. I knew there would be good protection, and besides, there was an American mess hall, I mean

DFAC, there, and their chow was revered throughout all American bases in Kabul! It would be worth the risk just to get away from our food!

Upon my return from the US Forces - Afghanistan Headquarters, I was walking near the air terminal on our compound and noticed a stretcher being unloaded. It was a wounded Afghani civilian who walked toward a command post's Entry Control Point (ECP) and wouldn't stop after repeated warnings. Everybody who's been trained in ECP procedures knows the drill. At a certain point, after repeated warnings, you shoot. He was lucky and they just shot him in the foot. He sure was howling a lot for just being shot in the foot! I know - it can hurt!

On 6 June my roommate Uso returned from the Jirga security mission, and was very subdued. He was tired, but had enough energy to howl about his wife sending gray and black underwear when he specifically asked for more colorful underwear. Then he was bitching that she sent an American battery charger for his camera that was useless in Afghanistan. But, having thought about it more, he said maybe it was good she sent the charger because it took up space that may otherwise have been used for another pair of gray underwear! "Ah hell" he said, "She is a good woman after all!" Definitely worth the price of admission! And then, like somebody pulled the plug, he was snoring in his chair.

If soldiers are like Marines, and we always say a bitching Marine is a happy Marine, then my roommate was the happiest Master Sergeant in the US Army! Hopefully we'd be able to relive some of this when we were both home again. He came in during Vietnam and had quite a balance of reserve and active service like mine. One of the last of a kind for sure!

Things weren't progressing satisfactorily on getting terminals in place and augmenting the bandwidth for our satellite program. On 13 June Lieutenant Colonel Arwood suggested, in the form of an order, that I personally visit every regional command to identify and crush any obstacles getting in the way of progress. At 58 years of age, I had very mixed emotions. By nature I was mission oriented, so this made perfect sense. I came in during the Vietnam era and served alongside of many Marines who had done combat tours there. It was common for servicemen to be killed in their first or last thirty days in country in the Vietnam days. I had survived an Iraq tour without a scratch, but the most danger came from travel, and this assignment would mean a lot of travel! In order to get to all the regional commands, it would take at least two or three weeks due to the lack of dependable air transportation.

I did almost everything via email, and would be off the net for all that travel time, so I had concerns about my CENTCOM liaison duties. This did not feel good, but I knew it had to be done and Lieutenant Colonel Arwood knew it would help - or he just wanted me out of his hair. Who knows for sure? So I walked over to the air terminal and signed up for my first flight to start my whirlwind tour of the beautiful land we call Afghanistan.

Back in Rocky Point, 2011

As the sun set lower, the air got cooler, and the run got harder, I suddenly realized I was in the latter part of the way back to my Hyatt room. If choosing to stay on, did I really want to go back to Afghanistan or was it time to get home, see more of Terri and our families and just stay put? It was difficult knowing that when I left active duty this time, my Marine Corps days would be over for good.

Chapter Twenty Two
To the Hills – Part 1: Jun-Aug 2010
Task Force 236, Afghanistan

Hurry Up and Wait!

It would be a week before getting arrangements for my first regional command visit. The first two sites were set for visits within a few days, but flights were cancelled and priorities changed. I had selected Bagram Air Field (BAF) first as it was closest and I thought it would have the most robust capabilities to latch onto. But Herat in the west and Mazar-e-Sharif (MeS) in the north were deemed more mission critical due to some gaps in their communications capabilities. Flights to those bases would be first.

On 13 June we had a rocket attack in the middle of the night. Three rockets were launched at our compound, but missed it entirely. Many of the guys in the tents heard the rockets go overhead and land, quite thankfully, a good distance away. Just an unneeded reminder that the bad guys were out there to do all they could to disrupt our operations and cause any casualties in the process. Again, the military and civilian personnel were very professional and well grounded and the daily routine went on without much notice.

The phone lines out of the country were still quite horrible. In order to call from my desk, I had to punch over 40 digits to get a single call to eventually connect me to the states. I estimated it took me over 600 digits to get a call through to Terri at 40 per call with about 15 failed attempts, and about 15 dropped calls. At least I could call. It wasn't that way in my early days!

Back Home

Hopefully my mother would be released from the hospital if there were no further complications from her gall bladder infection. I spoke with Dad on his birthday on 16 June and wished him a happy birthday and a happy Father's Day. Terri visited some of the Key Volunteers that she met in Chicago during my Iraq tour that still got together.

They were a great comfort to her during my Iraq tour and she found solace with them once again.

Kurt was busy videotaping dance recitals. His girl friend Jenny was busy with her job, but they had ideas for making my courtyard look good. Kristin and Mark were busy with work and raising three year old Dylan, and one year old Gavin. I enjoyed their pictures immensely and Dylan actually wrote his name on the computer for me last week! It will be so good to be with them all again!! I took advantage of being on the compound and bought the boys each an International Security Assistance Force (ISAF) teddy bear from the Dutch PX on the compound and got them in the mail.

Masar-E-Shariff (MeS), RC-North
On 17 June I finally got a lift on a Dutch C-130 to conduct my MeS visit in RC-North which was under German command and control. Terri and I would both be traveling on the weekend as she had a professional association conference to attend back home. I'm pretty sure her airplane didn't do the cork screw landing mine did! Security was always a concern for incoming aircraft in combat zones, and the C-130 is known for its agility. Someone mentioned it was a C-160 version of the C-130. No matter to me - it turned good! The Dutchman flying this one put it all to work!

The mountains were very majestic, but it was much hotter than our Kabul compound. The land was actually owned by the Germans, and they ran the base called Camp Marmel. The staff at MeS was extremely busy making preparations to house the impending massive growth for both German and American forces coming in as part of the Surge. I met the field rep from the intelligence agency and the US Forces-Afghanistan North J6 (Systems) officer. We worked together to find ways of expediting construction of a needed dish platform and to get the USC-60 communications equipment implemented to support voice and data communications for the incoming forces.

I returned to Kabul the next day. I would have to quickly organize many projects, and then head west to Herat to deal with another set of issues related to construction delays hindering our ability to get connectivity for critical Intel and command and control systems support. Getting air transportation to Herat was taking more time to arrange so I found time to keep all my wobbling poles standing and plates spinning before I left. Anybody who has tried to maintain forward momentum in a multi-national environment would know my pain!

At least I knew I was thought of on Father's Day and it was a great feeling! Terri sent a great card, Kurt sent pictures of what he and Jenny did to clean up and plant fresh flowers in my courtyard at the Sauk house, Kristin and her family sent another nice care package with artwork from the Grandsons. Every day would be like Father's Day when back in the good 'ol USA!

Herat, RC-West

On 21 June I traveled to Camp Arena near Herat in RC-West on a Canadian C-130 with one of the civilian 20 pound brains of Task Force 236. They were in desperate need of power and serious upgrades to their fusion center communications facilities. It was clearly a priority of the ISAF J2 Intel Team to get them working better. RC-West command and control was shared by Italians and Spanish units and they both had PXs.

There was a new building next to the existing communications structure and the Italians said they could have power in two weeks, but they had said that many times before. Like most Europeans, it was about the process, not the results. As long as things followed the prescribed procedures, it didn't matter how long it took. That didn't set well with this US Marine so I knew I didn't have to ask Lieutenant Colonel Arwood if we should wait for them.

It would take some out of the box thinking, which is what every member of Task Force 236 was known for, or they wouldn't be on the team. I met with Captain Gramling from the US Air Force Engineering and Installation (E&I) team assigned to the US Forces-Afghanistan. This guy knew what he was doing! Resourceful and mission oriented! Damn! Another Air Force guy that would have made a great Marine! We agreed to lie, cheat and steal to get the crap working, and get what we needed with whatever scrounging it took. Anything we got from storage areas would take six months or more for the sleepy bureaucrats to even know if anything was missing!

First things first, we rigged some temporary power and communications connectivity. We would enjoy a very effective working relationship over the next months to vastly improve the communications of a very important facility in a very important part of CENTCOM's area of responsibility. Captain Gramling made sure they got their work done and moved his team onto many other feats of heroism I'm sure.

They even had a PX tent in this remote area! I couldn't resist buying a couple more teddy bears for the boys. They had to be the only kids on the block back home with teddy's that said Herat on them! The bears actually served as my pillow for two nights in Herat. I just folded my spare uniform trousers neatly over them, clipped my reading light to the top bunk braces, and voilà!! Happy Marine! Dylan and Gavin would be honored to know their teddy bears were Gampa's pillows in Afghanistan! Of course, Terri got a set too.

The camp was divided between the Italian and Spanish side, and our hot, dingy tents were on the Spanish side. I was touched by a couple of memorial monuments nearby. There was a Madonna statue with a blue background which was lit at night. All the night lights there were shielded blue lights to minimize light signatures, and to not make it easy to identify for night attacks, and there weren't many of them. They also had a memorial listing every Spanish person that had died in service to their country in Afghanistan for the Global War on Terror. There was one helicopter crash that took many lives at once.

After a couple of days, we finally found a flight to Kabul via Lashkaghar and Kandahar. It was another Canadian C-130, probably the same one. The Canadian crew chief was a female senior non commissioned officer and quickly demonstrated she knew her duties and did them well. Because the small airfield at Lashkaghar didn't have exterior security, the Canadians had to load their machine guns and provide their own security when the ramp was lowered. That was quite a sight from inside the cargo bay as they opened the ramp with the silhouettes of two heavily armed crew members readied to run off the ramp and assume good security positions outside the aircraft while the engines remained running. The pallet they were to accept wasn't ready, so they got right back on and we quickly took off again. Definitely a reminder of my many infantry years!

In Kandahar, I settled back in and continued to read my book. Thank goodness for Nelson Demille on that trip! We had to wait outside the terminal under a camo net and it was hot. The Air Force staff inside didn't like us opening the door, so I found lots of reasons to go in and out. As was customary in Kandahar in those days, a rocket attack came in. I heard the sirens and the rocket and quickly determined it wouldn't land near us, so I sat right there, irritating the indoor desk clerks even more. This was fun! We finally got moved to a larger, cooled area inside the terminal and eventually got on a flight to Kabul. We arrived "home" around 9 PM.

Back at Home in the IJC

I now had two regional command visits behind me and had four more to go. Too bad my AAA card didn't work here! I was catching up on three days of email traffic and debriefing my superiors after my brief Indian Country travels. Terri was home from her travels as well, so I was relieved. I always thought it strange that family and friends worry about us in combat zones when they faced so much danger back home! I was very well protected here, but they were driving around on icy Wisconsin roads in the winter, had to dodge texting millennials on the hot summer highways, and who knows what could happen on civilian flights anymore!

    After sorting out how we were doing with things that had to be done for my folks, things in Washington, DC, Tampa, the ISAF Headquarters, and at the IJC Headquarters, I would go to RC-South in Kandahar for a day or two, and then maybe RC-Capitol/East in Bagram. Then I could focus on my fellow Marines at Camp Leatherneck down south. As was typical of Marines, there were no issues there. They had been working with me in advance, so there was no pressure at Leatherneck. My trip should involve putting my feet up on a stack of MRE cartons and vying for first place in a good Marine Corps sea story tellin' competition! All these other places were killing me with all kinds of problems! Why can't we all be Marines!

Trouble at the Top

In the middle of it all, General McChrystal resigned after being recalled to Washington, DC to respond to a Rolling Stones article where he spoke in an uncomplimentary manner about the President. General Petraeus would leave his post as the US Central Command (CENTCOM) Commander in Tampa and replace him at the ISAF headquarters in Kabul. I had many personal thoughts on the matter. Suffice it to say that I often judge the worth of a person by whether or not I feel I can trust them to keep watch when in a fighting hole in a high threat environment. I'd go to sleep without hesitation knowing General McChrystal would have my six. I wouldn't feel that way about any of those who fired him nor the reporter whose short lived day of fame brought a brilliant career to an end. My disgust and distaste for journalists stems back to the Vietnam days, and had now exceeded a level that I didn't think possible in the human psyche.

I've always said that the only reward for good work is more of it. Lieutenant Colonel Arwood's phone and emails were getting hot with people at CENTCOM and ISAF getting very nervous about how to get all of General Petraeus' systems over here without disruption. Gunnery Sergeant Powell and Master Sergeant Schaffner were our two top Task Force 236 non commissioned officers and they had been tapped to take charge of the transition and coordinate between Tampa and Kabul. They both worked on the Commander's Communication Team for the last three CENTCOM commanders. Gunnery Sergeant Powell led the transition between Iraq and Tampa when General Petraeus assumed command of CENTCOM. General Petraeus knew both the Gunny and the Top personally, so they were given the job of making it happen again. Gunnery Sergeant Powell was scheduled to leave within a week, after being here since December, and Master Sergeant Schaffner would take over.

Kandahar Air Field (KAF), RC-South
I worked hard getting all my ducks in a row so I could get back out on the hot, dusty trail. It was Saturday but that didn't matter much here. Somehow we still know that means it's the weekend back home. As soon as possible, my "20lb brain" civilian engineer and I would go back to Kandahar to meet with our teams working on our coalition network system. We came through there on our way back from Herat, and were waiting for our flight to Kabul. This time I was hoping to get a brief tour of the site, meet our folks, and get back as soon as possible to keep things rolling on all fronts.

On 27 June we caught a flight to Kandahar Air Field to meet the team working on our satellite terminal and coalition network. As was common at all the sites, there were power and cabling issues. What blew my mind was that their Flight Safety Officer declared our plans for our satellite dead because our planned signal trajectory crossed the airfield's runway. That would be a show stopper for sure! The safety concern was that our signal could set off the electronic counter measures (ECM) on incoming or outgoing aircraft.

I had sudden visions of a C-130 or C-17 coming in and firing off the ECM flares, intended to distract heat seeking ground or air missiles, just as it bursts into flames. It's a beautiful sight to see if you're watching the "Angel Flight" videos, but not when you want to see a safe landing! Our dish had to go up and the planes had to land safely. We had to resolve this one for sure! Just one more of many obstacles to crush...

We checked into the transient tents of KAF. It was huge with rows, almost acres, of bunk beds and was very depressing. The head facilities were separate. The walk in between was filled with the foulness of human waste and other decaying debris that was pumped into the adjacent sewage and garbage fields. Is this how they treat their guests? Anyone traveling through Kandahar would attest to the fact that it would be this way for many years!

It was just the transient area of KAF that was bad. They had an area called "Board Walk" where there were lots of shops built around a big square with actual raised sidewalks built of wood. It really was a pleasant place to relax and enjoy more shopping than anywhere else in country that I'd seen. Kandahar Air Field was huge, so they had a lot more shops than the four at Kabul Area International Airport (KAIA). They also played hockey in the middle of the square board walk, which was very popular to watch. The various countries had teams, and they were quite serious about it. I was not able to see what they used for a puck, but it rolled. Hockey on sand. Interesting!

Thankfully we only had to stay one night. The good news was that we got a flight back to Kabul the next day. The bad news was it would be via Herat to the west and MeS way up north. Talk about the long way home! It would be another MeS landing with another Dutchman pilot. Sure enough! The entire flight was filled with abrupt ascents, descents, and banks. We all learned to grab the straps around us at the same time. Was this a training flight or were they shooting at us? Anybody that has flown "nap of the earth" would surely understand.

No Place Like Home

Humble though it may be, I once again confirmed there is no place like "home." We were back on 28 June. After visiting only three regional commands, we had crisscrossed Afghanistan twice! We had been to Herat, MeS and Kandahar twice, each stop being just to get back to Kabul. We needed a new flight coordinator! Did I mention the Air Force hadn't figured out, after being there for 10 years, that people needed to move around Afghanistan?

Lieutenant Colonel Arwood and Gunnery Sergeant Powell were consumed by making preparations for General Petraeus and his team's arrival as it was top priority. Everybody in our Task Force would end up working in the ISAF headquarters in the next couple of days if necessary. There was a huge difference in the way the two generals communicated and operated, and our guys were the only ones on the ground that already knew what had to be done.

I'd covered all regional commands except the new one, RC-South West, commanded by Camp Leatherneck and my fellow US Marines. They had their ducks in a row, so I saved them for last. Lieutenant Colonel Arwood asked, "Why aren't you so worried about them as you are the others?" To which I replied, "They're US Marines Sir! They've already sent me plans for what they want to do and they've made arrangements to get it done. Plus, I've already worked with the same guys on a separate, but related effort to move large reconnaissance images from F-18's across a line-of-sight shot that we put in." He said, "Get your ass out there." I said, "Yes Sir!" Just like the rabbit begging the fox to not throw him in the briar patch!

"Pred Porn" Can Be Fun

Most anybody that spent grueling hours in operation centers watching drone feeds for any signs of useful intelligence knows about "Pred Porn." At all times they would have to maintain keen awareness and readiness to react to any situation requiring it. One of the most common feeds coming into operation centers is live camera feeds from Predator drones that you hear about in the news.

One day our IJC teams got to enjoy a good one. Two insurgents were digging holes to bury an improvised explosive device (IED). The normal notifications were made to units nearby to take appropriate action. It wouldn't be needed. An argument started between the young aspiring martyrs which escalated to the point of raising their weapons. It was a draw. They both shot at the same time and killed each other. I love self correcting problems!

War and Work at IJC

June was nearly done. We were on high alert again. Thanks to the good work of our Bulgarian's and Belgian's perimeter security skills and good intelligence, we were aware of a group of 19 suicide bombers planning a ground assault on our compound. Between them and our Turkish attack helicopters, we were able to stay one step ahead of them.

At one point things got pretty hairy. I was in my room ready to leave when the alarm sounded and it was not a drill. There were several of us in the barracks, but I was the only American. We were all armed. I gathered everyone and put together a hasty barracks defense plan. Everyone spoke English and was glad for me to make recommendations. Even they knew every US Marine is an infantryman. What they didn't know was that I had already done it for nine years! Within an hour the situation was resolved permanently, again by our good perimeter defense. Great way to meet the neighbors, huh?!

If I stayed the full 120 days shown on my orders, I was now past the half way point. If ordered back to Tampa sooner, I was even more past half way! It felt good to have some time and experience under my belt. There was a lot of work ahead, so I didn't think much about leaving. My satellite project called for a terminal in Kabul, and the agencies I worked with wanted to get started on it. Not much of an excuse was needed to delay another couple of days before going back "on the road."

It was sounding like General Petraeus was sailing through the senate confirmations and would be bringing quite a few of his trusted Tampa people. My contacts back there said that he just walked around, tapping the ones he wanted on the shoulder, and gave them just a few days notice to get here for a year! How would you like to be those families! At least I was already "deployed" away from my home when in Tampa. Many of them were there already so it wouldn't be long before the general's arrival.

A Family Fourth of July

I was thinking of my family and friends back home and what they'd be doing over the fourth. I envied Terri, Kurt and Jenny, Kristin, Mark and their little boys Dylan and Gavin. They were all going to Witwen for the parade. Witwen is a very small town west of Sauk City that draws thousands of people every year for their 4th of July parade.

After the town celebration, they would all go back to the place Terri liked to refer to as "Big, Bad Work!" I hoped to get more colorful pictures of the Grand Runts and their adventures. That was always a treat! In Kabul we were just hoping for no fireworks at all.

Support for the Generals

General Petraeus arrived just before the fourth of July and wasted no time taking over. He sent a letter to all of us in theater. It was clear he intended to keep our emphasis on minimizing civilian deaths and injuries while separating radicals from the general population, but would allow our own people to protect their lives. No permission would be necessary to return hostile fire! He came over to the IJC from his ISAF headquarters for a conference on the latest IED techniques. The insurgents adapted quickly to our defensive techniques and had an endless source of creative, new approaches to defeating our defenses. We gathered large groups of leaders from the forward operating bases all around for updates. It was a good chance for the general to get in front of them.

As of 6 July, Gunnery Sergeant Powell was officially named the head of General Petraeus' communications team until the new CENTCOM Commander was named and a new communications team could be assembled for him back in Tampa. He had hoped to leave 24 June, and we didn't know how long the transition would take. That's the life of a loyal Task Force 236 leader! Master Sergeant Schaffner took over his duties leading the Task Force 236 team. I remained focused on my satellite program implementation and a few other projects.

Once General Petraeus' communications team arrived, they still wanted Gunnery Sergeant Powell and Master Sergeant Schaffner to stay in charge because both of them had previous experience. The Gunny brought the team over to our shelter in the IJC compound to work on his fly-away kit. It wasn't working yet and it needed to get working fast! We had the needed brain-power on our team and a good test area. The unexpected ISAF change of command really made a dent in our Task Force 236 operations, and much of our priority and energies had to go that direction.

General Petraeus kept his work schedule up-to-date on long flights, which were frequent at CENTCOM, and would continue here. He'd have to go back and forth from Brussels a lot to stay in touch with NATO and there were always those cross Atlantic flights back to Washington, DC and the nation's flag pole. We felt bad for him. Even though it was what it was in Afghanistan, most everyone agreed the further away from the flag pole you were, the better!

Camp Leatherneck, RC-Southwest
It felt like I'd been in Afghanistan for much longer than just two and half months. Sometimes it felt like I never left Iraq, although the camps were very different in some ways, and very much the same in other ways. The heat, the sand, the dirt, the wind, the Hesco barriers, T-Walls, Jersey Barriers, shelters, and daily battle rhythm were very similar. I did miss the palm trees planted by the British in the 30's for their air base at Camp Habbaniyah in Iraq, even if they were always filthy dirty and sandy. But, here I had the mountains and their unique personalities each and every day. I'd never seen the mountains with the skies over them in the same mood, and didn't think anyone ever would. Mountains are like that, yes they are!

On 11 July I finally caught a flight to Camp Leatherneck. It was a flight returning a group of Afghani National Army recruits back to training from home leave. They would conduct these flights every two weeks to get recruits to their homes as much as possible. Imagine fighting in your own country and going home where there is also fighting. It was a night flight. The line to C-130 was reminiscent of my many infantry operations. Night time just seemed to lend an eerie feeling to it all. The fact that it was a line mixed with Afghanis in traditional garb and uniforms made it even more eerie. We filed up the ramp and into the rows of metal and nylon seats. We were all seated and buckled in when we learned there would be a minor delay due to cross winds.

Just then one of the young Afghani recruits in traditional garb was being very loud and struggling with his buckle. Any former Marines and soldiers know that C-130 buckles and CH-47 helicopter buckles are very clumsy to attach, especially when you're fully combat loaded or just scared. Or was he ready to attack? Was it time to draw my pistol?

I could see he was very bright and somewhat playful, but in his eyes was a lifetime of war. It was all he'd known at his age. Before the morning's dawn, he would be back in his uniform and training. Not long after that he would be in the mountains and fields of sand fighting what could easily be a friend or relative who chose the radical route of the Taliban or Al Qaeda, or any one of hundreds of other groups hardened in the radical, fundamentalism of the strictest interpretation of the Islamic religion. It all comes down to a lifetime of war, poverty, and 50 year old eyes in a 20 year old's face. I helped him with his buckle and hoped he would live to his next leave. I would never know for sure.

The Marine Staff Sergeant in charge of transporting the recruits didn't trust the young Afghani either so he moved us to the seats farthest to the rear of the aircraft, along with him. The good Staff Sergeant had done many of these flights and said Afghanis had a terrible time with air sickness. They never fly after all! The C-130s were very maneuverable with steep climbs, banks, and descents. He was right. The landing was too much for many of the young Afghani recruits. I'm glad we weren't sitting at the end of the row. There were plenty of garbage bags at the ready!

We arrived safely at Camp Bastion in Helmand Province at 0030. We were picked up by US Navy Chief Pintello, another CENTCOM Task Force 236 member. He gave us a field expedient debrief on the way to the adjoining Camp Leatherneck and dropped us off at the transient tent. It had all the qualities of a transient tent, only Marine Corps style. That meant no floor, no bunks, and no electricity. Ah yes. Home for the old grunt! It was just good to have canvas over my head!

There were a lot of Marines at Camp Leatherneck that I served with in Iraq in 2008 as well. They were part of the regimental headquarters in Fallujah back then, and had less than a year off before coming to Afghanistan for another 14 month tour. Higher headquarter tours were longer than infantry battalion combat tours, which were seven month tours, so as to maintain continuity. They would get a two-week rest and relaxation (R&R) break and could fly anywhere they wanted. That was reminiscent of the Vietnam days to me, and I was happy with my shorter tour! If only it would stay short...

Camp Leatherneck was very flat and characterized by many rows of tents and T-Walls (high Texas cement barriers). There were mountains in the distance, but it didn't have the elevation of Kabul so it was much hotter. It was the headquarters for the new Regional Command-South West. The RC-South in Kandahar was so big, and had the biggest concentration of insurgents, so a new one was created to allow better operational planning and control. It was commanded by US Marine General Mills, who was also the commander when I was in Iraq, and included British troops.

As promised, and just to prove to Lieutenant Colonel Arwood that the Marines were squared away, I made my trip very short, although the chow was great and I loved being around my brethren. I worked with the senior staff non commissioned officers to work out plans to fix a few power issues, shot the shit with my buddies, and bought a couple more teddy bears in the PX for the Grand Runts, and Terri of course. After some "rest" in the transient tent, we departed Bastion field at 0100. We would be in full armor and double time across a large, very dark open area of dirt and grass to our C-130 ready with engine running. Oh yeah! Memories again!

Back at the IJC
We got back to the now familiar tarmac of the KAIA early on 13 July. I kept my body armor and helmet on and carried my bag from the PAX terminal to my quarters, which was about the equivalent of three or four blocks, so there was no need to awaken the Top (Master Sergeant Schaffner) to pick me up in his cart. He'd been pushing hard, and there was no reason to roust him. I was dirty, sweaty, sandy, and tired for sure. I kept the door open just enough to have a little light in the room so as to not awaken the roomates either. I quickly unpacked what was needed for a shower and got in my nice bunk. I was keyed up enough to get out my book light and read a little. I allowed myself some extra sleep, but was back to our Task Force 236 shelter by late

morning checking on the three electronic junk yards (email systems) in the computer networks. Isn't one electronic junk yard enough!

The Search for Power

Thus far, power shortages were the common theme everywhere I had been. Today's headquarters were full of computers, network equipment, communications gear, and even satellite antennas. In Iraq, even our infantry platoon headquarters had at least five computers! Our regional commands at Herat in the west, Mazar-e-Sharif in the north, and Leatherneck in the southwest were all in desperate need of generators. There were no power grids, so all power would need to come from generators. The needs would be immediate as the sudden surge of people and equipment flowed in after six months of thoughtfulness at the White House chewed up logistics planning time. This is where lost time would be amplified.

The acquisition process was flawed and took far too long. We knew there were generators in lots around the country somewhere! We were contacting every major command but nobody wanted to give up such a precious commodity. I envisioned keeping every junkyard dog at every storage lot in Afghanistan barking at night trying to keep us out! Our logistics guy, Major Brian Jeter, had some amazing tricks up his sleeve and got a couple small generators to Leatherneck right away. The other needs were larger scale and would require more time.

The Dog Days of Task Force 236

By now, July was half over and I was within a month and a half or less of heading back to Tampa. My duties got more intense as time went on. Lieutenant Colonel Arwood was at The Hague for a NATO conference, and Gunnery Sergeant Powell was finally on his way back home. He would have to set up General Petraeus' office and his residence in Washington, DC, but at least he'd be in the States and be able to mix in some family time. Funny thing though, he didn't bother checking out all the way. He knew he'd be back, and it was so much easier getting a room if you never gave it up. What the barracks manager didn't know wouldn't hurt him!

Thoughts of Home

Things were picking up on my satellite project but some days it
seemed that everything I touched went bad. If there was anything to
learn about those days, it was to let them pass and don't fight it. I did
the only reasonable thing on a day like that and went to the Haji shops
on the compound, which were tattered tents with all sorts of local and
imported souvenirs, rugs, and clothing and got my Grand Runts a
couple of handmade Afghani toy trucks. Dylan's fourth birthday was
coming up but he got to open the last package from Grandpa while
little Gavin had a melt down because he wanted to help. They would
both be getting their own boxes mailed this time. The trucks are very
different and no doubt the boys would be the only ones on their block
to have one!

I got another handwritten letter from Dad. His leather-hard hands
that had been smashed by sledge hammers, burned by welders and
torches, skinned by slipping wrenches and frozen by Korean waters
were far too rough for even attempting to use a computer. It always
amazed me how much my own handwriting was so similar to his! I
realized it in my boot camp days when all we had were handwritten
letters. He also wrote much differently than he talked. His letters were
much more intimate and open. I was so proud to read every one of
them and would keep them forever!

Back to Rocky Point

As the Rocky Point run continued, I was consumed by the realities of
traveling in the suffocating Afghanistan heat and long delays at
Military Air (MILAIR) terminals. By this time in my mental journey,
the flashbacks were only one year old. If I stayed, did I really want
more of that? I was so glad to leave and I certainly did my share! My
memories persisted...

Chapter Twenty Three
To the Hills – Part 2: Jun-Aug 2010
Task Force 236, Afghanistan

Another International Conference

Another International Conference would be held in Kabul sponsored by the United Nations and the Afghan government. There would be representatives from 70 nations, and Hillary Clinton was expected to accompany the US delegation in her role as Secretary of State. Translation: Security would be very tight on the compound since we were virtually on the north side of the airport. We already had several rocket/ground attack drills, and it was expected that the local Taliban, Al-Qaeda, and various and sundry other radical fundamentalists, would definitely try to target some highly visible international figures to show they could operate effectively, even in the presence of all the powerless NATO forces.

With the discovery of a huge natural resource of minerals, there was also renewed interest in Afghanistan's economics. I thought it might be like oil was to Saudi, and with any luck, it would interest Afghani civilians, who were in a position to become more involved in the world economy and benefit from a civil form of government. Hopefully it would be harder to convince them to take the path of radical, fundamentalist Islam. It was much too early to know but it was an interesting and potentially positive twist to things in the Middle East.

Attempts to disrupt the meeting were expected. We heard a loud explosion one early afternoon but I never found out what it was. We didn't see any smoke anywhere near us or the airport. Lieutenant Colonel Arwood was due back from his conference at The Hague but he'd have to wait because the airport was closed to commercial traffic. One night, Master Sergeant Schaffner came through the Task Force 236 van's door and said that Hillary Clinton was at the PAX terminal in our North Kabul Area International Airport (KAIA) compound. It was a very small terminal, and he only saw her for a brief moment, but was able to bring back important information every Marine wanted to know. She had big ankles.

All the PXs and Haji shops were closed during the conference. All the shop workers were local Afghans or Third Country Nationals, affectionately known as TCNs. It wouldn't be smart to have them in the compound during such a sensitive time.

More Rockets

Several hours after Hillary's departure from North KAIA to the Embassy downtown, rockets started coming in. It made for a long night. A total of five rockets would come, spaced out just enough to get everyone tired of getting out of the tents into their assigned bomb bunkers. They just stayed in the shelters after the second or third one. Those of us in hard barracks were required to stay in our rooms. We would call Master Sergeant Schaffner on our ROSHAN cell phones for accountability to make sure everyone was okay and then just ride it out. Don't think you can sleep through a rocket attack? Wrong!

Transition Planning Continues

The satellite program manager I was working with in country had expressed some concerns about my departure and we were working on getting my replacement named to quell their concerns. They had been very good about showing appreciation for the progress the program had made since my involvement the previous November, which was a good feeling. I was planning on starting the checkout process on 25 August. That would take a couple days, then a couple more to get a flight back to Al Udeid Air Base (AUAB) in Qatar, then a couple days to turn in my weapons and armor, and then I would take a commercial flight to Tampa.

I planned to be in Tampa by 3 September, then leave there by the 20th for Quantico to process back to retired status, then drive home by 1 October, or so. I didn't know who back in Tampa they would replace me with but knew it wouldn't be pretty for whoever got tapped. It was a very complex project that I'd been carrying, along with many other projects that have come to the Task Force due to their high visibility, urgency, and lack of progress via the normal channels. That's what Task Force 236 was all about and no job was too small or unimportant to get done!

We truly had our hands full to ship, install, implement, operate and maintain the necessary systems and equipment to support the war fighters who require very sophisticated support systems to effectively and safely operate in the urban and mountainous terrain in Afghanistan. Many people think our satellites can do anything we want, where we want it, and how we want, and at any time. It's not true unless you're watching a movie or reading a spy novel. We had several very practical problems we had to deal with in order to provide effective Command, Control, Communications, Computers, Intelligence, Surveillance, Reconnaissance (C4ISR) support that is the lifeline of war fighters.

Lieutenant Colonel Arwood was back again and quickly getting up to speed. We all missed Gunnery Sergeant Powell but he was back in the states and we were happy for him. He had General Petraeus' Washington, DC home and office properly set-up to maintain communications as he traveled. Master Sergeant Schaffner had everything well under control on this end.

Task Force 236 had many changes coming up. It was only supposed to be in existence until October as the funding for all the civilian contractors ended on the fiscal year boundary (30 September). Based on the successes and by popular demand of the senior International Joint Command (IJC) systems officer and his staff, Task Force 236 was funded for another year. Our original mission was to establish a single network that every nation would use for email, phones, VTC's, etc. That mission was well underway and would be done by October.

The surge had completely over-run every major command's ability to respond quickly and effectively to rapidly changing conditions as units flowed in around the country and required space, billeting, and working communications systems. The Task Force 236 mission would change to more of what would become the IJC's 911 number to call when help was needed. Task Force 236 had also been commissioned to continue to implement the SECDEF's priority satellite program which I had been supporting.

Included in succession planning was Lieutenant Colonel Arwood's replacement, as well as my own. His replacement had been named and would arrive in Qatar by 6 August and then catch the first available flight(s) to Kabul. He was Army Colonel Duane Carney, who I knew from the US Central Command (CENTCOM). My replacement hadn't been named yet. I was getting calls from Washington, DC and the International Security Assistance Force (ISAF) headquarters about who the CENTCOM rep is who would keep the program going. Since Task Force 236 had been extended, I felt confident telling them that a new CENTCOM rep would be named and sent to join the Task Force 236 team soon.

Much of what I had started would be coming together by the end of September, so my replacement would be well positioned for success. The "new" satellite would provide information to the intelligence agencies and command and control elements that would operate well into the future, long after the bulk of conventional forces left. Thirty days was a long time in that environment, so I still had plenty of challenges in front of me. Every day brought new challenges and threats to the terminal installations going on around the country. I'd be working to the last minute, no doubt about it.

The satellite program team was also rotating their senior field officer in charge, and they came to meet me. We'd have most of August to bring him up to speed. Before they left, the guy I'd been working with for several months in Tampa presented me with the agency's challenge coin. That was truly an honor for me! He even made me do the handshake with the coin in my hand and made a big deal out of it. Because the coin tradition came about late in my career, and especially as a reservist, I didn't have many coins.

I informed the new senior field rep that the satellite program required a tremendous amount of energy to track, identify stalls, obstacles, and set-backs. They were constant, but somehow we'd been able to keep things moving. The timeline was critical, and many of the people that we needed support from weren't aware of the full background of what we were doing. They automatically tried to do what they could acting as if it was a recreational sport they could do when they had time. I spent most of my time explaining the background and showing them my credentials to snap them out of their delusions.

I had also developed a short burst of one-liners that brought the message home very quickly. In that regard, I felt like the main characters in W.E.B. Griffin's books where the OSS (Office of Strategic Service), which was the predecessor of the CIA, had officers running around Europe and the Pacific in WWII who would whip out their super-duper identification cards whenever they needed priority to get on a plane or get any kind of logistical support to run their operations. The new guy left well armed to move things forward and he did so with a flare!

Back Home

As July was ending, the days kept clicking by. My thoughts were geared toward returning home. I had received some great pictures of my Grandson Dylan's fourth birthday party! I will always remember how much I loved getting all those pictures to bring color into my life, which was otherwise a constant blur of sand, dirt, sun, wind, and bland colored buildings and vehicles to match.

My Dad always said that he never liked to see summers pass quickly but this year was an exception. He never wanted one to pass faster so he could see me get back to the soil of the good ol' USA. I felt the same way. I hated to lose a summer out of my life but wanted it to go quickly too, in order to get back home. This summer wouldn't be lost though. Even though it's Afghanistan, and all that goes with it, I can honestly say I enjoyed being a part of something good and something special. The challenges were constant and the pressure was unrelenting. Every day brought new obstacles, but just when I would begin to feel defeated, something I'd been working on would come together. This gave me the strength and confidence to crush them and move to the next step. It was an amazing love/hate story I guess.

Change of Plans

On 30 July, I was totally surprised to hear Headquarters Marine Corps (HQMC) sent extension orders for another year of retired recall duty and that my Afghanistan duty would be extended to at least the December or January timeframe! I had been asked previously if I'd stay on a while if they could get approval, and I said sure, never thinking they would never get the Marine Corps to keep an old Warrant Officer 4 for a fourth year of retired recall duty. It was rare to say the least!

How would I break the news to Terri, my family at home, and Tony at work? Again! What was I doing? Terri saw it coming and took it like she had done so many times already, with total love and support. Tony and the WPS crew dug in for another year of doing what I wouldn't be doing in my civilian job.

The days were grueling! Somewhere between the boredom and mind-numbing grind of 16 hour days was the constant pressure of doing the impossible with nothing. No days off. Bad chow. Danger. I missed Terri and our family. My Dad would really worry now! Would this be the end of my WPS job? Knowing I had the rest of my life not to be a Marine and not be a part of Task Force 236, which I took great pride in, I really did want to do this if I could. I just didn't think I actually could. The end of my tug of war between love of home and family and sense of duty would wait for another year as the War in Afghanistan raged on!

Now I knew why Lieutenant Colonel Arwood's replacement was named and mine wasn't. Those sly dogs back in Tampa! Army Master Sergeant McDuffie came to mind immediately! It would take a senior staff non commissioned officer to pull something like this off. I owed him a beer! I think…

Lieutenant Colonel Arwood was a rare officer of the same ilk. Whatever lies I told, he swore to them, so I never had to worry about that top cover not being there when someone complained to him. I knew the incoming commander, US Army Colonel Carney, and while he didn't have the aggressive personality of Lieutenant Colonel Arwood to back it up, he was mission oriented and I hoped to have his backing as well. It worked out well and we enjoyed many bad KBR meals together upon his arrival. He would go on to become the Task Force 236 Commander back in Tampa and this would be his christening.

I wasn't the only one extended. Every military member had been extended to the December/January timeframe. That meant Master Sergeant Schaffner would remain, as well as Staff Sergeant Sherwood and Sergeant Williams, among many others that would get us around and keep us safe.

Change of Command for Task Force 236
Colonel Carney arrived and we expected a very short turnover. Lieutenant Colonel Arwood and Master Sergeant Schaffner had him briefed and ready to hit the ground running in no time. After briefs

from each section, he was ready take his first full 30-inch step and began his Task Force 236 Afghanistan tour.

He soon gave his first newcomer's brief which was impressive. We had established a top notch reputation with whomever we worked with over here, and the only way to maintain that was to remember your sole goal of making the regional commands successful in their assigned missions. Before he was done, he had everyone's attention and they all knew they were a part of something very special (we take pride in what we do, and we take care of our own). By the next day the newcomers would be on C-130s to their new deployment sites throughout Afghanistan for the next six months.

August in the IJC

Tammy Baldwin, one of our Wisconsin Congressional Representatives, was visiting Afghanistan and would be dining in our new chow hall, I mean DFAC, on the first night it opened. It was a brick structure and nicer than what we'd been used to. I knew six delegates from Wisconsin and Indiana would be there at 1800 that night, so I thought I'd check on her since it is my normal meal time. Glancing over at her table, I realized she had no service members with her! I couldn't let my own Wisconsin Congressional Representative not have guests! It was a very nice visit. We stayed away from politics and got along just fine.

The delegation took a video of Tammy and me and I asked if they would send it to Terri via email. Terri would never see that but was impressed to at least get a picture. Anybody who can catch me with my eyes open should be issued an "expert photographer" qualification badge! I've got the only set of human eyes I know of that are faster than any single reflex lens or digital shutter!! It was a pleasant break from the grueling routine! Terri never received the video, but Tammy sent it six years later after it was mentioned when she and Terri sat next to each other on a flight from Washington, DC to Madison. That was above and beyond!

Doing the Impossible with Nothing

I was feeling the pressure once again. My orders originally ending in early August were extended until December or January. The Marine Corps would never have approved the extension of a retired recall

Marine a fourth year if CENTCOM didn't make the case, so I knew they had help from the interested agencies in Washington, DC. Whether it was the intelligence agencies or war fighting commanders that needed bandwidth, they needed it and they needed it bad, and we were making progress. They didn't want it stopped. I had to get back home for a short break to take care of some administrative and personal things to support my additional time in Afghanistan. Hopefully I would do that in September and get back to doing all I could by the December timeframe.

I had designs submitted to the French staff at IJC who could get the local Afghans to build a platform we needed to support a terminal going in to our own compound. It would go right above what would become our "Man Cave" when three of us were moved into it to make room for the incoming civilians to the Task Force 236 van. I thought that was poetic! Here I was trying to get terminals built in 13 forward operating bases around Afghanistan, and the one for the Capital regional command would go on my own roof! Life had its idiosyncrasies!

Thanks again to US Army Major Brian Jeter, we had two 250kw generators on the way to Herat to support their special work. We also had teams in five forward operating bases working on terminals that could connect with the satellite we wanted to take advantage of. My travels had been productive in that I was able to establish points of contact that I could stay in touch with and help them deal with the inevitable daily obstacles that would pop up. It was truly a daily battle to compete with the engineering and logistic support required to support over 30,000 troops and equipment pouring into country. We made progress, but I couldn't turn my head for a second or something would stop somewhere, and that couldn't happen!

More thanks to Major Jeter. He took over after I got my orders arranged for the trip home and got the platform up over my "Man Cave" in the IJC compound. He got power to my friends in Herat, Leatherneck, Kandahar, and saw to it that the good German engineers in MeS got their platform erected. Talk about someone who could get things done! He was active duty and I hoped his career would benefit from appropriate recognition of what he accomplished and how much he contributed to the Task Force 236 mission. I think he was related to Derek Jeter, the baseball player. In any case, he sure knew how to hit a home run! Must run in the family…

August was ending and my version of an R&R trip was at hand. We did have a little excitement with our guys in Bagram Air Field (BAF). They had a cobra in their quarters. All the cartoons and movies show them climbing straight up out of a basket to the sound of an Indian flute player or something like that. This one was nothing like that. Ornery little bugger. They took care of it in good order, but it did make you think twice about what you'll find in your room at night!

It was getting hard to think about anything other than R&R. I was adjusting pretty much to the extended tour of retired recall duty and extended deployment. It was voluntary and I knew I would have the rest of my life to not be "in the game." I'd bring enough sundries back with me to last until 15 December, and watch it all go down again like a marker of time. The big thing was my medications that weren't available there. Colonel Carney was saying that I'd be done in Afghanistan by then for sure, so I would have less than eighty some days to go, depending on when I got back.

My mother's birthday was 22 August, and we were able to talk briefly before losing our connection to a higher priority demand for our circuit. Terri and the family were looking forward to our visit and life was good!

Back in Rocky Point 2011
The now more recent memories of Afghanistan were flowing and the thoughts of going back were mixed as my run continued. If I was extended for a fifth year, there would be little doubt about going back to Afghanistan. Tampa would be fine if I could remain there and Terri and I could see each other regularly, but the uncertainty was wearing on me. The tug of war continued…

Chapter Twenty Four
Afghanistan Extension and R&R: Sep 2010
DeForest, Sauk City, Roxbury, and Lake Wisconsin

The Trip Home

On 6 September Staff Sergeant Sherwood drove me the long way around the runway to the civilian side of the Kabul Area International Airport (KAIA) in the only set of civilian clothes I had for my civilian flight to Tampa. I brought my pistol for the trip as you could never be too careful. The far end of the runway was basically Indian Country and vulnerable to attack at any moment. He took my pistol into custody until my return. This was another complication. Normally if you left Afghanistan, you had to go through Al Udeid to turn your weapon and armor in. This is where the brotherhood of Marines comes in. I wasn't going to waste a week of leave going through Al Udeid and waiting for flights! I would have only entrusted my weapon to another Marine or one of the Task Force 236 team members, and I trusted Staff Sergeant Sherwood and Master Sergeant Schaffner with my life, so trusting them with my pistol was not hard.

On the drive around KAIA, I had very mixed emotions. Terri and I loved our time together, my family wants to see me more, and WPS had been holding not only "a" job, but "the" job for three years already. But the reality was that what I was involved in was too sensitive and too important for me to leave right now. The agencies from Washington, DC and our US Central Command (CENTCOM) representatives had seen more progress on the satellite project in the short time I'd been there than the past year. I had already been deeply involved in the program last year from Tampa so I knew what they meant.

Even though the Marine Corps was way over strength, and Headquarters Marine Corps (HQMC) was being extremely stingy with bringing retirees back, the agency pressure on CENTCOM, and a by-name request from a general officer from CENTCOM carried enough weight to push it through. I was much honored in this regard, and only hoped to live up to all the expectations. By the time I would leave Afghanistan for good (hopefully) in December, the satellite we were putting in the terminals for should be pumping the highly sought after Command, Control, Communications, Computers, Intelligence, Surveillance, Reconnaissance (C4ISR) data that the intelligence community and commanders had been anxiously awaiting. We made progress getting the first batch in, and there would be several more for me to be involved in, now that I'd be around for another year, whether there or Tampa. Sure wish I knew more about satellite terminals!

Terri and I and our families and friends would soon enjoy many hours in our homes in Sauk and DeForest and, of course, all of our favorite places in between. My goal was to be home for my Grandson Gavin's second birthday, and my own. It made me think. Being 58 years old in a combat zone was hard. Why do we have to get older than 25? You can vote, drink, and insurance is as cheap as it's going to get! And you can run around with 120 pounds of armor and ammo like you're in a T-Shirt. Oh well, Terri said I was only 39 plus tax, shipping and handling! That helped!

I was looking forward to seeing Mom and Dad up in Wild Rose and sit at "The Bar Dad Built" in the Oak Wood Lodge, and letting the grand runts show me their toy collections in Sauk City. I was also looking forward to drinking beer, talking smart, cutting wood, and being somebody with Schuman and Denny. They thought the Marine Corps was behind me when they flew down to Tampa for my retirement ceremony in 2002. I was sure my old buddy Chief Warrant Officer 3, USMC(Ret) Ray Schara and I would find a time to meet at the Antler Bar too! And I hoped to connect with my WPS team.

I was ready for an Old Fashioned at the Dorf Haus in Roxbury and that would happen by the 11th if not the 10th! Monte - this would NOT be the time to run low on brandy!

The good Staff Sergeant got me to the civilian terminal, pointed me in the direction of the entrance, and I was on my way. My flight would take me from Kabul to Dubai, Atlanta, and then Tampa.

On my way to the entrance, young Afghani boys swarmed around me wanting to carry my bags. They asked for $40. I wasn't in a position to argue or haggle, so I gave them $40 and it paid off! I checked in at the counter and got my tickets but I still had to get through another station. When I got there, I realized I didn't have my International Security Assistance Force (ISAF) badge! Another shock! It had to be back at the last counter, so I turned to get back as quickly as possible. I'm sure they were worth a lot on the street and I would need it to travel! The same kid I had given $40 to noticed I dropped it and was following me! It turned out to be a good investment for sure!

Things went smooth in Dubai and I boarded my Atlanta flight to find a full sized Indian woman in my seat. She didn't speak English and I didn't speak her language, but it became abundantly clear she wouldn't be giving up her prized seat. Possession became 100% of the law in this case. It was another long 14 hour flight without being able to budge. I stretched regularly and eventually arrived in Atlanta then Tampa.

CENTCOM

I shaved, showered, got in uniform and headed straight for the base. There was Army Master Sergeant McDuffie, the one whom I became convinced shepherded my orders through the gauntlet of bureaucratic hell to get approved. He had been a part of the original effort to hastily build the International Joint Command (IJC) headquarters where I now worked in KAIA. He had a hell of a background in the Army and took a great deal of pride in his important role at CENTCOM. We had gotten to know each other and I knew he always had my best interest in mind. It was a good feeling to touch base again!

And then there was the travel claim office and another chance for the Barbarians of Bureaucracy to have their way with me. Apparently I incurred a debt to the government of $3,600! It was a glitch in the system that I had been overpaid. They were very convincing in their argument, and I found the money in my checking account after not having checked it for six months. I wrote a check and cleared the matter up peaceful like. I touched base with all the necessary admin and supply types to get ready for my return to Kabul and popped into the J6 Operations Division to get caught up with all those on the receiving end of my desperate pleas for support from Kabul.

I relished a couple days in Tampa running errands and enjoying the beautiful view of Tampa Bay and Rocky Point. I had learned to love it there and it really made me want to stay. Somehow my Kabul room didn't compare, even with my new roommates Dan and Ollie's friendship! They'd better not be taking over my desk and storage space dammit!

Home

I flew to Madison and met Terri at the airport. Oh she looked good! Our hug was all that was needed to realize I was really home and it wasn't another dream. We made a quick stop at the VFW 8483 Post near the airport. Sue Haack was there and we enjoyed catching up. She was a proud Vietnam veteran and most of us are quite sure she still thinks she's there! So many of my good friends who served in the Vietnam war era never really seemed to come home even though they survived combat and made it to their freedom flight.

I wished every Vietnam veteran could see what it was like now and feel the support! Every time I turned around, someone was thanking me for my service. If they were my age or a little older, I told them to make sure they thanked the Vietnam veteran that they threw garbage on back then. It depended on my mood and their sincerity of course.

Terri and I finished the trip home and settled into our own DeForest house bar. We thoroughly enjoyed just being together with our favorite drinks and some Enya and Dennis Kamakahi music playing in the background. Every second counted and we only had a couple weeks worth of seconds to use!

On 11 September, my promise was made good to make Gavin's second Birthday Party! Dylan liked attention too and I made sure to give him some. It was a great feeling to be with our family and forget about the war and Kabul. We headed for Roxbury and the Dorf Haus and I finally devoured that "Monte Old Fashioned" that was on my brain for nearly a month now! I had so many good memories there. Both of my wedding receptions were held there. Terri liked it as much as me, and she wasn't the kind of bride to be superstitious or self-centered. I always remember when both the Dorf Haus owner and parish priest of the Catholic Church across the street both had the name Vern Maier. Terri and I were seated with them for a dinner play in the Dorf Haus one night when they thought it would be fun to change jobs for a week. Alcohol was involved.

We stayed at our Sauk City house. Sometimes it seemed nuts to keep both houses up, but we both loved our homes for our own reasons, and it still seemed like as good an investment as any! With the Dorf Haus on the road between us, it just seemed to work! I had time to putz around on the houses, my favorite domestic sport. It sure wouldn't be worth having two houses if I didn't like taking care of them!

The days on leave were filled with visiting our favorite places on Lake Wisconsin like Fish Tales and Anchors Away. Schumann, Kurt and I got some golf in at Devil's Head in Baraboo. Our tradition for years was to golf one night a week. We'd never get any better because we had too much fun. We would arrive late in the afternoon and get a good deal on twilight golf. We were quite often the last ones on the course so we never had to worry about being pushed. I often thought they should pay me for doing all their trimming in the roughs! Schumann said that he liked golfing with me. He got to see parts of the course he never knew existed. On one hole a fawn came right up to us. We would always see deer, eagles, rabbits, squirrels, and all kinds of other wildlife. It would be a ritual that would continue for years, even after I got home for good. Kurt, and Denny's son Tim, would join us in the years to come.

I would get lots of Mom and Dad time too. Terri and I went up to Wild Rose and met them at the Oakwood Lodge for dinner. I enjoyed getting up there and doing that every chance I got, and this time it was even more special with me going back to Afghanistan. Dad was proud of me, but he understood the unexpected realities of war from his Korean War days. He was doing very well after we nearly lost him several years earlier to cancer.

We drove back down to Sauk City for my birthday. We had a good mix of fun and rest, touring all our favorite spots. My birthday was the 19th and we celebrated in the Sauk house. Schumann, my brother Ron, and I exchanged ideas of the highest order after quickly and soundly solving all the world's problems.

Mark and Kristin and the boys were there, as was my sister Tammy and her husband Bob. How can you go wrong with a crew like that! It really made me feel the heart strings tugging. I didn't have to be doing this anymore! I had done my share many years ago! It was there though – that desire to get away from the talking heads on TV who thought they knew more than our generals. I couldn't sit on the couch and listen to them when I could be with the generals. I wondered how those generators and platforms were coming along....

Terri in Tampa

After a last night back home in the DeForest house, Terri and I flew down to Tampa on 20 September. We used my birthday certificate at the Palm in Westshore for some free crab legs. We'd have nine days together. My flight back to Kabul was delayed because of federal budget timing. This meant waiting until after 1 October, the start of a new fiscal year. It was an unexpected opportunity to enjoy some more time together! The government is always full of surprises, some of them good!

We enjoyed all our favorite Tampa spots. I made sure to hit the Marine Central Command (MARCENT) supply hut to get some cold weather gear that would be needed as Kabul started cooling off. I also calculated my toiletry needs and bought the right amount of soap, shampoo, and toothpaste to use as a countdown calendar upon my return. When I got back from the supply hut, I mailed it all to my address in Afghanistan.

Terri left for home on 29 September. That was a tough one. Hopefully it would just be for a couple months, but if there is anything we learned about the Marine Corps and marriage, you couldn't count on anything. You had to hope for the best and be ready to accept the worst.

Back to the Business of War

My flight back to Kabul was finally arranged for 5 October. I returned to CENTCOM and prepared. Not having access to my Kabul email account, I did what I could to check on progress in Tampa and my friends in Washington, DC. On 4 October I ran my final errands and spent a lot of time in my room on the computer communicating with family and friends, and doing what I could to keep my personal financial affairs up-to-date. I declared one more laundry night. Stephanie at the Rusty Pelican timed out the drinks and dinner perfectly as I ran across to the Sailport for my wash and dryer times.

My flight left at 1745 on 5 October and would arrive in Kabul at 0700 on 7 October. Once again, I would miss the creature comforts of home and the Hyatt. I got a haircut, did my final packing, took my gear back downstairs for the guys to put in storage, and had a night cap with Joel in the Lobby Bar. I shot off a message to my team on the cleared network and to my Task Force 236 team to confirm my flight details, and in case my ROSHAN phone didn't work when I got back, to let them know I landed in the Kabul airport.

I would fly to Atlanta, then Dubai. Arriving in Dubai at 1950 local time gave me some time to kill. I did the only reasonable thing and found the Irish Pub. It wouldn't be a violation of General Order 1 to drink in Dubai, but I did have to remember where I was going. I ordered a drink and got to know a retired US Navy Chief working for a Dutch oil rig. The gig he had was impressive. Five weeks on, five weeks off, and traveling the airports of the Middle East regularly. I felt safe and ordered another one. Did I mention he was Navy? We had a few more….

We finally boarded and finished the last leg of a very long journey to Kabul. I knew Staff Sergeant Sherwood would be on the alert and would be there to get me. I got right through customs and carried my bags to the parking lot at the airport. There were some very tightly lipped American civilians in the parking lot. They all had khaki clothes and beards. Don't the Special Ops guys know that alone is a uniform? In trying to talk to them, it was clear they were there to pick someone in particular up and it wasn't me. Staff Sergeant Sherwood and Sergeant Alba pulled up, loaded my bags, and handed me my pistol, armor, and helmet. Being back brought instant clarity to what still had to be done. Let's get on with it!

A Fourth Year of Marine Corps Retired Recall Was Underway
I arrived back at the IJC compound and cracked the door open to see if Dan and Ollie tried to take over my territory in our small room. My space was just as I left it. Good guys! I had several days of beard to harvest by now and was ready for a hot shower. The only thing I hate worse than shaving is not being shaved! I immediately got a dose of the sulfur-like smell of the non-potable water, but it was hot and running. I again remembered, and appreciated, I was in a hard shelter barracks in Afghanistan when most of my team members were in tents with trailers for heads. I unpacked, put on a fresh uniform,

strapped on my pistol belt noticing I had to loosen it a tad, and stepped out into the compound to start Afghanistan Tour, Part Two...

Back to the Present, Rocky Point and the Future

I was sailing through my run now. Nothing hurt, much anyway... I was truly a world away in thought! I had covered nearly 40 years of trying to balance my love of family with the strong sense of duty of my Marine Corps service. I neared my destination of the Hyatt knowing I would go through this all over again if I stayed for another year. Would I be ready for that? What part of me did the "hell yah!" come from? It had to be the part that said there is no way the Marine Corps will ever approve a fifth year of retired recall duty when they were already starting to ask younger 20 year guys to leave early. Or was it the endorphins from the run? It sure wasn't the part that made me wonder what I would say to Terri or Tony and Mike back at WPS!

Chapter Twenty Five
Back to the War: Oct-Dec 2010
Afghanistan

A New Season Brings Progress

Fall was definitely making its way to Afghanistan upon my return. The days were still quite sunny, warm, and very comfortable. The evenings and early mornings were getting cool. The winds were strong though, and sandstorms were more common. One day I walked out of a nice refreshing shower after a workout right into a blast of wind and sand. The weather was clear as a bell when I came back from the "gym just minutes earlier!" There went that fresh, clean feeling and clean pistol! Again! As fall paved the way for winter, it would also turn cold very quickly and abruptly since we were at 6,000 feet.

My wall locker was now restocked and I'd again watch it go down like an hourglass marking my time. The malaria pill bottle on my desk was full again after it felt so good to see it empty before leaving. This tour should now only be a little over 60 days compared to what turned out to be 133 last time, so it would be less than half. Once again, we were off and running in Afghanistan!

Task Force 236 was making good progress everywhere. The coalition network implementations at the regional commands were going well and the satellite project I was working on made great headway during my leave. Three of the five terminals we were working on were operational as we had hoped. There were persisting problems in the north at Mazar-e-Sharif and right there at the International Joint Command (IJC) headquarters in Kabul, but they were all being addressed to my satisfaction.

Power remained our primary obstacle, and it was always very difficult to overcome because of the persisting shortage of generators. The complexities involved in getting generators and getting them operational were great, and mostly due to the very thing that most American leaders wanted - more international involvement. NATO is big on bureaucracy and process, and if you go by the book it could literally take months for the proper paperwork and approvals to get what was needed in hours and days. Every installation has some mix of nations involved, and the concern for politics and due process overrides the operational wartime urgencies. What should take one day took three days, and what could be done in a week could take months.

Our role was to cut through all that with a mixture of persuasiveness and, when necessary, the use of serious horsepower. I had been given a great deal of authority to "get things done." When hitting an obstacle that could potentially cause an unacceptable delay, I had backing that went to the very top in Tampa and Washington, DC. For the most part, however, my charm, persuasiveness, and debonair personality had been working. If you believe that we're going to be great friends!

Special News from Home

On 13 October, I received great news from Kurt that he and Jenny were engaged! Our family loved Jenny and heartily welcomed her to the fold. He popped the question in Wisconsin's Door County with a beautiful sunset and water background. Like the gentleman he is, he dropped to one knee and did it properly. Kristin and her family were also in Door County that weekend and between both of them, I enjoyed a lot of beautiful, colorful pictures of that day! It was so good to see such color and lush countryside after living in so many desert scenes the past three years! It was Packer season, otherwise known as football season to non-Packer fans. Win or lose, we love them enough to shovel snow off the bleachers before the games in the dead of winter. What other team has fans that do that!

Some Bandwidth for Kabul

On 20 October the team arrived in Kabul to install the terminal on top of our now cherished Man Cave. We had it all figured out. The umbilical cord would be routed through the existing underground tunnels between the dish and the special equipment that we would install in the existing equipment racks. That was important at every location. The umbilical cord was the lifeline that connected the circuitry allowing the dish to chase our "bird" around to maintain signal connectivity. Even though it was old technology, it was better suited to withstand the wind, rain, and sand than the new digital technology.

The Kabul winds of fall would make it interesting. The dish was big and made a great wind sail! We didn't have the special bolts to anchor it properly yet, so I had to "procure" some sand bags - fast! Gunnery Sergeant Powell was gone and Master Sergeant Schaffer was busy with his own highly visible and critical priorities. Using our Gator, I did some "shopping" around the compound. People really shouldn't leave loose sand bags lying around like that! It's been a long time since I man-handled sandbags, but by God, I still had it! The sand bags worked for now, but we knew we would have to do much better and very soon!

By the time we had the dish up and held down by sand bags on top of our Man Cave, there was a full moon, and the sandstorm had cleared to the point of allowing a view of the dish and the moon and stars behind it. A good day's work! The dish was up and would soon be producing the desired result. The International Security Assistance Force (ISAF) and IJC and other supporting units in Kabul would get some badly needed bandwidth that would help our intelligence efforts, and would give our commanders additional support for command and control activities.

The dish and starlight background gave me cause for thought of why I was here and why it was important. The full moon was a beautiful site hovering between the elevated guard tower on the berm forming the boundary of the compound and our shiny new SATCOM terminal. It really was a beautiful site. I told Terri it was very romantic. She liked my humor!

There was the remaining issue of holding it down with something other than the fruits of my sand bag shopping trip. Major Jeter to the rescue. Again! He worked a deal through the IJC logistics folks to engage some local Afghan welders already on the compound who had the necessary work permissions. They couldn't speak English, but that was okay because I couldn't speak Dari either! It was amazing how well we worked together by using gestures. Before I knew it, they were on top of the shelter securing the terminal to the platform, emitting hot sparks on all those walking underneath. I liked that!

Thanks to hanging out in my parent's machinery business in my childhood years, I had good knowledge of what a good weld looks like, and these guys did a super job! Most of the Afghan welders were not so skilled, and I made sure he understood we were very happy with his work. I was so relieved that Major Jeter pulled this off! I had visions of the vicious winds of the Hindu Kush Mountains coming down on us, like they do on occasion, and with the satellite dish acting as a sail, picking up the dish and our Man Cave van with Major Jeter, Dan, and I still in it!

I told them it would be great! It would be like Dorothy in the Wizard of Oz and we would be blown far away, landing on a mountainside in Pakistan somewhere. With any luck we'd crawl out to see Bin Laden's foot sticking out from the bottom, and the Tin Man, Cowardly Lion, and Scarecrow would skip us back to Kabul. We would then safely blast our way through the Taliban and Al-Qaeda bad guys with the knowledge, strength, and courage we got from the Wizard! I damn near got sent to the clinic for a PTSD check on that one!

It was definitely cooling off at nights. I would finally dig my field jacket out of my seabag. The days were still quite warm, when it was sunny, and the mornings were comfortably crisp. But as soon as the sun went behind clouds or went down behind the Hindu Kush though, it got cold real fast!

Planning Ahead

We pulled together the appropriate planners from around the world to start the planning for a new terminal site near a neighboring country border. Using the five sites I worked on while there as a model, I'd be still able to manage additional sites considered key to the area after leaving Afghanistan. I sure hoped so! The supporting units were getting a better idea of what was expected of them now. As long as they worked directly with the program manager's installation teams, it would work after my departure, which I most certainly wanted to do! I did most of my work from Kabul over the computer and phone systems anyway, so I was hoping for the best! The overall goal from Washington, DC was still to have 13 terminals up and running and we were well on our way.

The Fabled Rhino

I was fascinated by the "Rhinos" in Kabul. They were up armored buses used to transport large groups of military members between compounds within the greater Kabul area. I caught a group that was part of some incoming 10th Mountain Division who were being bused to Camp Phoenix, only a couple miles away, on a route with a significant IED history. I've never ridden on one, but I found them intriguing! I guess they had them in Iraq in big installations like Baghdad too, but I never saw them out in my forward operating base at Camp Habbaniyah. It is amazing how a group of radicals can change the complexion of a bus stop!

A Good Marine is Promoted

Any military officer will tell you of all our duties, some are arduous, some are painful, but some are a pleasure. One of the most pleasurable duties of an officer is to promote well-deserving Marines, soldiers, sailors, and airmen. Marine Master Sergeant Shawn Schaffner had been selected for promotion to Master Gunnery Sergeant, the highest enlisted rank in the Marine Corps. The "Top" achieved this prestigious rank in just 24 years of Marine Corps service. Being around long enough to know a good marine, I had no trouble seeing why. He was truly among the best!

It is tradition for an enlisted member to request who they want at their promotion ceremony, as well as who promotes them. He asked for General Petraeus to promote him, and for me, Colonel Carney, and Major Jeter, to join him. What an honor! General Petraeus did a great job summarizing Master Sergeant's career and the many experiences they shared during their US Central Command (CENTCOM) service together. When it came time to pin the new chevrons on the Marine Corp's newest Marine Master Gunnery Sergeant, General Petraeus asked me to give him a hand. This would be a very proud moment!

After his promotion, we all needed to remember to quit calling him "Top" and start calling him "Master Guns." This was hard. Pushups are traditionally involved for those forgetful ones to help instill the change, officers included. Even before he was promoted, he wasn't shy about asserting himself (understatement of the year). One night in the van, we had been fighting for chairs and places for our nightly meeting with Colonel Carney. The Colonel's Deputy, a civilian of GS13 grade, Dan Holz, which is like a Major/Lieutenant Colonel equivalent, tried taking the spot next to me that Master Gunnery Sergeant Schaffner normally occupied. The "Top" looked at him with one of his best snarls (I had been schooling him) and said, "Don't confuse YOUR rank with MY authority!" The deputy moved. I was impressed! He took it quite well too. They were buddies...

We celebrated with a fantastic meal at Camp Phoenix afterward. Colonel Carney hasn't forgiven us to this day for not including him. If you read this Sir, we are still sorry! It was Friday, Surf & Turf night at all American mess halls, I mean DFACs, in the Middle East, especially for those in harm's way. The crab legs at Camp Phoenix hung six inches over the tray on either end, and it was hard to find room for the steak, say nothing of the shrimp!

A Turn & Burn Flight

On 31 October, I participated in a one-day flight I would never forget. The senior agency field representative I was working with on the satellite program requested I join her and her team on a "Turn & Burn" one-day flight to Herat and Kandahar. I had been flying all over Afghanistan on the standard Air Force Military Air (MILAIR) flights and it was horrible. You never knew if you'd get on the few flights you needed, and the waiting areas were bad, very bad. She promised me the Intelligence Bird known as the "IC Bird," the aircraft used by their team, would eliminate all that and have me at both bases and back in the same day! She said that our teams in Herat who benefited from Major Jeter's and my work in getting them generators wanted to thank me personally, and they had other business in Kandahar that was none of my business. Who could turn down an offer like that? Even if it was in Indian Country!

The aircraft was a DASH 8-100 which looked like a very small C-130 and was very maneuverable. I would end up flying around on it on later flights and learned of its very amazing maneuverability! We were met at the Herat stop by the commander and a senior enlisted Navy Seal Chief. They were involved in insurgency, counter narcotics trafficking, and governance operations, and the generators improved their mission capabilities tremendously!

The commander was a Navy officer. His chief was a Master Chief Petty Officer (E9). They were obviously very key players in their assigned mission. The chief's uniform was very unique as it was a special variant of the Marine Corps desert utilities, but not actually a Marine Corps uniform. The Seals have uniforms for all environments, of course. He was temporarily assigned to Herat's Intel fusion center to guide them as they brought together all sources of intelligence to "fuse" them into coherent, actionable intelligence that our special ops and conventional forces in the West could act upon.

They gave me their Regional Command-West ID holder and Italian Command badge to put in it. I'd be the only one on the block back in Sauk City, Wisconsin to have them displayed, I was sure! The patch has the flags of the 11 countries operating in Regional Command-West. We couldn't know why it was so important to them, but the Navy Seal Chief pulled me aside and made sure I knew I should hold on to those simple items and pass them on to my grandchildren. You get good results with good intel! They hang with great pride in my Sauk bar today!

A Meeting of the Minds

November started with Colonel Carney and me attending a two day conference at the IJC headquarters. It was led by Army Lieutenant General Rodriquez who now reported directly to General Petraeus. You may remember me occasionally referring to "C4ISR" when describing how CENTCOM is organized or when referring to my duties. The extra "C" is Coalition when we combine international forces like we do here in Afghanistan. The full title becomes "Coalition, Computers, Communications, Command, Control, Intelligence, Surveillance, and Reconnaissance (C5ISR)."

There would be lots of high level players from all the countries involved. I was impressed by Lieutenant General Rodriquez' opening comments, "Our hardware now exceeds our headware." He may have made a good Marine too! It was so true. He meant we keep throwing more technology at things we should be putting more human thought into! The theme was to achieve regional command stability in the three legged stool of security, governance, and development. The conference was an effort to get the intelligence, operations, and systems people in the same room to take stock of the various intelligence platforms we had in country in order to maximize their effectiveness.

Those who read spy novels, or see movies where satellites can provide detailed, live imagery anywhere in the world on a second's notice, would be sadly disappointed to know the actual capabilities and limitations of the technology used in the defense of our country and world compared to the spy novels. It is good, very good, but not THAT good. The bottom line is we have to have good human intelligence and signal intelligence, and other forms of intelligence to help us focus our resources, in order to give us the kind of information that ultimately leads to actions by the commander.

Reminders of War and Thoughts of Home

On 12 November, the Rhino convoy was hit. We suffered two Afghan National Police killed in action. The lead vehicle gunner was shaken up, but there were no American casualties. Master Guns Schaffner and Gunny Powell were just two minutes behind them, and so were again very lucky. Gunny Powell had returned after his break back home and getting General Petraeus' home communications installed and secured. They did all they could to help out with the casualties, but they certainly returned with heavy hearts. We had so many reminders that we were in harm's way.

On 14 November we had another rocket attack alert, but it turned out to be nothing. I was just getting back from the gym and changing back into uniform in the dark and Dan was sleeping, when the siren went off. He woke up and asked what to do. Being an old hand now, I calmly said we stay put. If it was a real attack, we were in the safest place, but since we didn't hear an explosion, I said it must be a drill. It was confusing because "Big Voice" didn't announce "Exercise Exercise Exercise" like they normally do during drills over the compound speakers. Fully awake now, he said, "What?", and went right back to sleep. I finished dressing and went back to work. Another day, another rocket attack...

Such is a day of life in a modern combat zone, a three-star headquarters combat zone that is. Our infantry units endured danger on every street corner, on every hill, and on every road. It really had been quiet since August after we took about 40 well documented bad guys off the streets prior to the elections, and I personally believe there were some "deals" being made to induce other bad guys not to attack. We still had to remain extremely vigilant, because it is times like this when you're most vulnerable. My days had been much slower and I was getting caught up and reorganized. I wouldn't say boredom was an issue yet, and it wouldn't be anyway because it takes about two seconds to go from slow to overdrive. I was starting to think about that Freedom Bird flight though, and it was now only about 26 or 28 days away!

The War Persists
My next major event would be a trip to a remote base near a neighboring country border to lead a site survey for another satellite terminal. We wanted to get it installed by February to support a build-up of US and Afghanistan operations. NATO would soon be announcing the plans for Afghanistan operations for the next 18 months, and this area played a key role. I would be traveling around the 22-24 November timeframe, getting back just in time for a Thanksgiving meal that Major Jeter was planning. Did I mention he was probably the best logistics guy I ever met?

Life Goes on Back Home
Back home, Terri would attend the Association of Food and Drug Officials (AFDO) conference in Washington, DC. I'm sure if she got a chance, she would go out to the Marine Corps Monument (Iwo Jima Memorial). It was a reminder of 1995 when my new job was too demanding to keep up the reserves anymore, so I decided to quit. She called me just to say that I would always be a full-fledged Marine to her. She was now on the board of directors for AFDO and would soon be on her way to becoming the national president of AFDO. I was so proud of her! She could never know how that powerful act of kindness, love, and friendship back in 1995 would shape our lives for years to come, when it would be her turn to serve a higher calling!

My son-in-law Mark got a seven-point buck on opening day of deer season! I had hoped to spend some time at my deer hunting "spot" in Lodi where I grew up with Kurt when getting back home. I had my rock on a hill, and a couple guest rocks that Kurt and Schumann have shared with me through the years. Those are the things you live for when you're a citizen Marine!

Back to Indian Country

The hopes and dreams of home would have to wait just a while longer. Right on schedule on 22 November the senior field rep for the agency I was working with arranged to have me picked up by the IC Bird for a flight to Shindand for a site survey along with some systems engineers and my primary intelligence representative from CENTCOM J2 (Intel). We would fly the DASH 8-100 I grew to like. It was officially a part of Presidential Airways, a contractor.

We had to stop at a place called Farah on the way. It would be built up and become a base for the Afghani Army to contribute to similar long-term goals in western Afghanistan. It was very remote at the time, and only had a dirt runway. There were two buildings. One had a miniature weather station (weather vane and solar panels on the roof), and the other had a machine gun on the roof. A Farah Police Chief (I think) and a big shot, probably a Finance Minister dressed in very clean, white traditional Afghanistan garb, came over looking for a ride to Kabul. I was sort of taken aback by their clean clothes and relative fresh appearances! Their armed group was in the distance near the second building with a machine gun. I hoped they would get their ride elsewhere. He seemed anxious to be able to talk to Karzi's people as soon as possible. I was also glad his armed "party" stayed where they were! I had my pistol, but I suddenly felt the need for a little more firepower...

We took off from the desolate Farah stop without the additional passengers and landed without incident at Shindand. It was home to the US Air Force's 445th Air Expeditionary Advisory Squadron, and over the next year, would host a much expanded US, Afghani, and Italian presence. The living conditions were crude, but not too bad. I rather doubted they would ever improve much over the basic tent and wooden bunks they had then, but they were heated (and cooled), and overall, not too bad. It was the Air Force after all...

Home Sweet Home

We arrived back at the Kabul compound without incident. Even though the agency I worked with made me feel as comfortable and safe as could be expected in Indian Country, it was good to be back in the relative safety of my Kabul "home." Our mission was highly successful and I had every confidence the Shindand installation would go well after my departure under the guidance of the agency's new field rep. He was very capable.

I donned my armor and carried my bags the distance to my room, unpacked, got a nice, hot shower, picked up my laundry, and reported to the Man Cave to resume my routine duties. As I cracked the hatchway and looked in, there was a package on my workstation. Yes! It was Terri's Thanksgiving turkey cookies! They got here in time to compliment the real American Thanksgiving meal Major Jeter planned to bring from Camp Phoenix the next day!

Thanksgiving in Kabul

The Task Force 236 Thanksgiving meal was enjoyed by all. Major Jeter, and the usual traveling crew of Master Guns Schaffner, Gunny Powell and their team worked their magic with the Camp Phoenix DFAC and brought back some great thick and juicy ham! While they were gone, we set up a couple of tables in the shelter and readied for their return.

It may be the only Thanksgiving meal I ever get that was catered by an armed and dangerous team of America's finest! The roads and streets between KAIA and Camp Phoenix were just as dangerous on Thanksgiving as any other day. They risked their lives for this meal! My recommendation to load their M16s and M9s with bird shot and bring back extra Turkeys was unanimously and violently rejected for some reason! Do they even have turkeys in Afghanistan?

Colonel Carney gave some brief words of Thanksgiving praises and the feast began. I'd forgotten the last time I not only had an edible chunk of real ham that wasn't called "Gammon" to fool the Muslims into thinking they weren't really eating pork, but a delicious slice that even a plastic knife glided through! There were real mashed potatoes, corn on the cob, thick sliced ham, and macaroni and cheese. Pecan pies were for desert. My contribution was Terri's Thanksgiving turkey cookies. She used to love making them for the family back home but didn't get a chance anymore as the kids went to their mother's for Thanksgivings. This gave her a chance to make her favorite Thanksgiving treat for the Task Force 236 team and the cookies were greatly appreciated!

Back Home

I thought of Terri as she flew back to Hawaii for some rest. I knew Kurt and his fiancée Jenny would be enjoying their family gatherings and working on wedding plans. They worked together to get the Sauk house all spiffed up for the holidays! Kristin, Mark, and the boys would be spending their Thanksgiving day together and enjoying their families. While I missed being there, I knew I'd be home soon and sharing Christmas with all of them!

On with the Mission and Sites on Christmas

Colonel Carney declared a continuation of holiday celebrations and encouraged an early start to the Christmas holiday season a day after our Thanksgiving meal. Somebody set up a small Christmas tree. In less than a day it was adorned with some very creative ornaments. Colonel Carney's only guidance was that all decorations be rated PG13. We were definitely officially on the commercial speedway to Christmas in Afghanistan!

My last mission would be to join a small crew of agency personnel and engineers to Tarin Kowt for some preliminary planning work for things we'd be doing there in the January/March timeframe. We heard it had a real runway and was pretty well established, so we felt pretty safe.

Terri time was usually 10 and a half hours behind Afghanistan time, but now it was 14 and a half hours behind as she was in Hawaii again. I had to adjust my reminders to call hoping I could catch her. If she was more than twelve hours behind me, does that mean we're actually closer together if we could sneak around the world the other way? I'm like Andy Rooney that way...always thinking up dumb questions. I think it was noticed. Marine Lieutenant Colonel Gomez, my boss back in Tampa, told me to plan on taking some time off when I get back. I'm sure it was meant as a compliment. In any case, I would do just that! I rather suspected that once I got processed back in early December, he'd tell me he didn't want to see me until January. Another compliment! I think...

A Final Mission to Indian Country
It was time for my last mission with the agency folks that would
continue the task of setting up terminals to provide more bandwidth to
our command and control and intelligence folks. The plane crew
would pick me up in Kabul and fly to Tarin Kowt, conduct our
business, do a "turn and burn," and be back before nightfall. I really
didn't want to do this, but the IC Bird was the only way to fly into
Afghanistan! Even though the danger was certainly there, I felt as safe
with them as I did with my Marines in Iraq. They could and should
take that as a high compliment!

We boarded my now favorite aircraft in Afghanistan, the DASH
8, for Tarin Kowt. I was somewhat surprised by the dirt runway and
our corkscrew approach. It did make it much harder for ground fire to
hit an aircraft that way, I just didn't think we needed to worry about it
this time. We were picked up by Army Sergeant First Class White on
the sand flight line and taken to the Combined Team Uruzgen hosting
Task Force 34, Task Force No Mercy, the US 2nd Striker Regiment,
and an Australian contingent. They were truly in the middle of
nowhere, but they made the best of their environment. Their facilities
were quite amazing for such a remote forward operating base.

The Australians replaced a Dutch unit that included several
women that routinely sunbathed topless in a small designated area. I
don't think I need to elaborate on how much the Americans there
missed the Dutch, but the Aussies were a good bunch too.

Our site survey for the terminal installation went well. We
established good points of contact for the new agency's field rep. As I
felt with our Shindand visit, with what he would do in the field, and
what I would do to garner CENTCOM support back in Tampa, we'd
have a terminal operational as planned. This was a very good feeling.

Time for Checking Out and Going "Home"
I spent 4-6 December checking out of Task Force 236 at the Kabul
compound. Colonel Carney declared movie night on Saturdays at
2100 in the van. They had to have a holiday theme and must be rated
PG. They were very much enjoyed and appreciated!

The hunt was on for a flight to get me to Al Udeid Air Base in
Qatar from Kabul, always a challenge to do in less than two or three
days via MILAIR terminals. There were no direct flights. Master

Guns Schaffner contacted his old buddy who was still on General Petraeus' communication team to see if there were any Distinguished Visitor flights going to Al Udeid.

They were separate from MILAIR flights and had much nicer aircraft to support the travel needs for high ranking officers and dignitaries. I came over on one, and Master Guns Schaffner thought he'd check on the possibilities to get me out on one. His buddy said General Petraeus' aircraft was dead heading to Al Udeid to pickup Marine General Mattis, the new CENTCOM Commander, and some high level CENTCOM personnel and bringing them to Kabul. General Petraeus' aircraft was a Gulfstream and the Master Gun's buddy actually got me on the manifest!

What a deal! The Gulfstream would be three hours of a silent, relaxing flight without wearing armor instead of a six or seven hour loud, uncomfortable C-130 flight in metal and nylon cargo seats, if you could get one. As a backup I signed up for C-130 MILAIR Flight Torque 21 leaving at 1430.

I made good progress checking out once I had a couple flight options, and was so ready to go by now! They stamped my checkout sheet with all the necessary NATO symbols. Since I still had to have access for a day or two to compound facilities, they cut a notch out of my ISAF badge so it would still work and I could keep it as a souvenir. It hangs proudly in my Sauk house bar today.

Back at Rocky Point and the Three Mile Run

The Afghanistan tour took every inch of mental and, at times, physical endurance I could muster. It wasn't long when I looked at it in terms of months. It wasn't WWII style gruesome and enduring, it wasn't Korean style frozen and forgotten, it wasn't Vietnam style sweltering hot, atrocious, and surreal, but it was challenging in its own ways. As my Rocky Point run continued and I pondered what my fate would be, I wondered mostly if I would have to go back if my orders were extended for yet another year. I had a choice, unlike so many. In so many ways that made the tug of war between my love for Terri, home, family, and sense of duty worse. I hadn't suffered like WWII, Korea, and Vietnam vets, but how far should I press my luck?

Chapter Twenty Six
Homecoming and Mideast Unrest: Dec 2010-May 2011
Sauk City, DeForest, US CENTCOM, MacDill ABF, Tampa, Fl

Flying in Style

On 7 December, the Distinguished Visitor flight to Al Udeid that Master Guns Schaffner arranged was still scheduled. General Petraeus' flight crew would fly me and an Air Force Colonel to Qatar to pick up Marine General Mattis and his US Central Command (CENTCOM) team, proceed to Djibouti and return to Kabul. He had a dedicated Gulfstream for such purposes.

The Gulfstream was truly a stroke of luck and testament to the powers of the Master Guns! With room for up to twenty, the Colonel and I would truly enjoy this flight! He would be returning to Afghanistan after a meeting in Al Udeid. I had no standing orders to return, but with nearly 10 months left on my extension of active duty orders, nothing was certain.

I recognized the female Air Force crew chief. I had seen her in the compound gym tent several times over the months. She tended to our safety and treated us to breakfast and chatted with us while she prepared for what would be a much busier trip to Djibouti.

The flight was smooth, quiet and very scenic. I flew over most of Afghanistan in C-130s several times in the last eight months, but it was very difficult to see out the few windows they had. Our armor wasn't necessary and the wispy silence was a very nice alternative to the noise and discomfort of the C-130s. I enjoyed the scenery from the air, but enjoyed leaving it even more!

We arrived at Al Udeid Air Base, Qatar, and everything progressed quickly. General Petraeus' communication team boarded immediately with several large boxes of electronics that would support General Mattis on the return trip. It would all have to be set up and tested within minutes. Our senior generals and admirals are seldom out of touch.

I disembarked and made the familiar walk to the armory to turn in my pistol. I made sure it was good and clean before leaving. Marines are like that. Air Force Master Sergeant Breton from our CENTCOM Forward Headquarters (CFH) team picked me up and drove me to the supply section to turn in my armor and other gear. Within minutes I was done and would now be able to make the commercial flight to Tampa that had been scheduled for me early in the morning.

Once again, I spent the night in the Air Force barracks. I still thought they were like a cross between a college dorm and prison. Al Udeid hadn't changed. It was still flat and sandy. You'd think someone would change that! I walked the one mile paved walkway from the CFH towards the "Bra," the two white pointed tents that served as the command's recreational facility. I found out about a new Officers Club near the barracks along the way, so I thought I'd have my first beer or three there. Three was still the limit.

The new club was quite nice! I enjoyed my first beer alone then three Marine Corps C-35 pilots recognized me as a fellow Marine and snuck over. They were pilots from a reserve squadron in New Orleans. Marine reservists sure get around! They were on temporary orders and had flown over Afghanistan quite a bit. They were Marine pilots, and I was a Marine Warrant Officer that served in artillery, infantry, and now systems stuff. We had beer. Enough said! The humor was so welcome!

They too were struggling with the balance of their own love of family and sense of duty, but we sure knew how to live the dream. We had our three beers and returned to our quarters. I did my laundry and hit the rack for an early rise. I was still laughing...

I met my ride at the usual meeting place for transportation to the airport at 0430 hours the next morning. It was the smoking pit in front of the barracks and my flight would leave at 0805 hours for Dulles. The base security was always extremely tight with US and Qatar layers. Each included bunkers, barriers, weapons, and sand. The Qataris made us unload our bags and scanned everything. They were very stiff and quite arrogant. We got through in good order and the 45 minute drive to the Doha airport went smoothly. Flight UA1001 would be on time. Great news!

I was all excited about my aisle seat for the 14 hour flight to Dulles. But it wasn't to be. An elderly and very strong willed Arab woman in traditional dress that couldn't speak English pointed at the center seat next to me, obviously indicating that it was now my seat. Here we go again. Well, I wasn't going to blow my ticket home after how far I'd come. I shifted over peaceful like. Of course, it had nothing to do with the beautiful Pakistani woman in the window seat.

We arrived in Dulles right on schedule. We endured an hour and a half of immigrations and customs and went through several layers of security. The sights and sounds of American civilization were a welcome sight! I met a former Marine Lieutenant Colonel near the gate for Tampa and we hoisted a beer. He had done his share of service at CENTCOM as well and did much of what I had just done, and much more. It was a great feeling!

I'd be in Tampa within two and a half hours! I couldn't wait to see the water and plush greenery of Tampa and the surrounding area as we flew in! Thinking of my experience made me feel great, but I was very anxious to be back safe and sound. Terri got much more than she bargained for in supporting my sense of duty. She supported me far above and beyond normal expectations. Because of her love and devotion, I was able to serve at levels I never thought possible. It's truly great to feel I played a small part in contributing to our nation's security. But now it was time for her to have her husband back! In the States at least!

Tampa, Terri, and Christmas in Wisconsin
On Thursday, 9 December I checked back into CENTCOM's Tampa Headquarters. As promised by my boss, Marine Lieutenant Colonel Gomez, he threw me out of the office until Tuesday. He had a new project for me to add to my satellite project and would brief me on Wednesday. The only reward for good work is more of it! I couldn't wait! I spent the weekend getting my room set back up and getting my body clock readjusted. Terri and I made arrangements for her trip down to join me.

On 16 December, Terri arrived in Tampa. Marine Colonel Murray invited us to Maggianos in Westshore for a division get-together. Brigadier General Donahue, the CENTCOM J6 Director and creator of Task Force 236, was there and pulled Terri aside for quite a long private discussion. Terri said that he was very complimentary of my contributions to Task Force 236 and our contributions to the satellite program. He told her it truly had a national impact. Terri felt pretty proud. There were a lot of people there, but she got a good share of the General's time!

On 20 December, we made the flight to Wisconsin and then went to our home. Our first stop was at Madison's VFW Post 8483 to see our friends there.

When in Rome, do as the Romans. I was in DeForest and outdoor Christmas lights had to be put up. It was cold and nothing went right. The snow was deep and I was feeling bogged down by my snowmobile suit. At least it wasn't armor! I persevered. Our DeForest house looked wonderful at night with the clear skies and snow filled yard. That's what we work for! Terri and I loved it! We went down to the VFW to share more time with them. I'd never met a more dedicated bunch of veterans and auxiliary members!

I had one day to fix some important things in the DeForest house and do some Christmas shopping. And I thought my Task Force 236 duties were uncompromising! I fixed the faucet, closet door, and vacuumed. Then I was off to East Towne to do my Christmas shopping. I quickly and efficiently hit jackpots for Terri and the Grand Runts. All would have plenty under the tree!

Christmas Eve at our Sauk house had been the gathering place for Mom and Dad's family for quite some time now. Mom was so proud! We had 100% attendance again. Every leaf of every branch of their family tree showed up! My son and daughter changed their own Christmas celebrations to give us a little more time together which we very much enjoyed. We usually went up north (yes – there is civilization north of Madison) to Larsen to be with Terri's family on Christmas Day.

Terri was born two days after Christmas and always lamented on how her friends and family combined cards and gifts for efficiency. It cheated her out of what should be two special days a year. I resolved to resolve that! I always made sure to take her out on her actual birthday and give her a real birthday gift and not combine it with her Christmas gift. She loved Louisianne's in Middleton, so off we went! It was a very romantic underground atmosphere and we loved it! We spoke of our unknown future.

Would I be done that October, or would I be extended again? It was hard. I could always say no, but would I if they authorized another set of orders? I loved my home and family but didn't want to quit my Marine Corps service until there was absolutely no choice. We committed to staying together no matter what life threw our way. She was becoming unhappy with her State of Wisconsin service and soon there would be a time where she needed to do something different. When this came about, I would stay home and hold the fort down. It would become a reality in our near future.

The days after Terri's birthday were filled with fun with friends and Kurt. My buddy Denny, Kurt, and I went to Leland, a small town west of Sauk City, to Junior Sprecher's Bar. It was so much fun to go there and look over a rifle or pistol while you had a beer! The trip there was always interesting as well. On this trip, we encountered a large herd of deer crossing the small highway in front of us. The Marine in me joked we'd have to shoot our way through them if it was like this on the way back! Junior entertained us with his stories of the proper care, feeding, and training of raccoon hunting dogs. It was a memorable stop.

Christmas festivities gave way to New Years. Terri and I traveled up to Wild Rose to meet my parents and enjoy New Years Eve in the "Bar That Dad Built." I really loved that bar! We were home by 2300 and all were in bed except me. I sat at the kitchen table reflecting on whether I'd be home or back in Afghanistan next year. Terri came out at midnight for a New Year's Eve kiss and took my hand to return to bed.

Back to Tampa and Duty

Being home for the holidays was truly a treat. Again I reminisced about why I was doing what I was doing. The world was ruthless in its harsh realities. I had served 35 years of active and reserve service by now, ranging from the Vietnam era to the Global War on Terrorism. I wanted to stay home, but would continue serving as long as I was able to obtain orders to keep me with the people I trusted most to deal with the realities of Islamic Terrorism.

This was a war of ideology and I knew I had a unique opportunity to serve my country in the earliest stages that will continue for decades, if not ages. So, I would do my best until the last day.

Life at CENTCOM

Lieutenant Colonel Gomez and I were called up to Washington, DC to meet with the agency officials managing the satellite program for which I represented CENTCOM. Many of the High Value Target successes we had the past several months were directly attributable to the work we and many others had done there, which would continue to grow well into the future. The agency director personally presented me with a letter of appreciation along with a very unique coin heavily comprised of gold. It was a highly coveted item within the agency.

I also got a coin from the Air Force Lieutenant General in charge of the Intelligence Surveillance Reconnaissance Task Force (ISRTF). It was a very satisfying experience. It felt good be a part of something good! I've always said that I'd rather be a part of something good than on top of something shitty!

It was great to be back in Tampa with sunny weather, beautiful water views, lots of palm trees, and clean roads! I was really growing weary of so many sandstorms, T-Walls, bunkers, tents, trailers, and mess halls over the last three years. I was still quite certain there would be at least one more Middle East trip before my orders expired in September, but for now it was "carpe diem" (seize the day).

Crisis in Egypt

Events in Egypt had been heaped upon us on top of everything else going on in CENTCOM's area of responsibility. Youth group protests focused on legal and political issues, including police brutality, state-of-emergency laws, lack of free elections and freedom of speech, corruption, and economic issues including high unemployment, food-price inflation and low wages. When the new Africa Command (AFRICOM) was created, six countries in Africa were transferred to it, but Egypt was kept in CENTCOM's area of responsibility.

The Levant area includes countries bordering the Mediterranean from Greece to Egypt. It was always tricky to coordinate command and control because the European Command (EUCOM) controls the Mediterranean Sea, and CENTCOM controls the Red Sea and Egypt. We were maneuvering ships in preparation of mass evacuations, if it became necessary, and the requirement to coordinate every move between us and EUCOM definitely complicated things. We estimated there were 30,000 Americans that we would have to move, plus

20,000 others that we were obligated to help if necessary. We had a very impressive plan in place, but I sure hoped we wouldn't have to execute it!

We had stood-up a Crisis Action Team (CAT) for this purpose and we were all on call 24x7. Lieutenant Colonel Gomez was the communications lead for the CAT and was totally consumed by it, so the rest of us had to cover his normal daily duties. He covered me so I'd damn sure cover him!

NATO and Operation Unified Protector (Libya)

The unrest in the Middle East and Africa continued to keep staff officers in AFRICOM, EUCOM, and at CENTCOM extremely busy. If you followed Operation Unified Protector, you knew it was "led" by NATO. This comes as good news for those who think other countries should be doing more, and the US shouldn't be taking on the highest burdens of cost and force contributions. NATO is similar to the United Nations, but is comprised of European countries and is meant as a coalition to defend the North Atlantic region's economic and defense interests.

You may remember my observations regarding the NATO countries to the Operation Enduring Freedom in Afghanistan. My point then regarding Afghanistan, and now regarding Libya, was that even if NATO is involved, they basically have very little to offer. The fact NATO was leading the Libya effort, if you paid close attention, was that the US still had to do the heavy lifting simply because the other countries just didn't have it to give, even though they were truly "in the game" when it came to effectively dealing with things going on in the Middle East and Africa. Their choice to focus their spending on social programs and to maintain very minimal defense postures was becoming an increasingly difficult challenge.

They literally counted on NATO for their defense, and it just wasn't there. So, I wasn't as excited about NATO being in charge of Operation United Protector in Libya as were our diplomats and political leaders, simply because we were in a position of NATO officers being in direct control of US forces and assets, after they did little to plan for their own defense.

Yet another Additional Duty – ISR Surge

My participation in the planning process for an annual exercise conducted in Egypt called Bright Star had been scrubbed when we realized it was too late to get a country clearance. Not to worry, I was not overlooked when someone was needed for a new and sudden requirement in the Intelligence, Surveillance, and Reconnaissance (ISR) area. The Office of Secretary of Defense (SECDEF) wanted to get more ISR assets into Afghanistan - fast! This was an urgent "push" that would require a coordinated effort between CENTCOM's Intel, Operations, and Systems Directorates with matching staff officers at the SECDEF Office, the ISR Task Force in Washington, DC, and General Petraeus' International Security Assistance Force (ISAF) staff at Kabul. Lieutenant Colonel Gomez assigned me as the CENTCOM Operations Planning Team Lead.

My satellite program was still a key effort at CENTCOM, and it was rolling along pretty well. I had a couple of lingering obstacles to crush, but Lieutenant Colonel Gomez was successful in bringing senior officers from Washington, DC down to Tampa, and we were able to blast our way through them. So, what was once consuming my energies would now just be a matter of me tracking progress and raising hell with someone if it looked like they might miss a date. I was good at that!

I had plenty on my plate, and it would ensure my remaining months at CENTCOM would continue to be action packed. That's the way I liked it, but we'd see how I felt this fall!

Time with Terri

Terri and I had another great visit. She arrived on the heels of the last day of the meetings we conducted with the Washington, DC agency reps for the satellite program, and she was a very welcome sight when coming into the room. We had the rainiest day I can remember there, and the airport was shut down right when she was due in. I checked her flight status, and her flight had landed six minutes before it closed! I knew she was here and just had to finish my day and get "home" to see her.

I got out of the office as soon as humanly possible, but the rain was coming heavier than I'd ever seen. I wasn't going to let that stop me! In my infantry days, we had a saying, "It doesn't rain on

Marines." In order to back it up, we had another saying, "There is no such thing as rain, there is only liquid sunshine." Well, those days came rushing back as I stepped out of the sliding door, down the ramp, and greeted that liquid sunshine! I was completely soaked in one second on the 10 minute walk to my car.

My car heater still worked, so I cranked it up to 88 degrees during the entire 40 minute drive to the hotel. Our reunion hug was delayed slightly, but we had a great time from the moment we were together to the moment she left! After I got dry, we went up to Armani's for a special meal and some time with John and Joanie. The sun was out for the rest of her trip. We had a couple of nice days at Clearwater Beach, and our Cuban friend, Margot, the piano player at Armani's upstairs, took us to the Columbia Restaurant in Ybor City. She used to play there and knew the history and many of the employees and flamenco dancers.

Spring Offensive in Afghanistan

Just as the sun comes up in the morning and goes down at night, the mountains of Afghanistan will come to life as spring approaches. Both sides spent the winter planning their strategies, goals, and offensives. The trick was to isolate the insurgents already in country and keep others from coming in from Iran and Pakistan. That really was the bottom line.

If we could deny all Islamic radicals (not just the Taliban and Al-Qaeda) the mountainous no-man's lands routes to bring recruits, training lands, supplies, and finances we could keep them from spreading. If we failed in this, they would eventually be in the US with their IEDs and acts of terror, as the people of so many countries in Europe, Africa, Asia, and many parts of the world have already learned.

Easter Leave

Terri was back home and I was going home for Easter. I was looking forward to Easter with the "Grand Runts." My guess was that the pesky Easter Bunny would have gotten loose in my house and would leave a trail of jelly beans again! I would most certainly need some help picking up that mess! We'd also be celebrating their Mommy's new job as a Human Resources staff member at St Mary's Hospital.

Kurt was called to film the protests of a collective bargaining bill, education cuts, BadgerCare cuts and immigrant rights being covered in Madison by reporter Susan Modaress of PressTV. He and his fiancée, Jenny Haack, had been very busy preparing for their October wedding. The balance between love of family and sense of duty was easier when I was in Tampa, but it was never easy.

After a final day of tidying up my personal affairs and getting ready to fly back to Tampa, Terri and I enjoyed a night at our DeForest house. We loved eating in our family room and listening to Enya and Dennis Kamakahi's Hawaiian music. We cherished our time together, and the next day would mean parting once again. But not for long, as she'd come to Tampa in less than a week! We talked about her trip down there where we'd have ten more days together! It would be a record! So ended a great Easter leave.

Bin Laden

My trip back to Tampa went smooth and on schedule. I got my uniform ready, checked back off leave the next day, and went back to work. I was quickly updated on the status of my satellite program and my responsibilities to support the SECDEF's ISR Surge into Afghanistan. All was well, and Terri and I were temporarily back to our routine of being "together separately."

Having such a great family and good friends that understood my commitment to the defense of our great country, as well as my love for home, family, and friends meant everything to me. It was a real tug of war at times, but it was looking like it would be over soon, and I'd be content knowing that I truly did all I could. Not one inch of dedication, loyalty, or sweat was left on the table, as it all got used! I was extremely honored at being able to contribute, as Army Brigadier General Donahue told Terri upon my return to CENTCOM's Tampa headquarters from Afghanistan, "at a level of national operational impact."

On 1 May one of the fruits of our labor would become known to the world as Osama Bin Laden was located and killed. There were many other high value targets that we pursued with utmost urgency, but Bin Laden had become a point of principle with a nation that wanted justice. The mission was conducted the same as many others, on a daily basis by various special operators and conventional forces after massive intelligence reports were collected, processed, and disseminated and targeting analysis and approvals were conducted. But, as always, it was human persistence and intelligence that were key contributors to the ultimate success of the mission.

As I lied in bed watching the news reports with the rest of America, I felt good about having my small part in establishing the networks that supported the intelligence and command and control systems that brought it all together. I hoped my work helped the persistent analysts who were at the center of it all! I always said "we will win this war when we could find a piece of fly shit in a pepper bottle and remove it with minimal disruption to the rest of the bottle." We were getting closer everyday!

Can Our Troops Come Home Now?
Killing Bin Laden was a great morale booster for the country, but it was largely symbolic. I was pleasantly surprised by the President's willingness to take the risk, and he deserved credit for that. Too many times the civilian leaders put too much emphasis on the political aspects and too many times too many high level targets got away. I had it on good authority that he took quite a while on this one too, but at least he did it in the end. The question remained of what the degree of willingness to act would be to stand above political correctness to identify the real enemy, and lay out a plan to engage it in the future.

The radical movement has tens of millions of followers, and is like a cancer that has metastasized. We wouldn't kill it by cutting off its head. There was all kinds of silliness spewing from the intellectual giantry of the media, but the real reason we couldn't find him for so long is primarily due to the protection of millions of followers, none of which a 25 million dollar reward meant anything to. Their dedication to Salafist and Wahabbi style Islam meant everything.

If we truly knew who we were dealing with, a milking goat would have been a more effective bribe or reward. What our citizenry couldn't seem to comprehend is that only total submission and dedication to Allah and the law of Islam meant anything to the millions of followers, who would gladly martyr themselves in place of millions of US dollars or an entire herd of goats.

I thought back on what I had come to learn of the Middle East and Islam it made me worry about whether we would ever see a majority of mainstream Muslims willing to openly condemn the actions of the much smaller radical element of their religion. A key difference between a mainstream Muslim and a radical is whether or not Allah "abrogated" in his revelations to Muhammad. At the beginning of the long period of his revelations, Allah encouraged toleration of non-believers as long as they were monotheistic in their beliefs. A key pillar of the Islamic faith is the assertion there is only one God, Allah, and Muhammad was his prophet. Towards the end of the period of revelations, radicals believe Allah abrogated, changing his mind on the toleration of non-believers.

For the moment we could celebrate, but there would be lots of work ahead. I hoped and prayed it would be done there and not here in the land of the free, but worried for my grandchildren. The concern for political correctness in America could put us in serious long term jeopardy as the Muslim population increases. It was only two tenths of one percent in the US and the kinds of problems being experienced in Indonesia and Europe don't typically start until it gets to ten percent. For some time, it would remain an intellectual argument centered in political correctness here, but not forever. As the Muslim population grows in the US, the radical element will most certainly start asserting itself. I hoped our future leaders understood this and would get in front of it. The current administration clearly did not.

An Anniversary in Tampa

Terri had arrived for her ten day visit and we were enjoying our time together. I at least knew I would be there for our 15th anniversary on 11 May! Per tradition, I had gathered up a bunch of flowers and decorated the room for her arrival. She got there on a Friday and we enjoyed my off duty weekend time. I'd go to work during the week, she would enjoy Tampa at her own pace during the days, and we enjoyed our evenings together.

We finally had our anniversary dinner at Armani's! John, Joanie, Margot and the crew treated us like royalty as always and fun was had by all. It seemed much longer ago than one year that Terri came down for our anniversary after I left for Afghanistan with less than 10 days notice. They proved I wasn't needed for a fun anniversary celebration! I was just happy they let me be part of this one!

Chapter Twenty Seven
The Marine/The Citizen: Jun-Sep 2011
US Central Command, MacDill AFB, Tampa, Fl

A 40 Year/Three Mile Journey Ends

My Rocky Point run and journey back through nearly 40 years of my tug of war between love of family and sense of duty were both nearing their end. As I reached the entrance of the Hyatt, I realized I had just relived my entire military and civilian career in a three mile run! Boy was I tired! Never had my country needed my unique qualifications, experience, and abilities more than they did now, and never in my life was I happier with my home life. Having both wasn't practical, but Terri and I were doing our best to balance both worlds and keep our relationship intact. We were quite good at it, but it would soon get even more complicated.

Terri's Possible Washington, DC Assignment

Terri was becoming more and more disenchanted with her job in the Food Safety division of the State of Wisconsin's Department of Agriculture. During one of our Tampa visits, she got the announcement for a position she wanted to apply for at the state. Her boss of 19 years retired and she planned on applying for the job. It was a Bureau Director level position and definitely a good career progression opportunity. I'd never seen her so deep in thought and obviously not happily. They added a minor credential requirement that she didn't have. Even though she was a University of Wisconsin PhD in Nutritional Sciences with a minor in Food Science, and a long list of highly respected certifications, and even though she worked in the bureau for 19 years for the guy retiring, they told her she could not apply without it. Something smelled.

Did that stop her? Hell no! She got online and ordered what she needed to study and get the certification within 12 days! Much of our time together that visit was spent with her studying for the exam. She studied in my room while I worked. My room had a beautiful view, so that helped. Her shiny new Nook Color allowed her to study out on the beach when we went out there. Our weekend Clearwater suite was a perfect place for her to study as well. A little wine, a nice Hyatt robe, and a beautiful view helped take some of the sting off.

She took the test and passed it with flying colors and submitted the application on the Monday it was due. That's my Terri! I wished I could have been a fly on the wall when they got her application complete with the new certification! This political promotion had a new challenger!

They recovered quickly and simply cut her out of a second interview. She was crushed. In an effort to find some sort of distraction, she had reached out to her vast national network of food and nutritional scientists to look at her options. In doing so, she arranged to be selected by the Federal Department of Homeland Security to participate in a one-year inter-governmental program to incorporate state government expertise into the federal food safety defense. This would mean a year in Washington, DC starting in the October timeframe, just when I'd get home if I wasn't extended! In addition to the uncertainty of my fate at the US Central Command (CENTCOM), we were now waiting for a formal decision on her end! One thing was certain, I would support her in every way, just as she supported me for so many years!

Life at CENTCOM

By late spring of 2011, the entire Middle East had exploded into unrest that became known as the "Arab Spring". While the Africa Command (AFRICOM) was responsible for US Military operations in Libya, most of the other countries involved were in CENTCOM's area of responsibility, and General Mattis' CENTCOM staff was running ragged. They needed to keep the experience and expertise they had on hand, and they needed more help. I understood the need but I didn't know if Headquarters Marine Corps (HQMC) did. My current orders ended 30 September and our CENTCOM J6 (Systems) Chief of Staff was working hard to extend my orders for another year.

Leave, Bruised Ribs, and Terri's Tampa Visit

I flew home for a few days in July for my grandson Dylan's fifth birthday party, visit my parents, and of course, have some Dorf Haus time. It would also be a chance to take home a few things to lighten my load for driving home in September. I was sensing a higher probability of driving home in early October rather than flying back to Afghanistan.

It was a great leave! The boys lured me to the floor, ostensibly to play with their toys. Of course, the tickling started. The next thing I knew, they were using me as a trampoline! Early in the fight, the almost three-year old had me pinned about the head and shoulders, and I couldn't see the five year old circling back to the couch to set up his high jump onto "Gampa's" tummy. I took a significant hit to the ribs, but persevered. I got help from Grandma Terri, who saw the deadly swan dive, and we all still had lots of fun. It was so good to be there to play with them, but I was sure Kristin and Mark had to deal with some hyper activity at bedtime. What are grandparents for anyway?

My painful, bruised ribs would heal over the next six weeks, and I would be ready to reengage in battle if I could make it to Gavin's third birthday party in September, again reigning supreme in the continuation of our tickle fight! Some kids never grow up.

I met my civilian boss, Tony Konkol, at Wisconsin Physicians Service (WPS) at the VFW Post 8483. His wife's grandfather was one of the original post members and he'd hope to get a confirmed sighting of him. I also made contact with Mike Endres, one of our technicians who had been doing double duty to cover me, and let them both know where things stood. WPS had gone far and above the call of duty to support my recall and they had taken much of the burden of worry off Terri and me. They were more than ready for my return, but my job would still be waiting for me even if I'd have to stay for another year. To paraphrase Tony, "…it's our way of doing our part to defend the nation." To paraphrase Mike, "Get back here dammit!"

When Archibald Henderson, the first Commandant of the Marine Corps, left Headquarters Marine Corps during the Indian Wars, he famously left a note pinned to his door that read, "Gone to fight the Indians." Nobody at WPS seemed to understand that I would rather be with the Marines in a fire fight in the Middle East than sitting through another meeting there! Didn't they see my note?

Back at CENTCOM

The Middle East kept all of us on our toes. We lost 30 American special operators in a helicopter crash. Our operators would run dozens of these operations on a daily basis using the same techniques. This one ended tragically, and I knew it had to be especially hard for Admiral McCraven to take. He had just assumed command of Special Operations Command (SOCOM) here at MacDill Air Force Base and was previously the commander of the Joint Special Operations Command that led the attack on Bin Laden. I was in the same room with him a couple times in Qatar in 2009, and last year in Afghanistan. He was definitely a consummate professional. I knew he would take appropriate steps to ensure the small groups of special operators that would remain after the withdrawal of the larger conventional forces, would have the information and equipment needed to be successful and safe.

The transition of forces out of Iraq continued to demand a great deal of attention. This was especially tricky because of the known desire of some in the Iraqi government to maintain a US presence to offset Iran's intense interest in our leaving to assert their influence. Close eyes were always kept on Syria. We were standing by to set up a Crisis Action Team (CAT) in case the violence required us to step in to protect American lives and property. Iran always demanded a great deal of our time. We conducted exercises to rehearse different scenarios that could result from their growing influence in the region and their continued support of weapons and training to the Taliban and Al-Qaeda.

Regardless of practical military and political reasons to keep a force in Iraq, some of our politicians still wanted to end our presence in the Middle East. To me our mission was still simple. We needed to keep the improvised explosive devices (IED) off our own streets, our children free from hostage taking, our subways free from poison, and our country fairs and small towns free from explosions. If we didn't stop the radical Muslim elements where they started, we could expect them to start here in the States. Simply put, if we weren't there, they would be here.

Our conventional forces would likely be leaving and our special operations capabilities would need to carry on the mission. I was very proud to have a small part in shaping that future, keeping us safe at home until we got an administration that recognized the true threat of radical Islamic terrorists beyond the Taliban and Al-Qaeda, and was willing to have a backbone and treat it accordingly.

Futures in the Balance

Terri and I had been doing great seeing each other since my return to the States. She came down again after my leave for one of our coveted three day weekends. On my way out of the office one Friday, I bid Colonel Carney goodnight, and told him Terri was here for the weekend. He had returned from Afghanistan and assumed the J6 Operations Chief role. When he heard Terri was here, he ordered me not to come back to the office until Tuesday! He didn't have to tell me twice! We enjoyed a great Tampa weekend even if it was hot and rainy. It was just good to be together.

We were both waiting to see what our futures held next year. I was so proud of her! She was selected for a very important assignment at the national level and I supported her all the way, as she did me for so long! If we would have to have our dates at the Marine Corps Monument in DC next year, so be it! I would be honored to be asked to stay at CENTCOM to see the programs unfold and go operational, but was also very ready to come back home! Both decisions would come soon.

In my case, HQMC finally denied CENTCOM's request for another year. My CENTCOM team was sure it was because of the per diem costs. Having agreed to stay without per diem expenses, they put in a follow-up request to reconsider the disapproval back into the same "gauntlet" the original request went through. It would be at least 30 days to process the second request. CENTCOM requested an expedited process since I needed to process off active duty by 30 September, but I didn't think the word expedite was in the HQMC's vocabulary. These were some of the world's finest bureaucrats. Barbarians of Bureaucracy they were! Nothing could interrupt their rights to their breaks, lunch hours, days off, long weekends, meetings, and other creative time wasters that are difficult to fathom in the urgency of war.

I told Marine Colonel Turner, who was working the request, that if the request had any chance of approval, it would require General

Mattis' endorsement as CENTCOM Commander. He didn't think so. I started packing.

I planned on going home for good in early October. I had already completed my retirement physical and got my VA physical exams. It was tricky working with the VA not knowing when you're leaving! There was even a farewell party for me! My new boss, Army Lieutenant Colonel Paul Howard wrote and sang a song with his guitar called "The Gunner" about my "legendary" work in CENTCOM's Command, Control, Communications, Computers, Intelligence, Surveillance, Reconnaissance (C4ISR) areas, and how HQMC would be responsible for any trouble they got into after I was gone. It was hilarious and I was highly honored! This entertainment was enjoyed much more than a sappy speech.

For those that don't know the reason behind why they called me Gunner, it is because traditionally this is what they called all Marine Corps Warrant Officers. There are some of the new breed "Gunners" that dispute that, but I just tell them I was laying in defensive lines and designating targets when they were still playing with little green Army guys on the living room floor....

One of my counterparts, Army Major Tim Root, who actually lived in Lodi many years ago, got up and spoke of meeting me for the first time upon my return from Afghanistan. He remembered how I responded to him when he naively asked me what the "satellite program" was. He said my response will forever live with him. He then proceeded to repeat his version of it "verbatim." He basically took the famous "You can't handle the truth" scene from "A Few Good Men" where Tom Cruise goads Jack Nicholson into a tirade, changing the wording to fit what I did in Afghanistan. More laughter. Big time! I hoped to have both "gifts" recorded for my family and friends' listening entertainment. They were both definitely worth the price of admission! But, of course, I can't figure out for the life of me where they got the idea to associate me with Jack Nicholson... They gave me a flag that flew over the CENTCOM headquarters too. Good piece of gear!

Terri was still hoping to get her one-year inter-governmental program assignment with the Department of Homeland Security (DHS) squared away. They were trying to put the agreement between the State and DHS together. At first, the state wasn't going to agree to the assignment for financial reasons, which the DHS was working hard to overcome. Terri's credentials were important to them. Of course, they were working at the speed of resistance too, only it was worse. In her case we had the exponential impact of both state and federal government bureaucracies involved, resulting in near motionless productivity...

She was anxious to "get out and do something" after 19 years of the same job and boss at the State. The DHS was working on food safety defense to protect the country's food supplies from terrorist contamination. They wanted to incorporate state government experiences, taking existing programs into account, and bring different state representatives in for a year at a time. Terri would be the third or fourth one, and she was their top choice due to her extensive academic and professional background.

She had a PhD in Nutritional Sciences from the University of Wisconsin, had vast experience in state government, and was well connected with government and industry food experts from around the nation that were members of various professional associations. She was also to be the national president for the Association of Food and Drug Officials in 2013. I was especially proud of that one!

I was pulling for her all the way. Even though we would like to be together back home after being separated for four years, this was a great opportunity for her, and it would give us a chance to enjoy Washington, DC together on long weekends. She has always loved Washington, DC as part of her own patriotic fabric and this would be a great chance for us to enjoy the sites on our free time.

Orders Come to an End

As the clock struck midnight on 30 September 2011, I once again became a civilian. Terri was in back in Tampa, and we would enjoy a couple days of perfect weather there before we started driving home. The Marine Corps still hadn't responded to CENTCOM's follow-up request to retain me so there was still a very small risk that I'd need to come back. I was very confident that wouldn't happen at this point. From everything I was told about the status of the request, it was going to be disapproved again. What I didn't know is what the CENTCOM personnel folks had told the Director of Manpower at HQMC which could still change things.

It was still technically possible when the request hit his desk as the last stop in "the gauntlet," the Manpower Director at Headquarters Marine Corps could still approve it, but I had no reason to expect that he would. It was his responsibility at that point to get the Marine Corps active force count down from 202,000 to 186,000. It would be extremely difficult to justify keeping a retired recall officer on active duty as he was attempting to cut the regular count of the active force.

I put on my dress blues, Terri put on a beautiful dress, and we had dinner upstairs at Armani's. We were treated to free meals and drinks all night! We had a great night and heartily celebrated my return to civilian life.

Reflections of the Middle East

We enjoyed the two-day drive back to Wisconsin, visiting my old buddy Colonel Bill Hamerstadt and his wife Marilyn in Indianapolis. As my service was likely to end, a lot of time was spent reflecting on where things were likely to end in the Middle East.

My personal observation was that the then current revolts in the Middle East, dubbed as "The Arab Spring" by an unjustifiably optimistic and very naïve American press, assumed that the dictators and monarchs would be displaced, resulting in free democracies instead of theocracies or straight-up Islamic rule. I say this simply, but confidently, because the world's Muslim population was steadily outpacing Christian populations. If only one to five percent of the approximately 1.8 billion Muslims in the world were radicalized, it amounted well into the tens of millions.

It is quite evident that this radical element is far more hungry and willing to fight and die for their religious beliefs than the idealistic seekers of freedom and democracy in their Middle East countries. Iran also was investing much more in shaping and influencing the directions the revolutions were taking. The people of Iran themselves may have been for free democracy, but the puppet civil government and President were unabashedly, totally controlled by the Ayatollah and Sharia Law.

As I left my post, I predicted a much more dangerous radical Islamic-dominated Middle East than we'd seen since the period of global Islamic domination in 632-1500 AD. I also saw the mainstream, non-violent Muslims assimilating more and more into the world's major civil governments. Indonesia was already firmly established as the world's highest Muslim concentration; Europe was well on the way. The United States was still under two tenths of a percent and growing much faster than anybody was noticing due to their focus on our economy, jobs, and immigration issues. When people asked if we were almost done in the Middle East, my answer was always, "We haven't even started. The real battles are yet to come and will likely be fought on our own streets."

This could, and I believed would be, avoided when we have an administration willing to stand up to break the political correctness barrier and publicly announce "Radical Islamic Terrorism" as our enemy. Also, mainstream Muslims would have to take a stand at some point as the radicals would persecute them equally to non-believers for not following the true laws of Islam.

These would be the important first steps and mark the beginning of the true fight. It will become more obvious to the average citizen as our own Muslim population reaches the 10 percent mark as it has in many other parts of the world, and when the radical element starts asserting itself beyond the normal assimilative tendencies of a changing Muslim demographic. To paraphrase Sun Tzu in "The Art of War": "The wise general first wins the war and then fights it". It took me many years of experience after first reading that famous phrase to understand it. I certainly understood it as I prepared to leave CENTCOM.

The Final Word
Back home in mid-October, I received the final word from HQMC and CENTCOM on the follow up request for another year extension of my orders. I would be staying home this time. At last the uncertainty and agony of not knowing was settled! It was disappointing in the sense that I would love to have remained involved in the duties that were so intriguing, and continue to write history instead of reading it. But there was a sense of contentment to finally focus on home and family without the sound of distant drums to distract me.

I came through forty years of active, reserve, and retired Marine Corps service with cherished memories of the good, the bad, the easy, the hard, the adventurous, the boring, the successes, and the failures. I wouldn't trade it all for anything. Winston Churchill said something like "…success is the ability to go from one failure to another with enthusiasm." Boy, I sure accomplished that!

I looked hard at my combat boots before taking them off for the last time prior to leaving Tampa. They held up good, and they had walked one hell of a lot of ground in a lot of places! They were always comfortable, and all service men and women know how important it is to have good boots. Today's boots and uniforms are the absolute best I've ever had, and I had many over the years. As I took them off, I had vivid memories of sitting up in my racks and shelters every morning and putting on my "boots and uts," always counting how many days were left. It felt good to take them off for the last time, but I would miss them, and the feeling of reward that came with wearing them, and all the uniforms I'd worn over the last 40 years.

It occurred to me how lucky I was to be on "our side." I had a home, a job, a great family, and great friends holding my place in a great life back home while fighting to protect our way of life in faraway places. Many of our allies that I worked with, and certainly our enemies, didn't have that. War was their life, and there was no job back home. They were home. Their friends were scattered, and their families that weren't scattered were huddled in their homes with dirt floors. There were flies in their food and their clothes were shredded robes.

I always appreciated my home, my family and my friends. I've always known what it takes to make sure we can continue to do our fighting far away from them. I thought we'd done that for awhile, but great dangers lied ahead if we didn't stay vigilant and stay the course. I hoped our allies and friends could have our comforts someday, and hoped our future politicians would make sure we kept ours. I remembered that young Afghani soldier on that C-130 night-flight to Camp Leatherneck with a lifetime of war showing in his 20 year old eyes, hoping he'd make it and would have a good life someday!

A Wisconsin Wedding

Kurt and his beautiful fiancée Jenny were married on 15 October. It was a wonderful day all around at the Cross Plains Catholic Church and Rex's Innkeeper in Waunakee. They were a great couple and both families were very happy to have our new son and daughter-in-law. I was assigned to keep Dylan, our now five-year old Grandson, next to me during the church ceremony. We did pretty well. He was constantly chattering, but in a low voice or whisper because I said we had to be quiet in God's house. He kept me pretty busy, so I didn't get much out of the priest's sermon. Dylan's chatter was far more interesting anyway! Gavin, the now almost three-year old, ventured over by us a couple of times, but was also pretty well behaved. I promised them both we would raise holy hell later...

Jenny had invited me to wear my uniform to the wedding right after they became engaged. That alone told me all I needed to know of her character. She wasn't concerned about attention being diverted from her on her wedding day. She had brothers in the service and was also very proud of them. Kurt made mention of my permanent return from active duty in Iraq and Afghanistan during his dinner speech and I was overwhelmed by a standing ovation from the entire reception dinner crowd. Not every newlywed couple would want to share even a minute of the limelight on their wedding day. I was so proud and so honored to be there for their special day!

We stayed through the last dance and enjoyed the company of Jon and Peggy Schumann, Ron and Wanda Guenther, and Denny Diehl. Our entire family was there and many old friendships were rekindled!

Hawaii and Rest Under the Banyan Tree
Shortly after the wedding, Terri and I headed to Hawaii and our beloved Banyan Tree at the Moana Surf Rider Hotel's Beach Bar for some decompression. We loved our beach breakfasts at the Hulu Grill overlooking the beach. I would work out afterwards and spend the afternoons under the shade of the Banyan Tree to relax. That was our usual vacation spot. We were very much looking forward to getting back after several years of touch and go separation, and all the emotions that go with it. After Hawaii, we would attend the Marine Corps Ball in Tampa on 5 November, and would return home to Wisconsin on 6 November. I would take a final week to do a few things around the Sauk and DeForest houses and then return to my civilian job at WPS.

New Directions and Change of Roles

My job at WPS was everything it was when I left. After four years, I had the same office, same desk, same phone, and same headaches. Either I had one hell of a boss and company, or nobody wanted my job! I would eventually make sure WPS was well recognized by the Employee Support of the Guard and Reserve (ESGR). My boss Tony and my team were what made me tick there. They understood things. The company was changing fast though. New top leadership was brought in and any of us who were around for even just a few years knew we weren't what they wanted for the long term. It became very hard to feel relevant and take the kind of pride I did as a Marine, but it did pay the bills.

Terri's one year assignment to the Homeland Security was approved. She got an apartment in downtown Washington, DC and felt very secure, and made a friend in Kendall. Their friendship would endure for that year and beyond. We enjoyed our visits back and forth. Her return to the State of Wisconsin was as miserable as it was before leaving. She retired from there and took a job with the Food & Drug Administration (FDA) back in DC within a year and a half. She returned to the same apartment building, resumed her friendship with Kendall, and enjoyed her new job at the FDA. Terri and I would now enjoy resumed visits between Washington, DC and our DeForest and Sauk homes in Wisconsin. The roles had been reversed. I would see to the care and cleaning of our homes and she would serve our nation. It was only right and fittin'!

The Tug of War Ends

Terri and I established a comfortable routine of visits until she comes home for good. I would retire from WPS in 2016 and enjoy catching up on home life and golfing with Schumann, Kurt and Timmy Diehl, son of Denny. I also would become the Post Commander of VFW Post 8483.

We would say goodbye to Dad in June of 2012. Mom would come live with us in our Sauk house and we would continue to enjoy our special time together. At 85 she still worked three half-days a week and kept the big house in top notch condition! We lost Denny unexpectedly a short time after Dad's passing. Chris married Jill and they are doing an amazing job raising their combined families while honoring Cherie's memory. Little Kenzie joined Kristin, Mark, Dylan, and Gavin's family, and Little Katelyn blessed Kurt & Jenny's lives shortly after. And we all live in Sauk Prairie! The decision to come home to raise Kurt and Kristin back in 1980 was a good one! They both had college degrees and could have gone anywhere! It just proves that happiness is right inside of you if you just take notice.

It was one hell of a run! I had the rare and very unique opportunity to feel I've had a small part of things that had a profound impact on the history and future of our nation, with a lifetime of stories to tell. A cardinal rule of sea stories is that no "true stories" are allowed. They say the only difference between a sea story and fairy tale is that one starts with "Once upon a time," and the other starts with "This ain't no shit." Of course, I will embellish as necessary and appropriate while engaged in deep story telling at the VFW, Dorf Haus, and other bar room discussions. And, of course, my stories will always start with "This ain't no shit!"…

Our family story is the story of many other thousands just like us. No blood and guts, just a lifetime of good, faithful service served at the price of family and friends. All those who have served and their families could change the names and places of my story, but the tug of war between love of family and sense of duty would be the same for you. I only hope I told our stories well!

My forty year tug of war has ended. As I watch the world events unfolding since my military retirement, I am extremely proud of those who have seamlessly and selflessly assumed the watch. The quote on the back cover says it all! "Patriotism is not a short and frenzied outburst of emotion but the tranquil and steady dedication of a lifetime."

Glossary

AFCENT	Air Force Central Command (3-Star Component Command)
AFRICOM	African Command 4-Star Combatant Command
AO	Area of Operations
AOR	Area of Responsibility
ARCENT	Army Central Command (3-Star Component Command)
AUAB	Al Udeid Air Base in Qatar
BAF	Bagram Air Field in Afghanistan
C4ISR	Command, Control, Communications, Computers, Intelligence, Surveillance, Reconnaissance
C5ISR	Coalition Command, Control, Communications, Computers, Intelligence, Surveillance, Reconnaissance
CENTCOM	US Central Command (4-Star Combatant Command)
CFH	CENTCOM Forward Headquarters
CJOA-A	Coalition Joint Operations Area - Afghanistan
COC	Combat Operations Center
COP	Combat Outpost
EUCOM	European Command (4-Star Combatant Command)
FOB	Forward Operating Base
FOBBIT	One who stays inside the wire in a forward operating base. Transformed from the HOBBIT movies.
G-x	Regiment/Division Staff: 1-Admin, 2-Intel, 3-Ops, 4-Logistics, 5-Civil, 6-Systems, 7-Training, 8-Finance
HMMWV	High Mobility Multipurpose Wheeled Vehicle (Humvee)

Glossary (Cont'd)

HQ	Headquarters
HQMC	Headquarters Marine Corps in Quantico, VA
Humvee	High Mobility Multipurpose Wheeled Vehicle (HMMWV)
IJC	3-Star ISAF Joint Command Headquarters in Kabul for Day to Day Tactical Operations
ISAF	4-Star HQ for NATO International Security Assistance Force for Strategic/Civil Affairs Operations
J-x	Joint Staff: 1-Admin, 2-Intel, 3-Ops, 4-Logistics, 5-Civil, 6-Systems, 7-Training, 8-Finance
JCSE	Joint Communications Support Element
JIC	Joint Intelligence Center
KAIA	Kabul Area International Airport
MARCENT	Marine Central Command (3-Star Component Command)
MARFORPAC	Marine Forces Pacific Command (3-Star Component Command)
MILAIR	Military Air Operated by US Air Force
MRAP	Mine Resistant Ambush Protected Vehicle
MSR	Main Supply Route
PACOM	US Pacific Command (4-Star Combatant Command)
PSD	Personal Security Detail
RC	Regional Commands in Afghanistan
REGIMENTAL HEADQUARTERS	Regimental Command Team - 1 in Iraq
RIP/TOA	Relief in Place/Transfer of Authority
River City	Communications blackout until next of kin notified
S-x	Battalion/Squadron Staff: 1-Admin, 2-Intel, 3-Ops, 4-Logistics, 5-Civil, 6-Systems, 7-Training,
USFOR-A	US Forces-Afghanistan (4-Star Command Dual Hatted as ISAF Commander)

Made in the USA
Columbia, SC
01 March 2021

33729643R00139